Solveig Spjeldnes

Building Community Capacity

D0141248

MODERN APPLICATIONS OF SOCIAL WORK

An Aldine de Gruyter Series of Texts and Monographs

Series Editor: James K. Whittaker, *University of Washington*

Building Community Capacity

Robert J. Chaskin
Prudence Brown
Sudhir Venkatesh
Avis Vidal

ALDINE DE GRUYTER

New York

About the Authors

Robert J. Chaskin
Research Program Director and Research Fellow, Chapin Hall Center for Children at the University of Chicago.

Prudence Brown
Research Fellow, Chapin Hall Center for Children at the University of Chicago.

Sudhir Venkatesh
Assistant Professor of Sociology and Director of Research, Institute for Research in African-American Studies, Columbia University.

Avis Vidal
Principal Research Associate, Urban Institute.

Copyright © 2001 Walter de Gruyter, Inc., New York
All rights reserved. No part of this publication may be reproduced or transmitted in any form or by any means, electronic or mechanical, including photocopy, recording, or any information storage or retrieval system, without permission in writing from the publisher.

ALDINE DE GRUYTER
A division of Walter de Gruyter, Inc.
200 Saw Mill River Road
Hawthorne, New York 10532

This publication is printed on acid free paper

Library of Congress Cataloging-in-Publication Data
Building community capacity / Robert J. Chaskin ... [et al.].
    p. cm. — (Modern applications of social work)
    Includes bibliographical references and index.
    ISBN 0-202-30639-9 (cloth : alk. paper) — ISBN 0-202-30640-2 (pbk. : alk. paper)
    1. Community organization.   2. Community power.   I. Chaskin, Robert J.
II. Series.
    HM766.B85 2001
    361.3—dc21   00-046930

Manufactured in the United States of America

10 9 8 7 6 5 4 3

*No individual can live alone, no nation can live alone,
and anyone who feels that he can live alone
is sleeping through a revolution.*

—Dr. Martin Luther King, Jr.

This is the world as it is. This is where you start.

—Saul Alinsky

Contents

Foreword

Building Community Capacity by Robert Chaskin, Prudence Brown, Sudhir Venkatesh, and Avis Vidal speaks to a wide audience of readers concerned with promoting urban social change. It addresses the heart of the challenge faced by those working to strengthen and improve poor communities: how to repair and reconstruct a community's collective ability to address shared problems and capitalize on opportunities to improve community life. A broad range of people are engaged in this agenda, including practitioners, funders, and scholars from a range of disciplines, each of whom come to this work in different roles and draw on varied intellectual strains and traditions.

Of particular importance for this series, the book speaks to a lacuna in current social work practice theory: community change. Much work in this area of macropractice, particularly around "grassroots" community organizing, has a somewhat dated feel to it, is highly ideological in orientation, or—in the case of many "generalist" treatments of the topic—suffers from superficiality, particularly in the area of theory and practical application. Set against a context of an often narrowly constructed "clinical" emphasis in practice education, coupled with social work's own current rendering of "scientific management", "community practice" often takes second or third billing in many professional curricula despite its deep roots in the overall field of social welfare.

Chaskin and colleagues provide a wakeup call to revisit community-level processes, and the book rewards readers' attention to the issues raised. The authors bring to bear the perspectives of a variety of professional disciplines including sociology (Chaskin & Venkatesh), urban planning (Vidal), and psychology and social work (Brown), and provide us with new ways of thinking about "community" that are quite consistent with current theoretical perspectives in the social work field: the ecological perspective, the strengths or "social assets" perspective, the notion of partnership with clients, and "empowerment." The authors' focus is on community-based approaches to social change and economic development designed to improve both the current circumstances and life outcomes for people in poverty. Their particular point of departure is to try and provide more specificity and precision to that familiar, but elusive term "community capacity." In their own words:

> Like other vanguard terms used to catalyze and drive action in the field . . . , *capacity* and *capacity building* [emphasis added] at the neighborhood level are elastic: they lack consistent and explicit meaning. What, in concrete terms, does *community capacity* mean? What are its components? How can they be recognized, measured, and understood in action? What kinds of interventions can strengthen them? (pp. 1–2)

Drawing on extensive case study data from three significant community-building initiatives, program data from numerous other community capacity–building efforts, key informant interviews, and an excellent literature review, Chaskin and his colleagues draw implications for crafting community change strategies as well as for creating and sustaining the organizational infrastructure necessary to support them. The authors promote no panaceas and their thoughtful, critical analyses, while rich in implications for community-level practice, are not formulaic. Those favoring a cookbook approach to community change will be disappointed with this present effort. On the other hand, social work scholars and students of community practice seeking new conceptual frameworks and insights from research to inform novel community interventions will find much of value in *Building Community Capacity*.

Significantly, *Building Community Capacity* originates from two leading-edge centers of community analysis—The Chapin Hall Center for Children at the University of Chicago and the Urban Institute—wherein the tools of empirical research and a variety of disciplinary perspectives are brought to bear on complex urban issues. The resultant "conversation" is alternately rich and illuminating, and perplexing: much theoretical, empirical, and practical demonstration needs to be done before the field of social welfare has a definitive answer to the question, What is community capacity? Chaskin, Brown, Venkatesh, and Vidal provide fresh insights and perspectives that will inform and enrich the knowledge base for social work's community change mission in numerous ways. Their work helps to support a bridge between individual clients and the communities that both sustain and challenge them. Social work students, practitioners and educators, and the clients and communities they serve are in their debt.

James K. Whittaker
The University of Washington

Acknowledgments

The completion of this book was made possible by the hard work of many people. Research and writing was made possible by funding from the Ford Foundation and the Annie E. Casey Foundation, by the institutional support of the Chapin Hall Center for Children at the University of Chicago and the Urban Institute, and by the committed efforts and candid assessments of community residents, community development and service practitioners, sponsors, organizers, technical assistance providers, and researchers working on community building efforts across the country. In addition to those we have interviewed directly and whose work we have learned from through other sources, we would like to thank the following people by name for their insight and assistance in making this work possible: Janice Molnar, Ralph Smith, and Miriam Shark for their financial support and early guidance; Gina Barclay-McLaughlin, Paul Brophy, Susan Campbell, David Dodson, Ralph Hamilton, Mark Joseph, Langley Keyes, Mark Moore, Harold Richman, Richard Taub, Sherry Seiwert, and Rebecca Stone for their advice and thoughtful reviews of earlier drafts of this work; Amanda Toler, Jolyon Wurr, and William Mollard for their research assistance; and Hugh McIntosh and Anne Clary for their editorial help.

Introduction

Urban neighborhoods have been a recurring focus of social policy and organized social action in the United States at least since the Progressive era. From the settlement houses of the late nineteenth century, to the community center movement in the first decades of the twentieth century, and on to such service coordination initiatives as the Ford Foundation's Gray Areas Projects and the War on Poverty programs of the 1960s, such efforts have recognized the local community as the place where programs and problems can be fitted together.[1] The 1990s spawned significant renewed emphasis on community-based approaches to improving the circumstances and life chances of people in poverty. In the urban context, *community* has generally referred to *neighborhood*—a geographically defined subarea of the city, where residents are presumed to share both spatial proximity and some degree of mutual circumstance. Most clearly exemplified by the growing number of comprehensive community initiatives (CCIs) operating across the country, current approaches share a focus on comprehensive development within neighborhoods, as well as an emphasis on *community building* as a means to and a goal of neighborhood transformation.[2] The impetus for CCIs and other community revitalization initiatives has come largely from the philanthropies that have designed, catalyzed, and funded them. However, there is increasing activity in the public sector as well, from city- and state-driven endeavors to more than one hundred designated federal Empowerment Zones and Enterprise Communities.[3] Beyond these high-profile efforts, innumerable community-based organizations—from community development corporations, to settlement houses, to neighborhood associations and advocacy organizations—as well as a range of organizing efforts, coalitions, and technical assistance intermediaries also focus on community building as a central task.

Community building in all of these efforts consists of actions to strengthen the *capacity* of communities to identify priorities and opportunities and to foster and sustain positive neighborhood change. The focus on building community capacity as a goal of community-building efforts is both explicit and pervasive in the rhetoric, missions, and (to a greater or lesser extent) activities of these initiatives. However, like other vanguard terms used to catalyze and drive action in the field (e.g., *comprehensiveness*

1

and *empowerment*), capacity and capacity building at the neighborhood level are elastic; they lack consistent and explicit meaning. What, in concrete terms, does *community capacity* mean? What are its components? How can they be recognized, measured, and understood in action? What kinds of interventions can strengthen them?

This book addresses these questions. It provides a clear definition of community capacity and a pointed review of strategies intended to foster it. The book aims to help readers with a practical interest in strengthening poor neighborhoods in two ways: by providing a systematic framework to structure thinking about community capacity, and by exploring in some detail the choices and issues that those who seek to strengthen such capacity must confront.

The actors involved in community capacity–building efforts are tremendously diverse. They include members of community organizations and block clubs, bankers and businesspeople, advocates and academics, funders and government officials, residents and religious leaders, school personnel and youth workers, consultants and technical assistance providers, observers and activists. Each constituency comes to the task of community building in a somewhat different way, with distinct interests and roles in building and sustaining community capacity.

This volume is intended to shed light on the field of community capacity building in ways that may be of value to the full spectrum of participants and observers. This is not an easy task. Different actors in the field have different needs, and any single volume is unlikely to satisfy everyone. Furthermore, we lack a common language through which to convey our understanding of social change in general, and community capacity in particular, in ways that are relevant and helpful to the multiple audiences for whom engagement in these issues is important. We need better tools and processes to bridge concept and action, research and practice, evidence and policy formation.

We hope that this volume begins to construct such a bridge, understanding that different readers will take away different aspects of our analysis as more relevant to their work. For example, those with resources to allocate to capacity-building efforts, individuals interested in the history and conceptual content of such initiatives, and those responsible for structuring comprehensive initiatives may find it particularly useful to focus on how the elements of the framework can be actualized in practice. For them, key aspects of this process, such as the choice of organizing strategies or the decision whether or not to create a new organization may be most relevant. Practitioners directly engaged in community capacity building "on the ground" may find through this book that their experiences resonate with others across the country, and may gain some insight into the tensions and trade-offs faced by others. Although neither type of reader will find here a simple recipe to follow, both may take away a richer understanding of the complexities of this work, greater clarity about the mechanisms through which communities can "act," and a useful handle on some of the possibilities and limitations of community capacity building as a tool to promote social change.

The analysis for this book draws on four major sources: (1) case study data derived from in-depth implementation studies of three community-building initiatives, (2) documentary data from additional initiatives and organizations engaged in community capacity–building efforts, (3) additional key-informant interviews with a range of participants across the field, and (4) a review of existing literature.

Case study data consists of information gathered by one or more of the authors while participating in the documentation or evaluation of three CCIs. The Neighborhood and Family Initiative (NFI), launched in 1990, is a multisite CCI centered on the creation of neighborhood collaboratives as mechanisms to promote resident participation and organizational collaboration for a broadly based process of planning and project implementation. NFI operates in Detroit, Memphis, Hartford, and Milwaukee.[4] The Glades Community Development Corporation (GCDC), begun in 1991, is a single-site effort to create a community-based intermediary organization serving three rural communities in the western part of Palm Beach County, Florida (see Brown and Stetzer, 1998). The Consensus Organizing Demonstration Program (CODP), also begun in 1991, is a multisite organizing effort spearheaded by a national intermediary to identify and train local leaders and to develop capable new community development corporations (CDCs).[5] CODP sites are in Little Rock, New Orleans, and eastern Palm Beach County. These "core cases" are all multifaceted interventions that have employed some combination of the four principal strategies—leadership development, organizational development, community organizing, and interorganizational collaboration—used by community capacity–building efforts across the field. Data from these three cases include site-produced documentation, program and administrative information, and the results of extensive field research, including direct observation and extended interviews with both initiative participants and key informants (e.g., local government officials, directors of local organizations, and residents) not directly connected to the initiatives. Detailed descriptions of all three core cases are presented in Appendix A, and relevant information about them is presented throughout the volume when they are used as examples.

The use of these core cases allows us to explore the practice of community capacity building in some detail, with attention to the nuances of approach, process, and context that inform their implementation and condition their effects. Individually and in combination, the initiatives chosen provide a variety of useful perspectives and experiences on the dimensions of community capacity and on strategies for building it. These initiatives are not representative of the whole field. Nor are they intended to be seen as exemplary in the sense of best practice or proven models of success; collectively, they provide examples of both successes and failures. They do, however, illustrate the range of strategies, contexts, actors, and implementation issues being encountered across a wide spectrum of community capacity–building efforts. They are among the longest-running efforts of their kind and among the most thoroughly documented. Our intimate knowledge of them allows for a much more detailed exploration than would be the case with a more general survey of a broader range of initiatives.

We place our examination of these core cases in the context of the broader field of community capacity–building efforts by exploring (in less detail) some thirty additional efforts. We chose these additional cases both to provide more complete coverage of the universe of capacity-building approaches and to allow us to contrast and, to some extent, test the experience of the core cases against that provided by different approaches or by similar approaches structured differently. We base our analysis of these efforts on a combination of existing documentation and key-informant interviews; brief summaries of these efforts are presented in Appendix B.

We also conducted two rounds of interviews with key informants across the country. In the first round, we interviewed sixteen individuals with a broad overview of the field. These included foundation representatives, government officials, academics, and community development practitioners. In the second round, we focused more directly on work in progress—how initiatives were attempting to build community capacity in specific instances, and the successes and challenges they have encountered. Here, we interviewed thirty individuals directly engaged in efforts explicitly intended to build community capacity. These individuals were largely directors of community-based organizations or community-building initiatives and were not connected with the three "core" initiatives.[6]

Finally, we conducted a literature review covering both academic and applied research. The scholarly literature spans a number of disciplines and focuses on defining community capacity and on community structure and functioning. More applied literature describes the intent, structure, and activities of particular community-building efforts, including CCIs, CDCs, community organizing groups, neighborhood associations, community-based service providers, settlement houses, empowerment zones, and municipal efforts at building participatory, neighborhood-based planning mechanisms.

The book is organized into six chapters. Chapter 1 sets the stage by laying out a definitional framework for community capacity that draws on our understanding of how that term is used in the field. The chapter then demonstrates how the framework functions, using it to illustrate how communities generate and use capacity in the presence, as well as the absence, of formal capacity-building interventions.

Chapters 2 through 5 form the empirical core of the volume. They explore the major strategic approaches currently used by community-building efforts to develop community capacity. Chapters 2 and 3 consider strategies designed to strengthen the major building blocks of community capacity—individuals and organizations—by looking at approaches to leadership development and organizational development. The next two chapters discuss strategies intended to build a community's social capital—the networks of connection among individuals and organizations. Chapter 4 explores approaches to community organizing, focusing on relationships among individuals and between them and organizations that affect their well-being. Chapter 5 examines efforts to develop the organizational infrastructure of a community by fostering interorganizational networks and relations. Together, Chapters 2 through 5 articulate the field's implicit theory of community capacity building: Effective communities are distinguished by strong leaders, strong institutions, and strong networks among them that can, working individually or together, get things done.

Finally, Chapter 6 discusses the lessons emerging from field experience with the various strategies for building community capacity. It also explores the possibilities, limitations, and reasonable expectations for community capacity building as a tool for community change.

Our intent has been to review the state of the field (by synthesizing lessons from practice) and to propose a tool (the conceptual framework) with which to analyze community capacity–building efforts. We believe this combination will help support the planning, implementation, and assessment of these effects. The conceptual framework, the exploration of empirical cases, and the conclusions we reach regarding the possibilities and limitations of attempts to build "community capacity" are meant to provide a foundation rather than closure; through them, we hope to inform both policy and practice, and to provide the basis for debate as well as further investigation and action.

NOTES

1. On settlement houses, see, e.g., Davis (1984), Katz, M. B. (1986), Halpern (1995). On the community center movement, see, e.g., Fisher. On the Ford Foundation's Gray Areas Projects, see, e.g., Marris and Rein (1982), Ford Foundation (1964). On community action and Model Cities, see, e.g., Kramer (1969), Peterson and Greenstone (1977), Haar (1975), Frieden and Kaplan (1975).

2. For recent overviews of the field, see Kubisch et al., 1997), Kingsley, Mc-Neely, and Gibson (1996), Stone (1996), and Jackson and Marris (1996).

3. Congress established the Empowerment Zone/Enterprise Community program in 1993. In its first round in 1994, the program designated 105 communities—both urban and rural—to receive federal funding and, in some cases, eligibility for tax credits and waivers. The largest grants went to six urban and two rural empowerment zones, which are to receive $100 million in Social Service Block Grant (Title XX) funds over a ten-year period. Other designations were also made, including enterprise communities, enhanced enterprise communities, and supplemental empowerment zones, with various levels of funding attached to those designations. Designation was based on a competitive application process that involved demonstrable community input and a strategic plan for the proposed zone. Zones were defined as aggregations of census tracts that met certain poverty-level criteria. In a second round in 1998, the program designated twenty new empowerment zones, but funding has not yet been fully allocated for these sites.

4. For an extended analysis of the NFI, see the series of evaluation reports published over the course of its implementation by the Chapin Hall Center for Children at the University of Chicago: Chaskin, Chipenda-Dansokho, and Richards (1999), Chaskin, Chipenda-Dansokho, and Joseph (1997), Chaskin, and Joseph (1995), Chaskin and Ogletree (1993), Chaskin (1992).

5. For an extended analysis of this effort, see Gittell and Vidal (1998).

6. All quotations in the text that are not specifically attributed are from interviews with participants in community capacity-building efforts or with our key informants.

1

Community Capacity and Capacity Building

A Definitional Framework

WHAT IS COMMUNITY CAPACITY?

The word *capacity* includes the ideas of both *containing* (holding, storing) and *ability* (of mind, of action). Applied to a community, capacity implies that a community can *act* in particular ways; it has specific faculties or powers to *do* certain things. These capabilities may relate to a number of aspects of community functioning, but in the context of community building, they are all concerned with ways to help promote or sustain the well-being of the community and its components—individuals, informal groups, organizations, social networks, the physical environment.

Community capacity, in a general sense, is what makes communities "work." It is what makes well-functioning communities function well. As a starting point, we suggest the following summary definition:

Community capacity is the interaction of human capital, organizational resources, and social capital existing within a given community that can be leveraged to solve collective problems and improve or maintain the well-being of that community. It may operate through informal social processes and/or organized efforts by individuals, organizations, and social networks that exist among them and between them and the larger systems of which the community is a part.

At a fundamental level, the individual capabilities that make up community capacity are contained within the community, but they must also incorporate connections to and commerce with the larger systems of which the community is a part. But what does a community "with capacity" look like? Part of the reason the question is difficult to answer has to do with

7

the many ways community has been defined and the range of goods and services it is expected to provide (Chaskin, 1997; Sampson, 1999). On the one hand, community refers to a geographical area that is recognizable by a set of attributes tied to its physical location or appearance, such as natural boundaries, a recognized history, demographic patterns, or the presence and work within it of particular industries or organizations. On the other hand, community refers to social attributes and interests—such as language, custom, class, or ethnicity—shared by inhabitants and commonly used to designate them as a collective entity, regardless of geographic proximity. Often the two dimensions are combined, especially in many older cities where patterns of immigration and settlement have created geographically distinct areas within which a unique set of sociological characteristics is also shared (see, for example, Golab, 1982; Massey, 1985; Portes and Manning, 1986). In common parlance, the term *community* is often used interchangeably with *neighborhood* to refer to a geographic area within which there is a set of shared interests or symbolic attributes. In the field of community building—the focus of our exploration here— policymakers and practitioners either assume that sufficient commonality of circumstance and identity exists within the geographic boundaries of neighborhoods to develop them further as "communities," or deliberately select places to work where this condition appears to exist.

Communities so defined may be differentiated in many ways and assumed to contain a wide array of qualities. They are functional units for the delivery (and sometimes production) of goods and services. They are often considered to be natural political units around which collective action may be mobilized. They provide a physical context of spaces, facilities, and patterns of interaction. They may serve as a source and a nexus for interpersonal networks and be recognized as units of identity and belonging for residents.

Given that they are defined, experienced, and used differently by different people, it is not surprising that local communities are also described in different ways. Whereas treatments of community often stress affective aspects of community solidarity, increased population mobility and ease of travel and communication across large distances have allowed relationships to extend far beyond the local community, and most intimate ties are no longer bound to the neighborhood (Freundenburg, 1986; Wellman, 1979). Increasingly, communities are forged less out of geographic propinquity than out of common interests or social activities that bring a group of individuals together over time. Casual and instrumental ties continue to operate at the local level, however, though these again are experienced differently by different people. Relatively affluent individuals and those who are more highly integrated into the larger society (by virtue of age, education, employment, marital status, and other such factors) also depend less on the local community to provide their daily needs. For those who are less affluent and less integrated (e.g., children, women with young children, the elderly, people of color), the neighborhood is likely to be a relatively important source of goods and services, as well as the locus of a smaller set of instrumental, more frequently engaged relationships (Ahlbrandt, 1984; Campbell and Lee, 1992; Lee, Campbell, and Miller, 1991; Lee, and Campbell, 1993). Where the necessary facilities, institutions, and services are not available, however, or where there are serious barriers to engaging in networks of relationships within the neighborhood (caused, for example, by a fear of crime and victimization), residents may seek to concentrate activity and connections *beyond* rather than *within* the neighborhood (Furstenberg, 1993).

Local communities are differentially endowed with resources that residents can draw on—for example, services, physical infrastructure, housing, jobs, education, and income. This differentiation often corresponds with patterns of residential segregation by race and class across communities (see, for example, Jargowsky, 1997; Massey and Denton, 1993; Massey and Eggers, 1990). Communities are also dynamic: They have been settled by successive waves of populations. They have been used for different purposes and in different ways by residents in different time periods. And they have been the focus of shifting levels and kinds of investment (or disinvestment) over time. As the character of any particular community changes—owing to changes in residential composition, in the nature and quality of goods and services provided, and in the physical environment, organizational infrastructure, and political connectedness of its inhabitants—the "capacity" of the community will also change.

Given that the use and experience of local communities varies in these ways—across space, population, and time—is it possible to think generically about community capacity? What is a community that "works"? Will such a place look the same in the suburbs as in the city, among the affluent as among the poor, in heterogeneous contexts as in homogeneous ones, or across neighborhoods dominated by different racial and ethnic groups? Does it make sense to speak of "capacity" in the singular, or are there varying capacities that communities may possess? Finally, given the heterogeneity of communities, how would attempts to build community capacity in different areas differ? How would they be similar? In the exploration that follows, we suggest a framework that we hope will be useful in answering these questions. We also examine a range of formal capacity-building efforts, using the framework to illustrate how these efforts generate capacity in their respective communities.

Focusing on these specific capacity-building efforts relieves some of the challenge posed by the diversity of community types, because variation among the types of neighborhoods targeted by such efforts is relatively narrow. These neighborhoods tend to be poor and largely communities of color. Despite their poverty, however, they tend to have a set of identifiable "assets" on which to draw. Indeed, capacity-building efforts have attempted to build on such assets as a way to develop a process for improving and sustaining the well-being of families, children, and institutions.

Given the relative importance of such neighborhoods to the daily lives of their residents and the relative paucity (not absence) of the resources within them, community capacity in these communities tends to involve a more intensive and ongoing engagement with local resources—resident volunteers, institutions, organizations, relationships—than might be the case in more affluent communities. Affluent individuals have a greater array of personal resources to draw on to satisfy their needs in the larger marketplace. In affluent neighborhoods, community capacity exists in the individuals and normative institutions that are resident (and that tend to be better endowed with their own resources, as well as better connected to external resources) but that are only occasionally roused to collective action in response to particular threats or emerging needs.

A DEFINITIONAL FRAMEWORK

The literature includes relatively few attempts to systematically conceptualize community capacity. Some definitions concerned with community building focus on local reserves of commitment, skills, resources, and problem-solving abilities, often connected to either a particular program or institution (see, e.g., Mayer, 1994; Aspen Institute, 1996). Other approaches emphasize the participation of individual community members in a process of relationship building, community planning, decision-making, and action (for example, Gittell, Newman, and Ortega, 1995; Eichler and Hoffman, n.d.; Goodman et al., 1998). In some treatments, the concept has been developed to apply narrowly within particular fields—for example, public health—or the productive and organizational capacities of community development corporations (CDCs) (for example, Glickman and Servon, 1998). In others, based on the literature on related constructs such as community competence and empowerment, community capacity has been defined generally as "the community's ability to pursue its chosen purposes and course of action" (Fawcett et al., 1995) or as the aggregate of individual and community-level "endowments" interacting with conditions in the environment that impede or promote success (Jackson et al., 1997). Capacity has also been constructed as a set of specified "assets" that exist within and among a community's individual members, local associations, and institutions (Kretzmann and McKnight, 1993).

The relative stress placed on various dimensions of community capacity differs in these approaches. Some focus largely on organizations and some on individuals; others focus on affective connections and shared values; and still others are concerned primarily with processes of participation and engagement. Taken together, however, these definitions of community capacity do suggest agreement on at least a few factors: (1) the existence of resources (ranging from the skills of individuals to the strengths of organizations to access to financial capital); (2) networks of relationships (sometimes stressed in affective terms, sometimes in instrumental terms); (3) leadership (not always precisely defined); and (4) support for vehicles through which community members participate in collective action and problem solving. Less often discussed in the literature—and less a matter of consensus—is how these factors relate to one another operationally, through what mechanisms they are engaged, toward what particular ends they may be harnessed, or what strategies are available to promote or build a community's capacity.

Our definitional framework is intended to be comprehensive. It treats community capacity as dynamic and multidimensional.[1] We build on the existing literature on community capacity, the broader literature on components of community functioning, and the perspectives of practitioners engaged in capacity-building efforts. Our hope is that, by specifying how strategic social action can engage and develop the components of capacity, we can help those sharing a practical interest in building community capacity to think more effectively about capacity in their own work and communities.

Our framework has several dimensions and specifies relations among them (see Figure 1). Three dimensions concern community capacity per se: its *fundamental characteristics*, the *levels of social agency* in which it is embedded and through which it may be engaged or enhanced, and its particular *functions*. The fourth dimension concerns the *strategies* that may intentionally promote community capacity. The fifth describes context—the *conditioning influences* that support or inhibit capacity or attempts to build it. And the sixth focuses on particular *community-level outcomes* that may be the goals of community initiatives or of communities exercising their capacity toward particular ends. (Each of these dimensions will be elaborated briefly below.) In short, the framework suggests that community capacity is exemplified by a set of core characteristics and operates through the agency of individuals, organizations, and networks of relations to perform particular functions. It also asserts that strategic interventions can build community capacity—again by operating through individuals, organizations, and networks to perform particular functions. The effect of such interventions will be conditioned by both micro- and macro-level contextual influences and, when successful, such processes may lead to both increased community capacity and other, more tangible community outcomes.

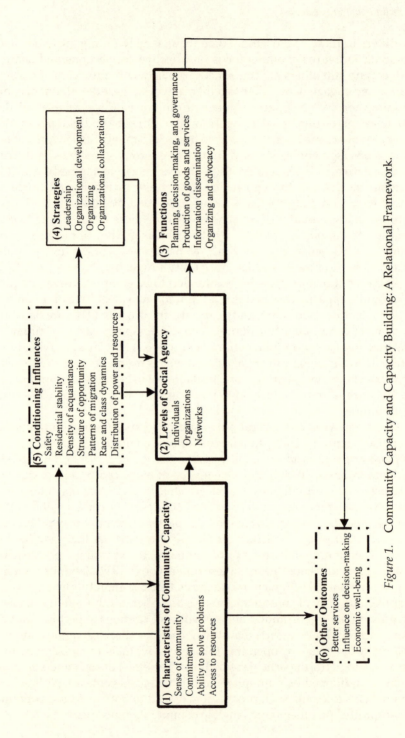

(5) Conditioning Influences
Safety
Residential stability
Density of acquaintance
Structure of opportunity
Patterns of migration
Race and class dynamics
Distribution of power and resources

(4) Strategies
Leadership
Organizational development
Organizing
Organizational collaboration

(3) Functions
Planning, decision-making, and governance
Production of goods and services
Information dissemination
Organizing and advocacy

(2) Levels of Social Agency
Individuals
Organizations
Networks

(1) Characteristics of Community Capacity
Sense of community
Commitment
Ability to solve problems
Access to resources

(6) Other Outcomes
Better services
Influence on decision-making
Economic well-being

Figure 1. Community Capacity and Capacity Building: A Relational Framework.

To elaborate, the dimensions of community capacity are related to each other in particular ways, and the individual components of each dimension can potentially have differential effects on one another. Thus, the characteristics of community capacity operate through one or more levels of social agency (Figure 1). For example, a "sense of community" (box 1) may be engendered at the network level (box 2) through the interaction of residents within informal relationships, and at the organizational level through the work of schools, community organizations, or businesses providing facilities and opportunities or sponsoring activities that promote interaction and exchange.

Similarly, activities that take place at one or another level of social agency can be geared to a particular function (box 3) and hence draw on community capacity with a specific aim in mind. If the aim is advocacy—for example, organizing the collective voice of the community to influence public policy around a particular issue—then problem solving that engages the commitment of residents and inspires a sense of community (box 1) can be activated through the involvement of individuals, networks, and organizations (box 2) toward that end.

A strategic approach (box 4) to building a community's capacity to respond in this way might involve community organizing in some fashion. But it might just as readily incorporate a leadership development component and seek to leverage the influence of local organizations, operating either independently or in some combination. Building and engaging community capacity for this particular purpose may in turn both enhance and sustain the community's ongoing capacity in other regards (box 1) and lead to other outcomes (box 6), such as influence on decision-making for the distribution of public resources that affect the community.

Finally, contextual factors (box 5) may promote or constrain the level of various aspects of community capacity, as well as the use to which it is put. The existence of a threshold level of safety within the neighborhood and a degree of residential stability and density of acquaintance among residents (which promotes knowledge, trust, and social interaction among them) is likely to support both a sense of community among residents and their access to mechanisms of problem solving (box 1) at different levels of agency (box 2). These factors enhance the likelihood that organizing strategies (box 4) will succeed. Enhanced organizing of the community, in turn, promotes the possibility of successful advocacy (box 3), helping the community gain the access to resources it needs (box 1), both within the neighborhood and beyond it in the systems it seeks to affect. If a threshold level of safety does not exist, however, or if residential mobility in and out of the neighborhood is high, successful collective mobilization may be more difficult to attain, since barriers of fear and potentially low levels of commitment will have to be overcome. Even in such cases, however, mobilization may be fostered in response to a clear and common problem or catalyzing agent, such as a shooting or incidence of racially motivated conflict.

Characteristics of Community Capacity

Overall capacity at the community level will be a function of the following characteristics that provide a foundation for action: (1) a sense of community; (2) commitment to the community among its members; (3) the ability to solve problems; and (4) access to resources. As we argue below, these characteristics exist along a continuum from less to more; different communities may have different levels of each, and the levels do not necessarily correlate with one another. That is, a community may have relatively little of one aspect of capacity (e.g., sense of community) and be relatively well endowed with another (e.g., access to resources). Although the existence of these characteristics is a matter of degree, threshold levels of some are probably necessary if the community is to accomplish particular objectives.

Sense of community reflects a degree of connectedness among members and a recognition of mutuality of circumstance, including a threshold level of collectively held values, norms, and vision (McMillan and Chavis, 1986). Although often described in affective terms, the existence of a sense of community may also be based largely on instrumental values—the recognition of shared circumstance based on investment (in housing stock, for example) or use (of a neighborhood school, park, etc.)—that allow people to come together in ways that support a common good (Crenshaw and St. John, 1989; Guest and Lee, 1983; Suttles, 1992).

Sense of community may vary by type and degree. For example, a community might "work" without a sense of community having any pronounced affective basis if the residents are able to draw on external resources. People in those circumstances may be bound together instead by instrumental ties. They might be involved together in constructing a park, reinvigorating dilapidated housing stock, addressing declining property values, or other efforts to resolve a problem or support a common good (Crenshaw and St. John, 1989; Guest and Lee, 1983; Suttles, 1972). Indeed, the sense of community shared by people in such a place may be quite impersonal, without real roots in concrete, everyday relationships with neighbors, family, and friends.

Areas of relative social disadvantage, in contrast, may be more likely to evidence a greater feeling of belonging and stronger ties of identity among residents (especially where other shared characteristics of the population draw them together), because hardship makes sharing and togetherness a matter of survival (see, for example, Stack, 1974). For example, in a community with endemic street gang activity and ineffective law enforcement services, residents may work with one another to provide safety. The scope of their relationships might expand to include a sense of investment in one another, fostering a more intimate association with their neighborhood. It should not be surprising, in other words, when residents exhibit a preference for and commitment to their community, despite its impoverishment (although this may not be the case in extremely poor communities or among the very poorest members of a community) (Briggs, Mueller, and Sullivan, 1997; Furstenberg, 1993). It may also be that a neighborhood does not possess the resources to allow this heightened sense of community to be translated into effective action, or residents may not be committed to act. Thus, a sense of belonging is never sufficient to produce a community that works; it must be joined by other characteristics of capacity. In the example given above, the long-term resolution of street gang conflict may depend on importing institutional resources from outside the community. Just working together may not be enough for residents to prevent conflicts, reintegrate youth into the community, or provide a permanent, more assured sense of safety in the neighborhood.

Commitment describes the responsibility that particular individuals, groups, or organizations take for what happens in the community. It has two essential aspects. The first is that community members see themselves as stakeholders in the collective well-being of the neighborhood; the second is the willingness of these members to participate actively as stakeholders. The distinction is an important one, as illustrated by one of our key informants, the director of a community-based organization:

> I think there's a difference between being a resident and being an active resident. . . . [People] have to be willing to invest themselves in some activity beyond just living from day to day. They've got to be willing to volunteer. They've got to be willing to help their neighbors. It could be as simple as helping your neighbor, as simple as helping an elderly person with their groceries or something. There's a sense then of community at that point that we're all in it together.

Those who participate in this way are generally a minority of the residents and often have somewhat higher socioeconomic status than most people in the neighborhood. They tend to have more active connections with local organizations (e.g., churches, youth centers), and they are frequently responding to some immediate issue, conflict, or crisis (Berry, Portney, and Thomson, 1993; Crenson, 1983). But the commitment to act may also be institutionalized within local organizations serving as vehicles for resident mobilization. These mediating institutions—from neighborhood associations to local service agencies to CDCs—organize resources for the local production of public goods and services and link residents with the broader systems of decision-making, production, and provision (see, for example, Berger and Neuhaus, 1977; Knoke and Wood, 1981; Logan and Rabrenovic, 1990; Williams, 1985).

The ability to solve problems—that is, to translate commitment into action—is an important component of virtually all definitions of community capacity, and was the element of community capacity most often stressed by key informants. In the words of one:

> I see a community's capacity as its own ability to take charge of and make decisions about what happens in the life of neighbors and residents in a community. In particular, in terms of people's own ability to impact funders and policymakers, as a collective group and not just individually.

Again, because communities are continually changing, how problems get solved can shift as communities evolve. Key individuals may leave, while organizations remain to take over their work. As institutions develop, the ability of a community to solve problems may no longer have to depend on the charisma or clout of any single individual. Most important is not the particular locus of a problem-solving mechanism, but that there are enough such mechanisms and that they function relative to the demand for them. They must also be able to endure or adapt over time, responding to or compensating for the impact of community change.

The final characteristic of a community with capacity is *access to resources*—economic, human, physical, and political—within and beyond the neighborhood. This represents the ability to make instrumental links with systems in the larger context (the city and region) and to access and leverage various types of resources located both inside and outside the neighborhood. Neighborhoods are embedded in the broader socioeconomic systems of the area around them, and their ability to achieve and maintain stable economic well-being depends largely on policy being made and implemented beyond their borders. Their well-being also depends on macrostructural developments taking place in the greater metropolitan area, such as the persistence of racial discrimination in the housing market or the massive loss of jobs due to industrial restructuring (see, for example, Jargowsky, 1997). However, there are also numerous resources within neighborhoods, including the skills and knowledge of individual residents, the commitment and activities of neighborhood associations, and the facilities and services of local institutions such as churches, schools, libraries, and community-based organizations. All of these resources can contribute to a community's capacity to address concerns and support the healthy functioning of its members (Kretzmann and McKnight, 1993).

The degree to which community capacity depends on instrumental linkages to resources outside the community is not a constant. It can vary according to the nature of the problem at hand, the demographics of the community, and the social and political organization of municipal and regional systems. As the following chapters illustrate, community capacity-building efforts face great challenges in trying to act on two fronts at once: striving to enhance the capacities of social and institutional actors locally while strengthening their relationships with actors outside the community. Especially for poor neighborhoods, which historically have been subjected to inequities in funding and services, enhancing internal capacities may not be sufficient to improve either the trajectory of neighborhood development or the quality of life of its residents. For example, the external sponsor of a capacity-building effort may be the linchpin of the initiative's success. But this may not become apparent until the funds are depleted, the program is over, and the now internally well-functioning community must try to replicate its ties to an external source of resources. In contrast, in a nonpoor neighborhood where residents are connected to broader networks through their own work and social life, engaging this existing capacity may be all that is required to accomplish a particular objective.

In capacity-building efforts such as those we are exploring here, the concept of a community's ties to the "outside" is usually defined broadly, without adequate differentiation among levels (municipality, region, nation) and types of external actors (corporations, governmental bodies, nongovernmental organizations). The resources a community can get through connections with private philanthropies or government agencies will differ in scope, intent, and the level of freedom or constraints placed on them. Also, engaging with local actors (private foundation or government) whose funding is targeted to a particular city will afford possibilities (and carry constraints) that differ from those of national funders. Communities of disadvantage tend to suffer from a lack of productive relationships with local agencies and organizations in their metropolitan region. Inadequate policing, sanitation, and transportation services, as well as poor economic development, are not without their national dimension. Often, however, such problems can be traced to inequities within the political sphere of the municipality, or the inability to address municipal inequities at the regional level. As will become apparent in our discussion in the following pages, community capacity-building efforts sponsored by national entities (federal government, private foundations) vary in their ability to cultivate relationships between local communities and citywide agencies and organizations.

The four characteristics of community capacity outlined above may exist to differing degrees in any particular community. A community need not possess a threshold level of *every* characteristic to be considered as having capacity. Consider, for example, a community in which a city council member lives. The council member may ensure that sanitation services are provided, that local businesses are vibrant, that parks and recreational spaces are adequate, and may be routinely available to aid neighbors as problems and concerns arise. A strong sense of belonging among members of the community may not exist in this scenario. Some of the population, such as students at a local university, may be transient and never develop a feeling of enduring attachment to the community. Commitment to the neighborhood may be minimal apart from the council member and a few select other residents who become involved in community affairs. In effect, we have endowed this fictitious community with only two of the characteristics of capacity: it has at least one method of solving problems—the council member, who also provides the community's primary tie to external resources. Does it have capacity?

The answer is probably yes and no. In the short run, the council member both fulfills a critical problem-solving function and serves as the necessary liaison to the wider world. Capacity concentrated in this way (in the work, influence, and political capital of a single person) has some advantages, although communities that rely exclusively on a single individual are rare (if they exist at all). Decisions can be made expediently and problems addressed efficiently without the need to convene community meetings or establish consensus. The trust invested in the individual—or simple indifference among the populace—may be the only mandate required. However, to the extent that the council member does not have the trust of the community, does not operate as its agent in addressing its concerns, or is not sufficiently accountable to it, what the council member is capable of producing in the community reflects less the community's capacity and more his or her own will and work.

Further, even if the council member is well connected and truly works on the community's behalf, in the long run the capacity he or she represents is unstable. If the council member leaves office or moves to a different part of town, the community's capacity will in all likelihood be reduced substantially. In contrast, potentially greater community capacity that is more sustainable over time may be found in a community in which many different people and organizations work for the well-being of inhabitants and actively mediate interactions with the broader society. The active commitment of one even relatively powerful person, while potentially sufficient to meet the community's needs in the short term, is likely to be less desirable over the long term than a widespread commitment that manifests in the ability of persons to recruit and engage others in their social network when needs arise.

The characteristics of community capacity in any given community may change over time. Capacity can be gained or lost. For example, communities may devise new problem-solving mechanisms (such as block clubs or community development corporations) to address particular concerns, or the arrival of new, energetic resident volunteers may revive existing organizations. Conversely, sense of commitment may diminish over time. For example, demographic changes may decrease residents' identification with their neighbors, or circumstances may improve in such a way that residents feel their active engagement is no longer needed, or residents may lose hope in the possibilities of community improvement.

The final point is in certain ways obvious, but it nevertheless merits attention. Maintaining community capacity in poor communities over time calls for continuous effort, and it can only be sustained through the work of community members. This labor has two aspects. It must be based on adequate communication and interaction among residents and organizations within the community, and a similar effort must be undertaken to strengthen ties between these actors and those in the wider world from which the community receives (material and symbolic) resources, services, and legitimation.

LEVELS OF SOCIAL AGENCY

Community capacity is engaged through varying combinations of three levels of social agency: individuals, organizations, and networks of association. These levels may also be points of entry for interventions such as training or leadership development, organizational development, or community organizing.

The *individual* level concerns human capital and leadership—the skills, knowledge, and resources of individual residents and their participation in community-improving activities. Investments in increasing the human capital of individuals can have significant influence on their ability to garner resources and improve their economic well-being, and the existence of human capital among a community's residents contributes to community capacity both through its availability as a collective resource and through specific, individual contributions. When individual community members use their human capital to act as change agents or to mobilize others and catalyze action, they exercise leadership.

The powerful city council member is one example of capacity operating through an individual. Another is the charismatic "informal" leader who could emerge from any of a number of places in a community. A church leader who mobilizes residents, a store owner who is active in media discussions about community problems, and a resident who attends city council meetings regularly are all instances of capacity grounded in individuals.

At the *organizational* level, community capacity operates through collective bodies, including community-based organizations (local business-

es, service providers, development organizations), local branches of larger institutions (banks, schools, major retail establishments), and smaller
organized groups (neighborhood and home owner associations, tenant
groups, and social clubs). Community capacity at this level is reflected in
the ability of such groups to carry out their functions responsively, effectively, and efficiently, connecting to larger systems, both within and
beyond the community, as appropriate. Criteria for assessing their "organizational capacity" may vary significantly from organization to organization, depending on the nature of the work involved (Scott, 1992). New
organizations are seen as mechanisms for creating community capacity;
criteria of organizational effectiveness are likely to go beyond a simple accounting of services provided or goods produced to incorporate issues of
constituent representation, political influence, and the ability of organizations to collaborate with one another (see, for example, Glickman and Servon, 1998).

Organizations can span the entire spectrum of formality. Many, including some neighborhood associations and economic development organizations, are legally incorporated. Some have broad name recognition and
may have received the "stamp of approval" from local governments, structured initiatives, or established funding sources to act as agents of the community. Other organizations may be far less formal, and virtually invisible
to the casual observer. These include block clubs, senior citizen social
groups, and card-playing and gambling associations that may come together in more formal ways only when circumstances dictate. Thus, the organizational resources of a community may not be fully visible until a
particular exigency requires them to change their guise and adopt a more
visible public presence.

Finally, at the *network* level, community capacity works through relationships among individuals, informal groups, and formal organizations.
Among individuals, networks of positive social relations that provide a
context of trust and support and that represent access to resources (information, connections, money) are known as "social capital" (Coleman,
1988; Putnam, 1993). The notion of social capital can be extended to relations among associational groups (block clubs, tenants' associations) and
more formal organizations, with each organization operating as a "node"
within the network. Such an infrastructure of relationships provides individual organizations with greater access to resources and a socially defined
context—normative rules and expectations among member organizations—that informs decision-making within organizations and helps
structure relations among them (DiMaggio and Powell, 1983; Laumann,
Galaskiewicz, and Mardsen, 1978; Powell and Friedkin, 1987).

Network ties differ in scope, strength, function, and use, and they are
not evenly distributed among actors (Mitchell, 1969). Two aspects of local

networks are particularly important influences on community capacity. One concerns the degree of network closure—the extent to which people know the people who know you. This is particularly important in supporting informal mechanisms of social control and support; youth, for example, are less likely to engage in delinquent behavior if their actions are likely to be reported to their parents, and watchful neighbors who know their circumstances are more likely to be able and willing to lend informal help. The second has to do with what are often called "weak ties"—casual or instrumental rather than intimate bonds—which can connect individuals to networks of association held by others and thereby provide access to information, resources, influence, and opportunities beyond their networks of close association. In poor communities, ties to relationships beyond the neighborhood are often particularly important. People or organizations that operate at the points of connection among different networks are able to wield significant influence and power within the community. They are often better able to negotiate transactions because they have greater access to timely information, greater control over information, and a better chance to take advantage of opportunities as they arise (Burt, 1992; Knoke, 1990; Laumann, Galaskiewicz, and Mardsen, 1978).

In practical terms, community capacity will probably always operate at more than one level of social agency at a time. Even in our hypothetical community with a single influential council member, we would find organizations, peer networks, and residents showing an active interest in the community's welfare. Conversely, even in very democratic settings, where community capacity functions largely through the broad involvement of individuals and organizations, it is often possible to find particularly charismatic people helping to disseminate information, motivate residents to action, and create consensus so that action can occur.

Some communities may be particularly well endowed with effective individuals working on behalf of the community, whereas others may have productive organizations and social groups. However, each illustrates the existence or building of *community* capacity only as far as it is connected to a collective agenda or to the realization of collective well-being at the community level. When this happens, the different levels of agency can be seen as the vehicles through which community capacity operates.

Consider, for instance, a high-rise public housing development as an example of a community of extreme social and economic disadvantage. In such a place, there may be few organizations beyond a tenant management board. Social networks may be strong, however, rooted primarily in ties among individuals and households where intricate systems of sharing and support have already been developed (see Stack, 1974). In a nonpoor community, such interpersonal and interhousehold networks may also exist. But that situation might differ from its disadvantaged counterpart in that the networks may not be directly involved in the realization of a collective goal. They may simply be used for friendship and peer support. In the public housing development, such networks might be routinely mobilized for rent strikes, protests, fund-raising for crime victims or evictees, and so on. A capacity-building intervention in such a setting, if it wins the confidence of residents, might succeed in using these survival networks as building blocks for broader action.

It is also possible for a particular characteristic of community capacity to be engaged simultaneously through different levels of social agency. For example, commitment may function through individuals (the block club captain, the neighbor who watches over kids playing in the street) and organizations (the social club that provides small loans to members, the CDC that leverages resources for local development). Similarly, mechanisms for problem solving need not be grounded in charismatic or influential individuals but may also exist in networks and politically powerful organizations.

Functions of Community Capacity

The third dimension of community capacity is function—the particular work that capacity enables a community to perform. In any community, individuals, organizations, and networks may fulfill many different needs. The functional dimension of the framework speaks to the *intent* of engaging specific characteristics (box 1) through particular levels of social agency (box 2) to perform specialized functions (box 3) such as planning and governance, the production of goods and services (such as housing or job training and placement), or informing, organizing, and mobilizing residents toward collective action. These functions lead to two kinds of outcomes: an increase in sustainable community capacity overall (box 1) and the achievement of specific other desired community conditions (box 6).

Community capacity may be engaged toward many different ends.[2] It may be called upon to perform normative functions, such as promoting shared values, socializing the young, or providing mechanisms of informal social control. Or it may be directed toward more specialized functions, such as controlling gang recruitment or promoting job development. In other words, the tasks may be routine, focusing on everyday maintenance and processes, or they may be driven by extraordinary needs and circumstances. Routine and specialized functions are deeply interrelated. Often in striving for the former, community-building activities will focus largely on the latter. Thus, a community that is trying to maintain control of the daily behavior of its youth (a routine function) may find itself collectively mobilizing to ensure adequate city park development or school funding (a specialized function).

In poorer communities, the weakness (or even absence) of institutions that perform basic everyday functions is one of the most telling signs that capacity is weak. For example, residents may be concerned that the neighborhood lacks safe play areas for children. If it has a variety of mechanisms for problem solving, the community will likely be able to galvanize successful action, either by developing a new mechanism (e.g., a task force) or by having one or more established institutions (such as the PTA or a coalition of churches) address this newly activated issue. In contrast, a community with few organizational resources—or with organizations that lack a track record of translating ideas into action—may never make headway on the identified problem. Helping this community realize its objectives is likely to require more than advocating for increased parks expenditures or refurbishing physical spaces; it will require investments in the capacity of the community to identify priorities and pursue a course of action.

Other Outcomes

As mentioned previously, the functions of community capacity (see Figure 1) lead to two kinds of outcomes. One is an increase in sustainable community capacity overall. The other is the achievement of other valued outcomes such as better services, greater influence on public policy decision-making, or more vibrant local commercial districts. These two kinds of outcomes are generated spontaneously through the normal dynamics of community capacity in communities that work: particular characteristics of community capacity (box 1) are engaged through levels of social agency (box 2) to perform particular functions (box 3) that, in turn, achieve specific goals (box 6), as well as build the overall capacity of the community (box 1).

Conditioning Influences

This element of the framework concerns those *mediating* circumstances that may facilitate or inhibit the development of community capacity and intentional efforts to build it. The development of community capacity never takes place in a vacuum. The processes of building community capacity operate within larger contexts—at the neighborhood level and beyond. These contexts include factors (box 5) that can influence the extent to which community capacity exists, as well as the potential to engage community capacity toward a chosen end.

It is clear, for example, that certain circumstances tend either to support or thwart the development of a sense of community in any particular neighborhood (Chavis and Wandersman, 1990). Residential stability is one such factor. Stability increases acquaintance networks, which in turn support a sense of social cohesion and enhance the likelihood that people will participate in local activities (Sampson, 1988, 1991). In addition, the existence of informal mechanisms of social control and a threshold-level sense of safety, again connected to stability and the existence of viable social networks, provide a framework within which a sense of community can more easily be fostered (Bursik and Grasmick, 1993; Sampson, 1999; Skogan, 1986).

Mediating circumstances may be located within the geographic boundaries of the community. Fundamental among these is the need for "safe space" or a "system of safety" within communities. This was often cited by our key informants as fundamental to promoting or inhibiting the growth or engagement of community capacity. In the words of one:

> To the extent that people feel unsafe, they become imprisoned in their homes and will not let anyone else in their home. . . . That sense of personal safety or that threat to personal safety is a disconnection from everybody else. At the same time, if you have no safe space because schools are closed at three o'clock and recreation centers are nonexistent—so there are no places for people to congregate to get to know each other, to discuss, to exchange, to argue, to debate—I think those things militate against your helping a low-capacity community move toward an enhanced-capacity community.

In much the same way, macrostructural factors—such as the structure of economic opportunity in the region, the influences of migration and racial segregation, or the unequal distribution of resources among neighborhoods—may constrain a community's ability to organize effectively or gain access to resources from systems intended to serve and support it (see, for example, Jargowsky, 1997; Teitz, 1989). In many urban areas, plant closings or sharp rises in unemployment have had a dramatic impact on local neighborhoods. When such events occur, capacity-building efforts are likely to have to be altered immediately, since the possibilities for residents to show interest and commitment have changed. Alternatively, conditioning influences can change for the better, such as when the regional economy expands. In these situations, opportunities arise for capacity-building efforts to draw on resources that were not previously available.

Power relationships, another important conditioning factor, generate strong undercurrents of influence that operate at many levels. Some power relations are macrostructural, such as political clout that may be skewed to certain ethnic, age, or income groups. Others may work at the level of daily social interaction, such as a lack of familiarity with the culture and language of bureaucratic institutions on the part of socially isolated constituencies.

Community capacity-building initiatives have little control over these larger systemic conditions, and it is unreasonable to place the burden of changing systemic inequities wholly on these efforts. However, the initiatives vary in the degree to which they take such factors into account in their work. A good understanding of regional economic shifts, segregation patterns, and other conditioning factors can influence the strategic directions taken by capacity-building initiatives, as well as the relationships they develop with community residents and other actors. For these reasons, we will try to emphasize the relationship between conditioning factors and the initiatives we examine, in terms of both setting the context for these capacity-building efforts and seeing how these initiatives affect broader structures and processes.

STRATEGIES FOR BUILDING COMMUNITY CAPACITY

In communities that work well, community capacity is relatively reinforced by the continual interactions of its three fundamental dimensions. In communities that work less well, or that face greater barriers because of resource or power inequities, capacity may be enhanced by intervention strategies that work through various combinations of the three dimensions both to increase community capacity overall and to achieve specific valued outcomes such as better services. These strategies constitute the different ways in which communities can work intentionally to increase their ability to maintain and improve the well-being of their members, respond to changing circumstances, and achieve collective goals.

Community capacity-building efforts tend to focus on some combination of four major strategies (box 4). *Leadership development* centers on the skills, commitment, engagement, and effectiveness of individuals in the community-building process. *Organizational development* includes the creation of new organizations or the strengthening of existing ones so they can do their work better or take on new roles. *Community organizing* targets the associational aspects of community functioning and the mobilization of individual stakeholders for particular collective ends. Finally, *interorganizational collaboration* builds the organizational infrastructure of communities through the development of relationships and collaborative partnerships on the organizational level.

Often, these four strategies are brought together under the umbrella of some sort of local governance mechanism, which guides initiative planning and implementation and tends to take on the more expansive role of speaking for and acting on behalf of the neighborhood (Chaskin and Garg, 1997). Capacity-building efforts may adopt a largely programmatic approach (job training and placement, structuring access to financial opportunities) or a more procedural one (voter registration, block club organizing). Efforts may operate through any of a number of mechanisms, including informal social processes (such as voluntary self-help networks); organized, community-based programs and processes (such as the work of community-based organizations and associations); or formal, targeted programs (such as externally catalyzed community-building initiatives). The strategies employed by these efforts to build community capacity are the subject of the remainder of this book.

CONCLUSION

We have defined community capacity as having four community-level characteristics (sense of community, commitment, mechanisms of problem solving, and access to resources) that operate through three levels of social agency (individuals, organizations, and networks) to exercise some set of particular functions (e.g., planning, collective decision-making, advocacy, production). Efforts to build community capacity seek to enhance the way communities operate in some or all of these dimensions through strategic intervention that aims both to increase community capacity overall and to achieve other specific outcomes within the targeted community—better services, greater influence on policy, increased economic well-being, and so forth. The existence of baseline capacity, as well as the effect of strategic approaches to build it, will be influenced by various conditioning factors such as the state of the regional economy or the quality of local race relations.

In the chapters that follow, we will explore the four major strategic approaches to building community capacity with reference to a variety of empirical examples. This exploration will illustrate how community capacity building is being addressed in practice. It will bring to light some of the assumptions that drive such practice and highlight emerging lessons about its implementation, possibilities, and limitations. We hope that together, our definitional framework and empirical explorations prove useful to researchers and practitioners striving to advance the theory and practice of building community capacity.

NOTES

1. A version of the definitional framework outlined here can be found in Chaskin (forthcoming).
2. In this sense, the functional dimension of capacity is not parallel to the other two dimensions; they are defined as each having a specified list of elements, whereas the functions of capacity listed in the model and discussed here are illustrative.

2

Leadership Development

Leaders are a core component of a community's capacity. They facilitate and give direction to the work of community organizations. They initiate activities that provide cultural, educational, recreational, and other opportunities for community residents to enjoy themselves and strengthen community identity. They advocate for community interests and catalyze the formation of informal groups to address emerging problems or capitalize on opportunities. The more active leaders a community has, the richer the body of activities the community can support.

Leadership development focuses primarily on individuals. It typically attempts to engage the participation and commitment of current and potential leaders, provide them with opportunities for building skills, connect them to new information and resources, enlarge their perspectives on their community and how it might change, and help them create new relationships. Leadership development often enhances the human capital of the individuals involved, but differs from conventional formulations of human capital development in being more focused: it attends to the subset of individual capacities that enable leaders and would-be leaders to become more effective in performing leadership functions, tapping appropriate sources of legitimacy, and engaging in the relationships that accompany leadership roles.

Leadership development is frequently embedded in other types of community capacity-building strategies that we will explore (community organizing, organizational development, and organizational collaboration) and has logical overlaps with them. Community-organizing efforts often seek out individuals with leadership potential and provide them with formal training, as well as opportunities to test and hone various skills that leaders need. In doing so, these organizing efforts are engaged in leadership development. To the extent that it focuses on the senior staff and board members of community-based organizations (CBOs), leadership development overlaps with organizational development. Efforts to promote collaboration among existing organizations may require leaders to develop

27

new capabilities for dealing with problems and organizational processes more complex than those encountered before. Such efforts are likely to include leadership development in a supporting role.

This chapter, however, focuses on community interventions in which leadership development is a central thrust. The chapter begins by considering the meaning of leadership, what leaders do, and how the community context shapes expectations about leadership. It then examines the range of strategies used to develop community leaders and discusses the relative merits of each strategy. The chapter next analyzes some of the thorny implementation issues that often arise in leadership development efforts. It concludes by returning to the definitional framework in Figure 1 to illustrate how and under what circumstances leadership development enhances community capacity.

THE MEANING OF LEADERSHIP

Leadership is fundamentally a *relational* construct. John Gardner emphasizes the seemingly obvious (but sometimes overlooked or forgotten) fact that "the most important thing to have in mind is that leaders need followers" (Gardner, 1990). The *Handbook of Leadership* (an encyclopedic review and synthesis of the vast literature on leadership) provides a useful definition:

> Leadership is an interaction between two or more members of a group that often involves a structuring or restructuring of the situation and the perceptions and expectations of the members. Leaders are agents of change—persons whose acts affect other people more than other people's acts affect them. Leadership occurs when one group member modifies the motivation or competencies of others in the group. . . . [It entails] the directing of attention of other members to goals and the paths to achieve them. . . . Effective leadership [is] the interaction among members of a group that initiates and maintains improved expectations and the competence of the group to solve problems or to attain goals. (Bass, 1990:19)

Within the context of building community and strengthening community capacity, what do leaders do? Often, individuals are viewed as leaders because they formally head an organization—the principal of a school or the pastor of a church, for example. Many people think about leaders as individuals who are "in charge" or who "get things done." More formally, leaders are said to mobilize a constituency and catalyze action. Devising effective leadership development strategies, however, requires a more detailed understanding of what leaders *actually do* to accomplish these things.

The literature on leadership is extensive, and observers and authors from different contexts and vantage points have described the central aspects of what leaders do in diverse ways.[1] A distillation of some of this work suggests that leaders do the following:[2]

Define Objectives and Maintain Goal Direction.   This is often described, especially in community-building settings, as articulating a vision. It is part of the task of motivating group members, thus providing an impetus to work hard, try again after disappointment, and risk engaging in new activities and unfamiliar roles. It is also the task of keeping the group "on track," for example, reminding members of a working group that their discussion has strayed from the agenda.

Provide and Maintain Group Structure.   This can mean maintaining a formal structure, such as a board with officers and committees. But even very informal groups have a role structure that enables the group to function smoothly. Leaders reinforce those roles but can also modify them if doing so will improve the group's well-being. For example, a leader may be instrumental in facilitating the inclusion and acceptance of new members by assigning or suggesting particular roles to them.

Facilitate Group Action and Task Performance.   Groups form and endure for a reason. Leaders facilitate constructive interaction among members to ensure that the group accomplishes its aims. Therefore, leaders need to have "people and process skills." For example, the head of a tenants' association may chat with other residents in the hallways to build support for a gardening project. Resolving conflicts and managing the structure and pace of the group's work are also important aspects of this part of the leader's job.

Represent the Group to External Actors.   This may entail representing the group or its constituents in a governance sense, and it is often an important activity of individuals who head community organizations that participate in comprehensive community initiatives (CCIs) or other systems-change interventions. But it also includes the more common task of serving as a group's main point of contact with key external agents and agencies. The president of the PTA, for instance, is this group's link to the school principal and the community at large.

Facilitate Adaptive Work.   This task is critical when the group faces problems that cannot be solved through familiar structures and strategies, and when solving the problem requires the group as a whole to find new structures, strategies, and behaviors. For example, an informal group formed to oppose construction of a garbage transfer station in a neighborhood experiencing numerous problems—such as low-quality housing—

may consider whether to disband, to adopt a new cause, or formalize its existence and take on a broader community improvement mission.

The community context for this discussion of leadership and leadership development is critical. Much of what has been written about leadership and much of the way people think and talk about leaders and leadership assume very different contexts—for example, national politics (Queen Elizabeth I, Franklin D. Roosevelt), social movements (Gandhi, Martin Luther King, Jr.), large corporations (John D. Rockefeller, Lee Iacocca), or the military (Alexander the Great, General George Patton). Those contexts and the types of issues and problems implicit in them provide examples that are not particularly helpful in a community context. They suggest a focus on men (and occasionally women) who are "great," somehow larger than life.

But community capacity–building efforts are not seeking to discover and groom the next Abraham Lincoln or Winston Churchill. Rather, they seek to bolster the ranks of local individuals who are willing and able to assume some responsibility for the community's well-being by being "out front" to initiate and facilitate action. In so doing, these efforts presume that most neighborhoods include enough people with adequate leadership capacity and interest to make the community function well *if* they can be identified, engaged, encouraged, trained, and supported. For people used to thinking about leadership in the "great man" tradition, this may sound strange. But most communities appear to function reasonably well by relying on the efforts of ordinary people—moms and dads, shopkeepers, clergy, school principals, home owners, tenant activists, elected representatives, and so forth—who take responsibility for the day-to-day activities that support community life.

Leadership is a contextual construct in more ways than one. People play different roles in different settings. The person who chairs a community-based organization board, for example, may be just another parent participating in the PTA. Even in the same setting, roles shift and are exchanged in different cases for different purposes; a collaborative member in one Neighborhood and Family Initiative (NFI)[3] site was fond of a T-shirt that read "I'm a Leader" on the front and on the back "I'm a Follower." Thus, the chair may take the lead in setting a board's direction in most instances, but the group may defer to another member who has acknowledged technical skills and expertise on a particular issue (e.g., law, finance), who is viewed as being wise about how to handle certain kinds of problems (e.g., dealing with the diplomatic legacy of an old political battle), or who is seen to have legitimacy to speak on behalf of a particular constituency (e.g., public housing residents or a particular ethnic community). Thus, the various members of the board exercise leadership in varying degrees and under varying circumstances.

STRATEGIES FOR BUILDING LEADERSHIP

Efforts to develop leadership may focus on one or more strategic approaches that attempt to harness and build the community capacity that resides largely in individuals and their relationships. Differences among these strategies generally result from basic choices in two key dimensions: process (formal training or informal learning "on the job") and target (individuals or groups).

Formal Training versus "On-the-Job" Engagement Strategies?

Some efforts to strengthen community leadership are explicitly labeled *leadership training programs*, whereas others seek to cultivate leadership talents and behaviors while participants engage in other activities. *Training* is structured to convey information, build confidence, or cultivate particular skills. In contrast, *engagement* approaches bring people together to learn "on the job" while working on activities that benefit the community. The differing strengths and weaknesses of the two strategies lead to their being used in combination in a variety of ways.

Training Strategies.   Training strategies are direct attempts to build the skills of individuals or groups of individuals. Their aim in a community capacity–building context is to enhance participants' ability and commitment to engage in community activities and use their skills to improve the quality of neighborhood life. Leadership training programs typically focus on one or more of the following:

• Information dissemination, in which classes or other vehicles inform participants about such matters as community conditions (both problems and assets), how other communities have handled similar issues, or how city government works.
• Personal empowerment / self-esteem building, in which training focuses on strengthening confidence, self-knowledge, and self-presentation.
• Building skills useful for civic participation, which may include instrumental skills (writing, organizing, public speaking, finding and analyzing information), as well as process skills (running meetings, solving problems collectively, navigating a city bureaucracy).
• Cultivating behaviors and perspectives specifically tailored to performing leadership roles, either informally or formally, which might include teaching adult leaders of youth groups how to integrate the principles of positive youth development into their activities and informal interactions with young people; helping heads of organizations to "think smart" about organizational strategy; or sensitizing participants to the process skills

needed to create a climate in which a group can find new ways to think or act in order to address significantly different or complex problems.

Training approaches have a number of advantages. Compared with engagement approaches, training approaches are well defined and structured. They are an efficient way to transfer information and build specific instrumental skills and are relatively straightforward to plan and manage. And because the four types of training listed above can be offered either singly or in varied combinations, training can readily be tailored to suit the needs of particular clients or localities.

Training programs vary in intensity. More intensive programs can provide broader and more extensive training, but they place greater demands on participants in terms of both time and, often, money. Programs also vary in the degree to which they emphasize individual growth or focus on participants' leadership roles in particular organizations, as illustrated by the following three examples.

The NFI collaborative in Memphis adopted a leadership development approach that focused on basic skills. The collaborative's program, called Leadership Orange Mound, offers a series of training classes in which a cohort (or "class") of neighborhood residents convene periodically over a twelve-week period. The sessions focus on providing basic information on neighborhood and city resources and processes for addressing issues (e.g., agencies responsible for particular services, numbers to call to file a complaint) and on developing particular skills (e.g., organizing a community event, running a meeting).

Neighborhood Leadership Cleveland (NLC), a program of the Center for Neighborhood Development at Cleveland State University and the Greater Cleveland Neighborhood Centers Association, is somewhat more intensive, and its training is more customized to the interests of individual participants. NLC uses speakers and workshops to provide information on issues, such as homelessness or crime, that participants identify as important to them, as well as on available resources such as neighborhood data technology. NLC staff work with participants to develop their individual goals for the next year and help them implement those goals, even after the training session has ended. This might be done one-on-one or through the Neighborhood Forum, a group of NLC graduates who regularly meet to network and share information and experiences. Like Leadership Orange Mound, NLC positions participants to engage more effectively in whatever group setting they choose.

Kansas City Neighborhood Alliance (KCNA), an organization that seeks to support community development through a combination of home ownership training, the development of rental housing, and leadership training, offers a more intensive program that seeks to increase the capacity of members of the city's numerous neighborhood associations. The alliance's nine-month LeaderShip training program works to develop a "critical mass" of trained neighborhood leaders who can effectively plan and implement projects that will strengthen their neighborhoods. Weekend classes are designed for members of legally incorporated groups that have completed a successful community project, so they have some experience in which to ground their training.

KCNA limits each session to four to six groups, with five people from the same neighborhood association in each group. This arrangement keeps the session to a manageable number and ensures that each group has enough members to do the amount of work required.

KCNA's program blends all four of the training approaches listed earlier as it walks groups through the process of creating an organizational strategic plan. The training is designed to build both individual skills (such as networking and stress management) and group skills (such as team building and cooperation). It provides structured opportunities for groups to think about their organization's vision and the importance of thinking and acting strategically on an ongoing basis. It seeks to build confidence and self-esteem by requiring regular presentations to the other participants. And it provides information about other KCNA programs and resources that are available to help participants implement their strategic plans. The program director cites word-of-mouth publicity as the major source of applications and a primary indicator of the program's usefulness.

Some features that make training an attractive option, however, also contribute to its limitations. In particular, self-contained training can be difficult to link to ongoing community change efforts. In Milwaukee, for example, the NFI collaborative developed a different kind of leadership development class (the Development Shop) focused less on information dissemination and training in particular skills and more on self-presentation and self-esteem building. It did not contribute much to the community's capacity because it did not connect newly trained "leaders" to the broader community development activities of the collaborative. In fact, as a result of an attempt to turn this program into an income-generating activity for the collaborative, neighborhood residents (many of whom could not afford the training) ultimately comprised only a small proportion of participants.

Engagement Strategies.   Engagement approaches can be divided into two broad types: (1) structured participation in *policy processes* (e.g., planning, governance, decision-making), and (2) direct involvement in *program work*. In both cases, leadership is developed mainly through the process of "doing something" rather than through formal training. Process issues commonly receive heavy emphasis (relative to direct transfer of skills and information), especially early in the intervention.

Collaborative governance, such as that employed in the NFI sites, is a prime example of strategic participation in *policy processes*. Although the details differ from place to place, each of the NFI collaboratives brought together a combination of recognized city leaders, heads of organizations serving the target neighborhood, and neighborhood residents with no formal positions of authority. This group was charged with establishing a governance structure for the initiative, planning what should be done, and setting policy about implementation priorities and agents.[4] Establishing working governance structures and developing strategic plans typically took several years, since the initiative placed full responsibility for providing structure on the participants themselves.

Although this approach was problematic for the NFI collaboratives in several ways (discussed later), collaborative members—particularly residents—gained skills, knowledge, and connections through their involvement. Skills in problem solving, strategic planning, and meeting facilitation developed as residents assumed progressively greater responsibility for collaborative planning and oversight activities, such as serving as committee chairs, making presentations for funders and at public forums, and coordinating or directing collaborative-sponsored projects. In some cases, residents developed technical knowledge about development practices, such as loan fund management in Milwaukee, and familiarity with the opportunities and requirements entailed in receiving funds from public programs, such as the Job Training Partnership Act (JTPA) in Detroit and Hartford. Finally, some residents acquired valuable personal relationships and influence with corporate executives, high-level city officials, or other people in positions of power. The number of individuals who benefited in this way was small, but their engagement in collaborative governance opened important new opportunities for them and increased their involvement in community activity.

The Consensus Organizing Demonstration Program (CODP), in which volunteer members of each CDC board played a hands-on role in developing real estate projects, illustrates an intensive form of the hands-on engagement approach in grounded *program work*. Start-up activities (establishing a governance structure and completing a neighborhood plan) were highly structured by CODP, so most CDCs completed them fairly rapidly (within about six months after the neighborhoods were selected). Volunteers devoted the bulk of their time and energy to actually "doing development." Board members in each neighborhood were responsible for doing all the planning work for the initial development of the projects, including investigating the ownership of prospective sites, conducting marketing surveys, and learning about and applying for various types of funding. They also negotiated the purchase of properties, selected architects and contractors, supervised their work, and marketed the housing units constructed. This demanding but carefully structured set of activities pressed volunteers to gather and assimilate new information about their community and the development process, learn and practice new skills (both process and technical), articulate and solve problems together, and interact with external agencies (mortgage companies, city community development departments) that were initially unfamiliar to most volunteers. But this was done as part of the core task of moving the real estate projects forward.

A second program-work approach operates through *staff recruitment* strategies, in which residents serve as paid staff or are trained as volunteers, ultimately to assume staff responsibilities. This approach may rely heavily on technical assistance (TA) or may include tactics such as "parallel staffing," in which a community resident, for example, may serve as costaff with a professional (e.g., an "executive on loan") who is expected to serve for a transitional period only, until the job can be accomplished by the apprentice. Alternatively, it may rely more on coaching, focusing on such skills as assessing complex situations and developing strategies and tactics rather than emphasizing more technical aspects of the leadership role. The line between coaching and TA, however, tends to blur, especially in practice, so many cases are actually a mix of the two strategies.

Relative Advantages and Disadvantages.   Engagement strategies for leadership development have some distinct advantages. Most obviously, an engagement approach allows an intervention to make a more immediate connection to a community capacity–building agenda. Participants gather information and build skills when these are needed for community-related work; this connection to a specific need boosts motivation for learning. If effectively managed to assure that residents experience success (especially early in the intervention), active involvement also gradually builds trust and confidence among group members, which makes their work go more smoothly and helps them weather setbacks and mistakes.

For example, the volunteer board members of each new CDC in the CODP initiative became engaged very early in planning and conducting a town meeting to introduce their CDC to the community and elicit community input about what the group's priorities should be. A formal session on how to conduct a community meeting might have helped some groups (or individual volunteers) avoid wasting time or hold a more "professional" meeting (and, in this sense, be more efficient). But for most groups, the benefits of learning by doing went beyond the topic-specific information and skills of planning, publicizing, and conducting a public meeting. Volunteers began to learn how to work together as well as to increase their understanding of community concerns. They learned they already had skills important for the success of their work. They gained legitimacy in the community and confidence in themselves and one another. And they began construction of a visible, shared record of accomplishment.

The engagement approach also has the virtue of being much better suited than formal classes to adult styles of learning; lessons are usually better internalized by participants and hence last longer. This approach also provides group members with a shared set of experiences and, over time, a history that can be referred back to as a way of reinforcing lessons learned earlier, sometimes in very powerful ways. For example, about a year after CODP began, Palm Beach County staff informed the CDCs that their planned projects were ineligible for Community Development Block Grant (CDBG) and HOME subsidies, in effect making the projects infeasible as affordable housing. Faced with this threat to the success of their primary activity, the CDCs decided for the first time to work together. With help from CODP staff, the CDC presidents mobilized key supporters and ultimately succeeded in getting the county's policy changed. This victory taught the volunteers, especially the CDC presidents, an important early lesson about the value and power of collective action (exactly the type of lesson commonly produced by leadership development done in a community-organizing context, discussed in the next chapter). When CODP ultimately ended and CDCs faced the choice of whether to form a coalition or to continue independently, the memory of this victory had an important influence on their decision to unite.

Engagement strategies can also create situations in which group members can work together *as a unit* to create something—a vision, a strategy, an agreement, a shared understanding, or an organizational format—that enables the group to move forward in a new way. (Although individuals sometimes have a personal "breakthrough" or other moving learning experience in a training situation, it is unusual for an entire group to do so.) In the early phases of a capacity-building intervention, those responsible for implementing the initiative may have to create opportunities for doing this type of group work. As indigenous leaders gain new skills, they can be groomed or coached to assume responsibility for this role.

For example, the leadership development approach MDC uses commonly (as it did with Vision to Action in the Glades) facilitates this kind of development. MDC is a nonprofit intermediary organization in North Carolina with significant experience in community planning. In their work, community members from various walks of life met in periodic retreats over a number of months to analyze their community and develop a shared vision for its future development. Initially, the trainers facilitated the group's work, helping to create a "safe" setting in which diverse individuals could share experiences, ideas, and information about themselves. Since they were selected so the group would encompass the community's various racial, ethnic, and economic diversity, the group members came to understand one another in the context of the personalized histories of these various segments of the community. The skills they acquired, the knowledge they developed, and the strategies they crafted for effecting change were grounded in this common bond; together, these qualities position them to act with greater insight than the planning activities alone would yield. They continue to function, both individually and together, as change agents with shared values and a common vision.

The advantages of engagement approaches come at a price, however: they are much more challenging to implement than training activities. They typically involve substantial numbers of people, many (sometimes most) of whom have little or no experience working together or have not even met one another previously. Participants often have limited prior experience working on community revitalization, and the work takes place in the field, rather than in a controlled setting (such as a classroom or training facility). Because of this, those responsible for implementing the intervention have less consistent ability to assure that the group enjoys the sort of "safe space" that trainers commonly create in a classroom to facilitate openness, risk taking, and experimentation with new viewpoints. External events in the target community, such as a local crisis (e.g., a shooting) or sudden shift in policy (e.g., welfare reform), proceed in ways that may intrude on the initiative—with or without warning—while lying outside its influence. Finally, the intervention is "real" in a way that formal training typically is not, and participants correctly perceive the stakes to be higher. This perception tends to make them more wary and cautious.

The difficulty of implementing engagement approaches has implications for participants' substantive learning. Their ability to gain information, learn process skills, become more self-confident, and develop positive relationships with one another is largely a product of direct engagement that participants perceive as successful (i.e., positive, constructive, part of a process that is likely to lead to valued outcomes). Given the number of participants, the difficulty of their work, and the complexity of the context, "successful" on-the-job leadership development depends directly on the initiative's success in planning for implementation and managing a dynamic process in which "many balls are in the air" at the same time.

The contrasting experiences of two Palm Beach County CDCs created through CODP illustrate the potential benefits and problems of engagement strategies. The first public activity for each newly formed CDC was a "town meeting" in which the board members (in effect, self-appointed leaders seeking validation from the community) introduced themselves and their goals and solicited input from community residents. This is a relatively straightforward task, but CODP's expectations for it were high, and doing it well was a complex task. Pleasant City CDC held the first town meeting and accomplished virtually all the program's goals. These included (1) conducting varied and intensive outreach to assure good attendance, (2) presenting a representative and diverse board, (3) having the predominantly African-American board members clearly in charge of the meeting, (4) getting broad participation by residents at the meeting, (5) handling all logistics smoothly, and (6) getting the attendance of influential individuals (e.g., the mayor, the head of the Economic Council), who were clearly impressed by the new group. Volunteer board members left this meeting with a happy, proud sense of accomplishment.

A later town meeting held by Delray Beach CDC was a disappointment. The organizer had not built a large enough board, and those recruited did not meet their commitments concerning outreach. As a result, attendance was poor, board members felt embarrassed and deflated, and the meeting neither gained the group good visibility nor generated enthusiasm. Failure to perform well a challenging but manageable task sent this group (and its community organizer) back to square one; board members elected to hold a second, better-organized meeting to gain legitimacy for their new roles in the community.

This is not to say that participants in engagement strategies for developing community leadership cannot learn from mistakes and unanticipated events, which are inevitable (Pressman and Wildavsky, 1973). For example, when the board members of Limestone Creek CDC in Palm Beach County selected their first president, they chose an individual who their community organizer doubted would be a good leader for the organization. During the weeks prior to the election, the organizer had spoken with individual board members about the qualities they felt would be needed by the new officers and about which members seemed to have those qualities, but the volunteers elected a local minister, based on his position of respect and formal authority in the community.

The minister proved to be a poor choice: He did not observe the procedures the group had learned and adopted for their board meetings (e.g., he never prepared an agenda), and he declined to give his phone number to other members of the board to facilitate communication between meetings. The CDC quickly fell behind in its work. As it became clear that the president was unwilling to change, other board members became frustrated, and within a few months they used the CDC's bylaws to force a new election and select a replacement. The group had lost time, and in the process, opportunities to learn public-meeting skills and to engage in neighborhood planning were delayed. Board members did, however, learn other lessons—that they could use formal procedures to accomplish important objectives and that they shared a commitment to their community that was powerful enough to provoke them to challenge authority.

Nevertheless, mistakes can leave scars. They are also likely to be especially troublesome if they occur early in an intervention or if the mistakes are large. Significant mistakes, regardless of their real cause, too often are confused with (or give rise to) actions or events that confirm some participants' preexisting prejudices and expectations. Developments of this kind can quickly cost an intervention hard-won credibility and undermine its claim to be a vehicle for meaningful change.

Combining Approaches.   These examples begin to suggest the advantages of combining training and engagement approaches. Learning while doing through engagement approaches can produce powerful lessons but tends to be inefficient for conveying factual and technical information. In interventions that require participants to have much technical information, on-the-job learning can lead to significant problems: it lengthens the amount of time required for participants to see clear signs of progress, easily fostering frustration and reducing participation (not to mention trying funders' patience). Targeted formal training can ameliorate this problem, and engagement approaches typically have the flexibility to incorporate such training when needed. For example, CODP provided each group of neighborhood volunteers with formal training to guide them through the process of incorporating as CDCs. Several meetings with a lawyer gave community residents the knowledge and skills to move through the incorporation process much more quickly than they could have if they had had to research the legal issues on their own. Similarly, materials provided periodically by the TA provider helped them structure their work and created a series of benchmarks that motivated engagement by providing clear, achievable goals and a series of tangible victories to celebrate.

Training can also be used selectively to help some participants get "up to speed" on issues that are already familiar to others. This approach can be especially important in preparing residents to participate *as respected equals* with initiative participants who have particular technical skills or who are used to being in positions of authority. Without this type of preparation, community residents can feel awkward and reluctant to participate. As a resident NFI collaborative member explained:

> Everyone's encouraged to speak, but sometimes there are people like myself who are hesitant to talk because you're not sure what you're talking about, sometimes they talk in language that is a little bit over my head. I don't know whether that's because I don't have the education or I'm just not familiar with what they're talking about. And that may be the perspective of some other people of the collaborative, so we kind of hold back a little bit, but they do encourage us to voice our opinions, and they'll tell us if we're in left field.

Successful engagement, sustained over time, solves some of these problems, but training can also play a role. For example, the NFI collaborative

in Milwaukee was committed to providing residents with meaningful decision-making roles in the operation of their new revolving loan fund. To
perform this role well and have their opinions treated with respect, residents needed to understand the business and financial issues involved in
individual loan applications and in the operation of the fund itself. A combination of training and intensive TA accomplished this. The approach was
time-consuming and costly, but it generated effective, engaged resident
leadership on both the board (which set policy) and the loan committee
(which made lending decisions). This leadership was not problem-free.
The loan committee made loans to some businesses that subsequently
failed (as staff had predicted). The most significant difficulty, however, was
sustaining effective participation over time; as resident members rotated
off the board and loan committee, mechanisms for ongoing training to
bring new members up to speed proved hard to maintain.

Conversely, formal leadership training, such as that done by MDC and
KCNA, is strengthened by building in curriculum elements that help participants link what they are learning to their work on behalf of the community. MDC does this by having teams work through a nine-step
planning model that starts by identifying the important issues in their community, and moves through data collection and analysis to creating a vision for the community and writing a plan to implement that vision. MDC
teaches skills and points to models and resources the participants can learn
from, using the participants' own work in the community as their learning
laboratory. Similarly, KCNA helps the participating groups develop a realistic and useful organizational strategic plan and teaches them the skills
they will need to put it into action. The groups can then apply for a small
grant from KCNA's Neighborhood Self-Help Fund to implement a piece
of their plan; this possibility forges a direct connection between the participants' training and their work in the community. The link to community
issues helps motivate participants and positions them to transition more
smoothly from training to action.

Combining training and engagement approaches is, of course, subject
to its own pitfalls. Seamless integration is not easy to achieve. For example, the CODP effort in New Orleans had considerable difficulty recruiting
local real estate TA providers. As a result, all the TA providers did not join
the effort at the same time, and their training and orientation to CODP
were uneven. CODP recommended to TA providers that they use an approach that breaks the development process into a structured sequence of
steps and gives volunteers information only for the step they are about to
take. One TA provider in New Orleans, however, chose not to follow this
approach. Instead, he prepared a comprehensive flowchart of the entire
process for the board of Gert Town CDC. The magnitude of the task ahead
completely overwhelmed the volunteers, who decided that CODP "ex-

pected too much." Participation on the board dropped off, and the group ultimately disbanded. This TA mistake was not the only factor contributing to the group's demise. But the mistake was nevertheless quite costly, even though it involved only one apparently small aspect of a complex program.

Individuals versus Cadres

Leadership development strategies used in efforts to build community capacity tend to focus either on strengthening *individual* leaders or on cultivating leadership *cadres*. Leadership has long been considered as something exercised solely by individuals, and capacity-building efforts may adopt a strategy focusing on individuals because that is presumed to be the only option for leadership development. However, as the difficulty of effecting meaningful change to benefit disadvantaged groups becomes more widely apparent (making collaborative approaches seem more promising), community capacity–building initiatives are giving greater attention to the strategy of preparing groups of individuals in a community for leadership roles.

Cultivating Individuals.   Efforts to groom *individual* leaders have a long history in politics, education, the military, and the corporate world. Comparable efforts tailored to developing leadership in low-income communities are much more recent, but nevertheless well-established. These are primarily training programs intended to build the human capital of individuals, facilitate their professional development, or strengthen a particular field of practice. They are not part of explicit community capacity–building efforts, but are available as tools for those efforts. Among the oldest and best-established providers of such programs are the Industrial Areas Foundation (IAF) and the Development Training Institute (DTI). IAF, a national network of organizers founded by Saul Alinsky, has long offered leadership training for participants in community organizing efforts, and for nearly twenty years, DTI has offered intensive training specifically targeted to executive directors and directors of real estate development in CDCs. DTI's year-long program includes short, intensive, on-site training sessions and workshops interspersed with longer periods of work in the home organization that includes implementation (or more detailed planning and development) of a project designed during the training. Many other organizations offer programs that also seek to enhance a wide variety of skills and capabilities of community development practitioners, both paid staff and volunteers. This training ranges from individual workshops or short sequences of classes offered by such groups as the Enterprise Foundation, Neighborhood Reinvestment Corporation, and Tufts University's Management and Community Development Institute, to degree or certificate programs such as those offered by New Hampshire College. Topics addressed in these offerings may include technical subjects, process skills (such as facilitating productive meetings and discussions), or a combination of subjects and skills.

Other approaches that focus on individuals emphasize developing better leadership skills and behaviors in the context of direct involvement in community work. Coaching is one form of customized leadership development, as illustrated by the earlier example of the CODP community organizers who coached emerging resident leaders about how to select good officers for their CDC boards and how to prepare well for their town meetings.

Efforts to cultivate individual leaders have numerous advantages. Existing leaders in positions of authority (e.g., executive directors of CBOs, the heads of major divisions within a nonprofit organization, or a board member taking on a specialized role) may require skills and perspectives that are distinct to their positions in their respective organizations; training in those skills can sometimes best be provided for a group of similarly situated individuals. The DTI training program described above is a good example. Such programs also offer opportunities for networking among peers who can share lessons from practice and serve as resources for one another over time. These programs can provide an opportunity to get existing or would-be leaders into new situations that facilitate growth. They can also give participants "space" to grow and rethink without sending conflicting signals to subordinates or undermining their authority with their organizations.

Individual leadership development can also be effective in on-the-job venues. As illustrated in the earlier examples of coaching and parallel staffing, assistance can be customized to a specific organization or community. It can help to strengthen the ranks of a wide range of community organizations and associations. It can also be a low-cost vehicle for cultivating new leaders, as promising individuals and development opportunities arise in the course of community activities; such efforts help to diversify a community's leadership, support more activity, and renew the ranks of active leaders when individuals move or curtail their participation. For example, the staff and board of the Glades Community Development Corporation (GCDC) in western Palm Beach County frequently identify emerging leaders and provide support, ranging from informal assistance to nominating individuals for board positions throughout the community and engaging them in various community initiatives. Chicanos por la Causa, a CDC based in Phoenix, pursues a related strategy, recommending young community leaders for positions on boards or task forces that will give them experience and exposure in the broader Phoenix community. This strategy provides the individuals with the personal development that Gardner argues is cultivated by "boundary-spanning" experiences. And it simultaneously provides the Latino community with stronger links to external sources of opportunity and influence.

Cultivating Cadres.   Efforts to cultivate *cadres* of individuals as leaders appear to be less common but show considerable promise in a community capacity–building context. An example from our core cases is the Vision to Action Forums carried out in partnership between GCDC and MDC. The Vision to Action Forums exposed thirty-two people to a year-long series of intense retreats designed to help individuals from diverse backgrounds and philosophies listen to each other, discuss the issues, and reach consensus on the vision, goals, and specific strategies that would comprise a long-range strategic plan for the Glades. The group assignments required participants to work together between sessions to gather, analyze, and synthesize information. Once a set of strategies was agreed upon, the group spent months reaching out to various parts of the community to solicit input and build support for the agenda, which is now being implemented through a follow-on program (Acting on the Vision) with the help of an additional 150 to 200 volunteers.

Several of the leadership development efforts described earlier work with cadres of community members. KCNA enrolls a small group of members from each neighborhood association participating in a leadership training session. Together, the three to five members of each group constitute a large enough number to make a real impact on their organization when they share a vocabulary, outlook, and process skills. In addition, they work together on a project for their organization, so their participation in the leadership training positions the association well for its next major activity, thus producing something of value to the entire organization, even though only a few members have done the training. CODP expanded on the cadre notion in two directions: In each site, it organized several CDCs that shared a common approach to community development, making it easier for them to work together. And it educated local funders about the community development process so they, as a group, could better support the new CDCs.

Relative Advantages and Disadvantages.   The advantages of cultivating cadres of leaders are fairly clear, and they extend far beyond the "power of numbers." Leaders with a shared language and vision are able to support one another in their work, providing encouragement and help with strategy when that work is difficult. If several respected people in the community voice similar viewpoints, their message is reinforced and becomes more likely to receive attention. If the leadership group is diverse and broadly representative of the community, that message will receive a broader hearing. In addition, the fact that a *diverse* group, whose members might be expected to have varying interests and points of view, delivers a *common* message can give that message greater weight and create a constituency for reforming entrenched practices and norms. In addition, a cohort of leaders in varied positions in the same community or system (e.g., the school system) has the potential to provide multiple points of leverage from which to work for change. Finally, a group leadership development process with a diverse group provides an excellent opportunity for that group to engage in the kind of adaptive work that can lead to fundamental organizational or systems change.[5]

The Empowerment Evaluation Workshops, cosponsored by GCDC and the National Civic League, a nonprofit organization dedicated to strengthening citizen democracy, exemplifies many of these advantages. The workshops trained a cadre of residents to analyze how well local community-serving organizations were carrying out their missions and to hold them accountable to the community. The fact that diverse individuals understood this issue deeply enabled them to place the issue of accountability for meaningful community service squarely on the table in discussions of how to improve programs and services. For example, the local technical college that was training people for jobs that did not exist was willing to review its curriculum and assess what changes were necessary to prepare Glades residents for the technical and managerial jobs that had been largely filled by people who lived outside the community (such as those in the prisons and welfare department).

Like direct engagement, cultivating cadres of leaders has costs and limitations, however. Because it is more complex than working with individuals, cultivating a cadre of leaders typically requires greater commitments of time and energy from participants. It is likely to be more expensive, as well. These higher costs in time, energy, and money—particularly in very intensive training programs like those developed by MDC, which require participants to be away from home for several long weekends—may make participation problematic for certain types of individuals, such as single parents and workers who have either very limited paid vacation or limited control over when they can obtain time off from work. Leadership development opportunities for individuals, on the other hand, can be made much more widely and flexibly available, allowing residents of various communities (not just those that might be targeted by a formal initiative) to develop their talents and contribute to community life.

CHALLENGES FOR LEADERSHIP
DEVELOPMENT PROGRAMS

A number of important issues and challenges cut across the basic approaches to leadership development. These include making a good early reconnaissance of existing and potential leadership; deciding whose leadership will be developed; adapting to the changing circumstances and expectations that confront capacity-building initiatives, particularly those using an engagement strategy; and building legitimacy for new leaders. Each of these issues is taken up in turn in this section, which concludes with a discussion of the need to prepare leaders outside the target community to interact effectively with leaders inside that community as its capacity increases.

Assessing the Leadership Landscape

Capacity-building efforts take place within a context of existing leadership—individuals who view themselves or are viewed by others (community members, perhaps outsiders) as community leaders. Whatever leadership development approach is planned, it is best undertaken in light of an understanding of the existing leadership structure and how it is changing. Mapping this landscape is an invaluable up-front investment. Mapping gathers information about existing and potential leaders that is helpful in selecting a site for an initiative and choosing individuals with whom to work. The information may also be used to position the initiative locally, customize it to the local context, and thus maximize its effectiveness.

The existing leaders who are easiest to identify are in positions of formal authority. These include clergy, elected officials, executive directors of CBOs, and presidents of neighborhood associations—people who are "in charge" or "at the top" of the organization and are considered leaders by virtue of that position. Some may have been selected by the community, others may be self-appointed, while still others (such as parish priests and school principals) may have been assigned by outside agents. Among these people, some are likely to exercise leadership more broadly (i.e., outside their organization), either because of the nature of their organization (say, a large church) or because of their personal qualities. Other existing leaders may be influential without a formal position of authority, for example, because they are known as "the person to talk to" or as "somebody who gets things done."

This leadership context is unlikely to be static. Any of the above-mentioned types of leaders may be secure in their positions of influence or viewed as vulnerable. Some so-called nascent leaders may be widely viewed as candidates for positions of authority; others may be virtual unknowns.

If the capacity-building initiative is an ambitious one, the relevant leadership structure may extend beyond the bounds of the target neighborhoods, since leadership at the city or county level may be important to program success. For example, the stance of public-sector leaders clearly shaped the conduct and experience of CODP. In Palm Beach County, the initiative was positioned extremely well from the outset, owing to the willingness of the chair of the private-sector Economic Development Council to become the first chair of the initiative's local advisory committee and to the favorable response of the chair of the county commission to CODP's plans. Similarly, strong support from the city manager of Little Rock helped smooth early relationships between the city and the new CDCs, giving new neighborhood leaders good access to staff in charge of the city's housing and community development programs. In contrast, the patronage politics of the mayoral administration in New Orleans led CODP staff there to keep their distance from the city until a reform-minded mayor was elected.

Deciding Whose Skills to Develop

Effective leaders have influence—they affect what and how things get done in a community. Much depends, then, on whose leadership skills get "developed." Equally important from a capacity-building perspective are the related questions of who makes this decision and what criteria they use. In purely training efforts, these questions may attract little attention because who does or doesn't participate in a training program may not be widely known in the community. Efforts that involve on-the-job engagement strategies will likely have a higher profile, and the issue of how choices are made may be subject to more discussion. How controversial these discussions are is likely to depend on what is perceived to be at stake, and how well the choices conform to community views about who "should" participate in the effort. Both of these factors are generally subject, to greater or lesser extent, to management by those who design and implement the initiative. What is perceived to be at stake will likely increase to the extent that the effort seeks to stimulate important change and the extent to which that fact is known and taken seriously.

Selection Process.   Candidates for leadership development efforts can be identified in various ways. At one extreme, whoever is responsible for the community capacity–building initiative may hand-pick individuals who are "promising" by some set of criteria, anointing particular individuals as leaders or prospective leaders; the initial NFI collaboratives and the early Vision to Action Forums in the Glades are examples of this approach. At the other extreme, the effort may be open to anyone who volunteers and makes a commitment to participate in the initiative; NLC and Acting on the Vision in the Glades operate in this way. One intermediate approach is to have a committee (using a group or consensus process) hand-pick candidates from the pool of initiative participants (NFI's approach to restructuring the collaboratives when they became boards of new nonprofit organizations). Another intermediate approach is to use a broad outreach or application process, followed by a more specific candidate selection process based on particular eligibility criteria and the availability of resources for leadership development (as KCNA does).

The choice of selection process will condition what can be done and what must be done to position candidates for success as leaders with actual influence and acknowledged legitimacy. This is an issue neither for NLC, which recruits individuals and helps them find a good way to use their new skills, nor for KCNA, whose trainees are already in positions of authority in their respective neighborhood associations and are presumed to have legitimacy already. However, for interventions in which the would-be leaders will "represent" their communities, helping them establish legitimacy requires attention from the time they are selected. Capacity-building initiatives commonly designate an individual or a committee to hand-pick a representative group of resident participants for leadership development. Since this process, in and of itself, has no political legitimacy, the results of the process must be convincing enough to stand on their own. Hence the need for broad outreach, careful screening, and good judgment.

The CODP experience illustrates how this type of selection process can be done well. Clear program design, good program management, and tough internal standards largely account for this success. Community organizers were clearly charged with creating volunteer CDC boards that were not only diverse and representative along lines of race, ethnicity, and gender, but also inclusive of each of six major neighborhood networks or interest groups: renters, home owners, businesspeople, service organizations, religious organizations, and major institutions (e.g., hospitals or schools). The stated goal was to be able to hold a well-attended town meeting in each neighborhood and have every community member present be able to identify at least one or two board members as individuals they knew and accepted as legitimate representatives of the community who would have its interests at heart.

Once the CDC boards began to take shape, a local coordinator monitored their composition weekly, helping and pressing the organizers to "round out" the boards. Organizers were also held responsible for making sure that town meetings were well attended; if attendance was poor, both the organizer and the board members received clear signals from CODP that they had not lived up to their responsibilities and improvement was expected. This "tough" stance was adopted partly as a matter of CODP operating philosophy, but it also reflected the awareness of senior CODP staff that strong, diverse boards were critical—as a matter of principle, as a means of gaining respect for the new CDCs and the initiative, as assurance that selected projects would be accomplished and have acknowledged value to the community, and as insurance against any political challenges. The absence of such challenges over the life of the initiative is one indication of the quality of the board members chosen. They were perceived from the outset, both in their communities and among outsiders, as being broadly representative of their respective neighborhoods.

The Vision to Action Forums in the Glades also hand-picked its participants, making a comparable effort to include all segments of the community. Two public officials who were invited to participate initially declined. However, once the training program was under way and those officials realized that the effort might really amount to something, they contacted the program to say they had reconsidered. Their request was denied to avoid disrupting the team-building process that was already under way—an early signal to participants of the program's integrity.

Selection Criteria.   The decision to screen and select candidates for leadership development within a community capacity–building framework immediately raises the question of what selection criteria to use. Virtually all capacity-building ventures seek to be inclusive in fostering participation, and they work to develop leadership groups that are representative and diverse. But decisions about whether or not to work with particular individuals require a more fulsome set of selection criteria.

The two most commonly articulated selection criteria are connection and commitment to the community. Indicators of connection include a deep knowledge of the community and a network of relationships with one or more important subgroups—for example, African-Americans or local businesses. Together, these indicators flag individuals who bring to their community work information about the lives, problems, and perspectives of the neighborhood, as well as the ability to tap those connections to gather and disseminate information. Such individuals are valued because they provide some assurance that viewpoints they express also represent the viewpoints of others in the neighborhood. In communities that are racially or ethnically diverse, identifying individuals with ties to each group in the community lies at the core of promoting diversity.

Commitment to the community is a more multifaceted criterion. The core aspect of commitment is whether a potential leader has the energy and willingness to participate in community-serving work. Beyond this, community capacity–building initiatives commonly look for individuals who are willing to "put themselves out there" and assume responsibility for making something happen. Some initiatives appear to assume that an interest in participating is evidence of such willingness. Other initiatives, aware that assuming responsibility for making the community a better place carries risks (e.g., that the effort will be perceived as a failure or that the volunteers might be perceived as "selling out" the community in return for a position of influence) are more cautious. As one neighborhood resident and collaborative member said about her concern that the NFI collaborative succeed:

> It took me years to build my reputation, for people to trust me. This is my livelihood. If we don't have our stuff together and come out here, it could be detrimental to a lot of us. If [the needs of the community] fall through the cracks, I will get hurt the most because I am more connected. . . . It always comes back to your relationship with the community.

As noted previously, CODP relied on its community organizers to select the resident volunteers on whom the program's success would ultimately depend. Since the organizers were themselves new to the program, they had to be trained for this task. As a result, this intervention had to be very explicit about the qualities the organizers should look for and how they should determine whether any prospective volunteer had those qualities. Toward this end, CODP linked the notion of commitment to two additional, related criteria: personal integrity and agreement with the initiative's goals, values, and strategy. (Many initiatives value these same qualities but typically do not articulate their selection criteria and may not give these two qualities the same primacy.)

The criteria of personal integrity, which emphasized identifying volunteers of scrupulous honesty and good character, supported the program goal of winning immediate respect for the new CDC boards. Staff appreciated the fact that volunteers would derive personal satisfaction from being active and useful and from any acknowledgment they received for their work on the neighborhood's behalf. In this limited sense, presumably all volunteerism is self-interested. But staff were very clear that they were seeking commitment to the common good, not involvement by individuals who might expect to receive personal benefits from the program, such as getting a salaried job or helping relatives get an affordable home. This emphasis was a matter of principle; it was also viewed as insurance against the risk that inappropriate actions of one individual might discredit one of the CDCs or even the entire initiative.

Agreement with the initiative's goals, values, and strategy—CODP's other additional criterion—served several purposes. It gave resident volunteers (many of whom had never met) a common point of departure for their work together. When volunteers became discouraged or uncertain about priorities, these shared goals provided a foundation the organizers could use to help reestablish motivation and direction. Finally, since a core program principle was that volunteers would control their CDCs in exchange for assuming responsibility to use it to help the community, this "buy-in" to the initiative's principles provided a mechanism to hold volunteers accountable for their actions.

Interestingly, inability to find "enough" candidates or "good" candidates does not appear to have been an important issue in the examples considered in this volume (although in some cases, most notably CODP, neighborhoods were prescreened for the presence of good prospective candidates). One reason for this was the criteria themselves: if energy, commitment, connection, and integrity (as opposed to formal credentials or technical skills) are the criteria, many communities, including very poor ones, are well endowed with talent. The other reason was the initiatives' commitment to aggressive, one-on-one outreach to identify qualified individuals who might not see themselves as activists, never mind potential leaders. This is a time-consuming, labor-intensive process, but it is key to broadening the community leadership base.

Choosing New or Existing Leaders?   The distinction between existing and new leaders is a simplified one, as noted earlier. But it is useful, nonetheless, because extreme examples of these types of leaders illustrate important program design trade-offs. In practice, of course, people may be recognized as leaders because they hold positions of authority, are new or "emerging" leaders, or manifest some aspects of both types of leadership.

Integrating existing leaders into community capacity–building efforts has several advantages. If they join, these leaders can lend legitimacy to the capacity-building effort—a particularly valuable contribution if the effort is spearheaded by people or institutions seen as "outsiders" and hence suspect. Most existing leaders have organizations behind them, so they presumably have a base of influence they can use to help get a change process moving. And they have the skills and resources that helped them reach their current positions.

In addition, electing *not* to work with or through existing leaders can create problems, since those who are left out may take offense. For example, in Memphis, the long-time head of the neighborhood civic association was not invited to participate in the NFI collaborative until several years into the initiative. He eventually signed on, but not without hard feelings. Similarly, in Hartford, the collaborative did not invite the participation of a local businessman who was well connected with the West Indian–Caribbean community (and the city); this omission created bad blood vis-à-vis a portion of the community the collaborative was otherwise taking great pains to include. Clearly, efforts of this sort need a strategy for dealing with those not chosen.

Nonetheless, there are good reasons for cultivating new leaders rather than working with existing ones. Sometimes the decision to reach beyond existing leadership is fairly clear-cut. For example, when CODP considered New Orleans as a prospective site, the initiative director identified numerous neighborhoods that would benefit from a new CDC, plus several neighborhoods with existing CDCs. The leaders of existing groups had strong ties to their respective city council members and had received regular awards of CDBG money—but they did not appear to have accomplished anything. Senior CODP staff realized that the integrity of their initiative would be seriously compromised if they were to "throw in their lot" with politically wired organizations that were not delivering for their communities.

The most basic reason to engage prospective new leaders as part of community capacity building, however, is to make the leadership ranks more numerous and responsive to community priorities. Some capacity-building efforts give priority to developing new leadership on the grounds that if the community already had effective leaders, more constructive activity would be taking place. However, the decision to focus on new leaders need not grow from such an unfavorable view of existing leadership; it can also develop from the belief that fresh talent is needed to add vigor to community efforts and to allow more and different kinds of improvement activities to move forward.

Cultivating new leaders is generally more costly than relying on existing ones, since the former are likely to require some investments in skill building that the latter would not need. In NFI, for example, the collaboratives worked in many ways like boards of directors. Although the professional members of the collaboratives were quite comfortable with this, many low-income residents serving on the collaboratives had little experience with these types of processes and deliberations at the outset. There were ongoing debates about how the collaborative should operate—as a "working board" in which members engage in all aspects of planning and implementation, or as a "policy board" providing broad direction to the staff. Ultimately a good deal of TA was provided to enable the collaboratives (all but one of which finally incorporated) to operate as policy boards of nonprofit organizations, and resident leaders to understand their legal and fiduciary responsibilities as members of such boards. Some board members also needed considerable help with matters such as how to conduct meetings, organize a committee, and use a committee structure. A more experienced or professional group would have needed considerably less help.

Community-building activities that tap new leadership make either conscious or implicit choices about the best way to bring together new neighborhood leaders and existing leaders from outside the neighborhood. CODP and NFI provide an interesting contrast. NFI brought residents and external "resource people" into the collaboratives at the same time. Residents, who in most cases initially made up a minority of the collaboratives, came to these meetings at a disadvantage that was both real and perceived. Other participants were often better educated, more sophisticated about development issues, more polished in presenting their ideas in front of a group. The residents, however, had to learn these skills by practicing these activities "in public"—hence the quotation, cited earlier, from a resident NFI collaborative member about initially feeling "hesitant to talk" and "a little bit over my head."

In CODP, on the other hand, resident volunteers were guided through careful preparation before any CDC contact with influential people outside the community. This process started with the town meetings (the CDCs' first public event in their neighborhoods), which were thoughtfully planned to send consistent signals that these were residents' meetings—planned by residents, with residents in control of the agenda and conduct of the meeting. Most of these meetings were conducted well and enjoyed good attendance, evoking positive responses from the "outsiders" who attended; these included program sponsors, public officials, and some funder representatives. Similarly, when each CDC was ready to apply to CODP for predevelopment funding, or later when they sought bank financing, CODP staff coached volunteers as they prepared their materials and practiced their presentations; sometimes a small number of CODP local advisory committee members were invited to these practice sessions to provide technical advice and give volunteers practice answering the kinds of questions they were likely to face. In each case, the goal was to make each CDC encounter with external "movers and shakers" one in which the volunteers were poised, confident, and competent; this was a deliberate strategy to combat negative stereotypes and win respect for the CDCs. It succeeded: members of both the public and private sectors were typically surprised, but impressed, by residents' effectiveness in presentations and public meetings.

Adapting to Initiative Evolution

Any leadership development effort that includes an on-the-job component includes some element of unpredictability. When people engage in the community, their activities are necessarily shaped and influenced by community events; therefore, people must be prepared to adapt, and so must the enterprise that seeks to make them better leaders. The early phases of most initiatives typically have a structure, or at least a strategy that has been devised in advance, and can therefore be planned for. However, the longer the activity extends, the greater the likelihood that emerging leaders and program supporters will face unexpected developments that the initiative must respond to if it is to succeed.

Sometimes, initiative designers and managers can anticipate such developments and structure the intervention to take them into account. In CODP, for example, the program design called for a *series* of training sessions on real estate development for resident volunteers. Each session could be offered when volunteers had completed (or were close to completing) the steps in the process that they knew how to conduct, and each session presented only as much material as the volunteers would need to move successfully through the next phase of their project. The goal was to make the process challenging and motivating, but not overwhelming. This process worked well.

This type of design is elegant and sets a high standard, but it is difficult to achieve. Even in CODP, the fact that volunteers had different degrees of aptitude for development activities complicated the delivery of training, as well as the conduct of the activity the training was designed to support. This situation posed an ongoing challenge to both staff and residents, and required staff to find new ways to support some residents and cultivate patience in others.

Sometimes the need for initiative adjustments will be created by a discrete, unexpected event such as a fire, a shooting that attracts much attention, or the loss of an election by an important political ally. More frequently, however, community capacity–building efforts encounter occasions when individuals who appear to have been performing well are confronted (either suddenly or gradually) with new expectations about what they should do—including things they may not have expected to have to do or for which they are not adequately prepared.

In NFI in Milwaukee, for example, when the collaborative decided to establish a small-business loan fund (an event that could not have been anticipated), neighborhood residents on the board and the loan committee of that fund needed considerable help to take on new roles; intensive training and TA specifically for that purpose prepared them for these roles. Supervising staff for the first time is another common event for which initiative participants might need similar assistance.

In contrast, as CODP phased out, resident volunteers were expected to shift from roles in their individual CDCs that required direct engagement in project work to roles as delegates (representing their CDCs) in the emerging coalitions. Those new roles required them to develop and refine new political and organizational relationships, determine the qualities they needed in an executive director, hire and supervise that individual (as well as delegate work and ask for accountability, which also meant learning to exercise newly acquired power), and set policy and organizational priorities—all while acting as agents of their CDCs, itself an unfamiliar experience for most. The initiative design assumed that the volunteers could move successfully into this complex new role without assistance. That proved not to be the case, but the need for greater help was not identified until too late. What volunteers needed was a combination of TA and coaching, preferably from the initiative staff with whom they already had relationships. But since the initiative was phasing out (a fact CODP staff decided couldn't be changed) those staff members were not available. Both coalitions eventually folded.

Institutionalizing Leadership Development

In general, a very small proportion of any community is actively engaged at any given time as leaders or participants in community processes. Voluntary participation in such processes takes time and energy. Because capacity-building ventures typically try to be inclusive and process-sensitive, the time costs are likely to be especially high. Participation may potentially cost volunteers money and put their reputations at risk (for example, if the activity fails or comes to be viewed negatively in the community). At the same time, many residents lack clarity (and sometimes faith) about the likely benefits of such participation—which are, in any case, likely to appear at some undetermined time in the future (unlike the costs, which are immediate). All these factors work against broad resident participation and make recruitment of new participants challenging and potentially time-consuming. They also reinforce the tendency to engage only a small and already involved core set of resident leaders. For those leaders that are engaged, burnout is common. As part of a process for building sustainable community capacity then, leadership development strategies need to include ongoing outreach to steadily expand the pool of potential participants and to keep information flowing to the community at large. This sounds simple. It isn't.

Community capacity–building interventions are rarely *just* about building capacity. They are about building capacity as a means to accomplishing other community betterment goals. Those goals attract, energize, and motivate participants—so both formal training and on-the-job leadership development work best when structured to help participants pursue those goals effectively. However, the felt urgency of addressing community problems, sometimes abetted by pressure from funders to demonstrate "concrete" results, easily becomes an impetus to give process issues short shrift.[6] Thus, activities like mentoring, reaching out to find new talent, and investing the time and energy required to give new people access to leadership opportunities are commonly crowded out.

The best community leaders internalize these outreach processes as a priority and build them into their regular pattern of activities. They do so not only to avoid burnout, but also to enrich the stream of talent working on the community's behalf and to sustain the legitimacy of their organization or activity as being genuinely community based. GCDC, which has adopted as its mission the task of building leadership and organizational capacity in the Glades, provides a powerful example. GCDC has consistently resisted the temptation to become a direct provider of services and programs, preferring instead to create new capacity in the community to take on new community improvement activities and to draw progressively more people into various community service roles. More modest programs, like Neighborhood Leadership Cleveland, perform a very useful service by providing individuals who are self-starters with the opportunity to acquire the skills to be effective volunteers for groups that may or may not have institutionalized outreach and leadership development. In contrast, most CDC volunteers in CODP did not develop an appreciation for the importance of this issue. As a result, most of the CDCs lost board breadth and strength over time. When board members dropped out, either they were not replaced, or the remaining members recruited acquaintances—people like themselves—as new board members.

Developing External Leaders

Community capacity–building efforts that include hands-on leadership development consistently focus their energies on residents and other neighborhood stakeholders. External participants in the initiative, if any, are presumed already to be leaders and to possess the basic capabilities they need to participate effectively. Examples include the "resource" people (those with various professional skills or useful networks of contacts) on the NFI collaboratives, and the local sponsors and funders of CODP.

This exclusive focus on people within the neighborhood is unfortunate. External leaders may be excellent at what they do professionally, but that does not guarantee that they are knowledgeable either about building community capacity or about how best to strengthen poor communities— which are both very difficult processes. In addition, they may or may not be experienced or comfortable dealing with representatives of poor communities of color as partners. Therefore, some way of helping external leaders move into their new roles might be quite useful. Furthermore, if capacity-building efforts are successful, particularly at helping poor communities link more effectively with external agents, those agents may themselves experience pressure to change how they do their work in order to accommodate their new constituencies.

How much existing leaders (and their organizations or constituencies) are willing to change is an especially difficult issue to address, since it may not be at all clear during early stages of an initiative that it will require external leaders to change. They are likely to see themselves as part of "the solution" rather than part of "the problem." Even people who genuinely want conditions in poor neighborhoods to improve and want residents in those neighborhoods to have more control over their own circumstances may, in fact, behave in ways that turn out to be inconsistent with the success of a community capacity–building effort.

Members of CODP's Palm Beach County Local Advisory Committee, for example, sitting by invitation on the screening committee for the new executive director of the CDC coalition, believed one of the African-American candidates to be completely unsuitable for the job. But they were unwilling to mention their lack of confidence in him to the volunteers on the committee. In part, this was reluctance to speak in opposition to an African-American candidate. In part, it reflected their failure to understand that expressing their opinion would not violate the spirit of community control; in effect, the Local Advisory Committee members did not trust that the volunteers could hear advice and still form an independent opinion. But their failure to speak out also illustrated the committee members' reluctance to assume responsibility for the success of the venture they were funding. They had been assured at the outset that the quality of the program would be high because they (and their peers) would always be in a position to insist on quality. But when the time came, they were not prepared to do so.

The issue of responsibility merits emphasis because it is so commonly evaded. Outside agents seeking to build capacity in vulnerable communities and to stimulate investments and risk-taking by community residents have a certain responsibility to those communities and those who agree to participate. So do their partners. The nature of this responsibility is often not articulated, but left implicit by the initiative. This omission is often for convenience, since it can sometimes ease the initiative's task of recruiting participants. But it can also leave participants unprepared to play important roles, as the preceding example illustrates. In contrast, external leaders who make the effort (and are accorded the opportunity) to learn about community development and capacity building—and who are willing to accept the responsibility—can support capacity building and community change in unexpected ways. Consider the following example:

The Economic Council of Palm Beach County, the most prominent association of local businesspeople, hosted the CODP effort there, providing senior initiative staff with space in its offices. Staff members spoke frequently with the council director, who was intrigued by the initiative, and the national CODP director spent considerable time talking with him about the initiative's approach and strategy, for which he developed a keen appreciation. This investment of time proved to be a good one, since it enabled the council director to be uniquely helpful. Combined with his extensive knowledge of the key actors in both the public and private sectors, his understanding of the initiative made him a reliable source of strategic advice that was highly valued by the local CODP coordinator.

The council director contributed in other informal ways, as well. For example, the county proposed to widen a dirt road in the tiny Limestone

Creek neighborhood to two lanes, pave it, and connect it to the county road system. The director, however, learned that the proposal included acquiring a four-lane right-of-way, which would enable the county to later build a four-lane through road that would bifurcate the community. He and the local CODP coordinator could have dealt with this threat using their network of contacts. Instead, they helped Limestone Creek CDC volunteers prepare testimony to give before the county commission supporting a two-lane paved road but opposing a four-lane right-of-way. The volunteers won a very energizing and motivating victory that was possible, in part, because the council director appreciated the importance of having local residents take the lead on behalf of their community.

Poor communities and the capacity-building initiatives that seek to serve them could use more outside allies like this—but such allies, like effective resident leaders, require cultivation. Sometimes this is best accomplished by identifying promising candidates and spending time with them one-on-one, as in the example above, and gradually encouraging them to become more engaged. In other cases, as in the Vision to Action Forums in the Glades, business and political figures were included in the leadership training group, along with a variety of lower-income residents. External agents and neighborhood residents all learned community leadership skills together.

LEADERSHIP DEVELOPMENT AND COMMUNITY CAPACITY

Developing individuals' leadership skills does not necessarily translate directly into community capacity. Those individuals must be willing to employ their skills in ways that benefit others (including the community at large) and that encourage others to play an active role in community life. That is the primary rationale for screening prospective participants in leadership development efforts for their commitment and connection to the community. It is also one reason that some initiatives try to engage people who are already active in community organizations or activities: they have a track record for working on the community's behalf.

Community leaders increase their contribution to community capacity when they learn and practice a style of leadership that is inclusive and collaborative. Practicing this type of leadership can include seeking ways to mobilize people who are willing to participate (and helping to persuade them that they should); spreading and delegating tasks so that as many people as possible can contribute, even though they may have different interests, skills, and available time; looking for opportunities to connect people who have something to offer the community with venues that enable them to do so; and being generous with praise and credit when groups of people make good things happen in the neighborhood. In diverse communities, it will also include working effectively across lines of difference such as race, class, and culture. More broadly, community capacity will be enlarged when community leaders are sensitive not only to specific activities or services that residents may need or enjoy, but also to the other components of community capacity itself (see again Figure 1). This means operating in a way that supports and builds the credibility and effectiveness of organizations in the community (not just the organization a leader may happen to head). It means adopting a style that extends and works through networks of association. It means making efforts to strengthen the community characteristics that lie at the heart of capacity, including efforts to build and reinforce residents' sense of community through specific activities, as well as through the style in which they are carried out; to identify constructive ways of solving problems, rather than ignoring them or sweeping them under the rug; and to reach out from the neighborhood to connect it to resources and opportunities beyond its boundaries. And it means being mindful of the types of functions that effective communities perform, such as sharing information and giving residents effective voice.

It seems likely that additional benefits will be gained when leadership development efforts are conducted in ways that encourage or reinforce the other three community capacity–building strategies. Developing the leadership talents of those who serve as senior staff or board members of community organizations is an obvious example. Less obvious but equally advantageous are leadership development activities carried out in the context of community organizing, which commonly emphasizes the kinds of strategic thinking and relational skills emphasized above.

It is also worth noting that a leadership development approach by itself may not serve all poor communities well—in particular, communities where a core disadvantage is simply the low level of organized civic activity. Too few tenants know each other well enough to organize a holiday party for their building; too few parents are active in the PTA to mount a good Halloween fair; not enough people are organizing safe, entertaining, developmentally beneficial activities for kids and teens (Littell and Wynn, 1989). Neighborhoods like these need more people with the confidence and skills to "put themselves out there" and make new things happen. By itself, leadership development is probably insufficient to enable this to happen. New activities require safe spaces, residents who trust one another well enough to work together, and much more. Nevertheless, leadership development has a role to play in making even these communities better places to live.

NOTES

1. Classic and widely cited examples of this literature include Burns (1978); a comprehensive summary and assessment of the literature is contained in Bass (1990). More recently, some authors have devoted serious attention to constructs of leadership that are more appropriate to a community context and that emphasize the importance of collective problem solving. Examples include Heifetz (1994), Lorentzon (1986), and Chrislip and Larson (1994).
2. This list of leadership functions is derived from Bass (1990) and Heifetz (1994).
3. See Introduction for a brief explanation of NFI and the other two initiatives (Glades Community Development Corporation and Consensus Organizing Demonstration Program) used as core case studies of this book. See Appendixes A and B for more complete descriptions of these and other examples used.
4. For a discussion of governance approaches in community-building initiatives, see Chaskin and Garg (1997) and Chaskin and Abunimah (1999).
5. This approach bears many similarities to "collaborative leadership," which actually involves the creation of a collaborative organization, with members drawn from all relevant sectors of the community to do adaptive work. See Chrislip and Larson (1994).
6. For a more extensive treatment of this "process/product tension," see Kubisch et al. (1997).

3

Organizational Development

Our framework for understanding community capacity suggests that organizations are key vehicles through which such capacity can be built. Strong organizations can provide needed goods and services to community residents. They can be important vehicles for solving community problems, and for helping community members find common ground and take action in the service of shared goals. They can be a forum for building leadership and social ties among residents that reinforce a sense of community and commitment to that community. They can function as important links to resources outside the community and as important power bases for representing or advocating the community's interests in the larger environment.

Nearly all initiatives to build capacity in a community work in some way with and through organizations, whether they are churches, businesses, CDCs, social clubs, organizing groups, arts organizations, or human service agencies.

Organizational contributions to community improvement efforts take a variety of forms. For example, a business association may work with its membership to create new jobs and training programs. A CDC may help build block clubs and tenant patrols to enhance neighborhood safety. A settlement house may sponsor an ongoing community forum to improve relationships among residents and build a common community identity cross different racial and ethnic groups. Or a local political organization may mount a voter registration and education drive to increase political participation of community members and, ultimately, enhance their influence with elected officials.

Organizations can also be the target of community change initiatives. For example, residents may join forces to improve schools, protest practices at the local welfare office, or increase their access to a hospital in their neighborhood. Similarly, an organizing group may demonstrate outside a business perceived to discriminate against residents or may pressure a major employer to set aside a certain number of jobs for community residents.

The ability of a community organization to get things done on behalf of local residents is integrally related to other levels of social agency through which community capacity works—the individuals (leaders and organized groups of individuals) and social networks of the community that strive for common goals.

This chapter focuses on the three primary strategies through which capacity-building efforts foster organizational development in the community: strengthening existing organizations, helping existing organizations take on new functions or roles, and building new organizations. (A fourth option, changing the ways in which organizations relate to one another, is the subject of Chapter 5.) We begin by reviewing the different roles or functions that organizations play in a community. We then look at three different but related strategies through which community capacity–building initiatives aim to increase the strength of a community's organizations. We identify the intended outcomes of each strategy and discuss some of the implementation challenges or tensions. The chapter ends with a discussion of the relationship between the strength of the organizations in a community and the community's overall capacity.

ROLES OF ORGANIZATIONS
IN THE COMMUNITY

The organizational landscape of a community is composed of many different kinds of organizations that contribute in different ways and in varying degrees to community capacity. Organizations differ in size, age, mission, culture, stability, political clout, and access to resources (Schein, 1992; Cummings and Worley, 1997). There are nonprofit, public-sector, and private for-profit organizations. Some community organizations are freestanding (a local neighborhood association, a day care center); others are embedded in larger systems (a school that is part of a larger school district, a branch of a bank that is headquartered outside the community). Some organizations have broad constituencies or consumer bases in the community (a community center or a neighborhood council); others have a much more targeted or limited reach (a building's tenants' association or a service program for chronically ill children). Some have individual memberships (a block club or a PTA group); others have an institutional membership base composed, for example, of block clubs or schools.

Organizations also differ in the degree to which their operations are formalized. Many organizations, like a tenants' association or a cultural group, may operate without formal tax status, articles of incorporation, or other legal and financial apparatus. Our focus in this chapter is on the more formal end of the organizational spectrum because these organizations are more likely to represent permanent elements of a community's capacity and because the more-informal groups are discussed in Chapter 4.

Organizations located in the community differ in the degree to which they are *community-based:* how much they involve residents and other community stakeholders in their governance; what vehicles they use for incorporating and reflecting community needs and priorities; and what opportunities they offer for community involvement. A CDC that uses ongoing outreach and a board composed largely of community residents to determine its priorities may plan or implement projects differently than a CDC whose strategic planning is driven largely by outside development professionals or funding opportunities. A church whose membership is composed largely of neighborhood residents may play a different role in the community than one that is physically located in that community but draws its primary membership from outside the area. Similarly, a business that targets its sales to community residents may have a different relationship to that community than one whose customers come from all over the city. Further, a business owned by someone who lives in the neighborhood may contribute to the availability of capital and political influence in a way that differs from one whose profits leave the area.

Depending on its particular characteristics, an organization can play one or more of the following roles in a community:

- **Produce needed goods and services:**   Organizations make loans, build houses, manage parks, provide health care, educate children, and put on plays and concerts. They offer forums for worship, for obtaining needed job skills, and for organizing a block party. Some organizations, such as credit unions and food co-ops, provide services that explicitly aim to keep capital and other resources in the community.
- **Provide access to resources and opportunities:**   Organizations provide employment. They also provide information about and access to resources outside the community, including such support as informal job networks, referrals to services, and specific information on how to negotiate larger city, state, and federal systems. A branch library, for example, can provide reference materials and Internet access to identify a vast array of goods and services, ranging from products for sale to free cultural opportunities; a local employment service can tap into a regional network of job listings.
- **Leverage and broker external resources:**   Organizations can leverage and broker resources for the community. A civic organization can make the case for channeling resources to particularly distressed areas, a settlement house can contract with the city to operate various service programs, a local church can become a participant in a national faith-based organiza-

tion or community development program. Both public and private funders use community organizations as vehicles through which to operationalize their investments in local communities.[1] Sometimes funders go so far as to create new organizations in a community so that there will be vehicles through which they can channel their money for work in that community.

• **Foster development of human capital:**   Some community organizations, like training and educational institutions, are explicitly devoted to fostering human capital. Other organizations also provide residents with skills and experiences that contribute, directly or indirectly, to their taking on leadership roles in the community. A parent who coaches in a sports league, a participant in a church-sponsored clean-up campaign, and a local businessperson who joins a merchants' association may develop the skills, desire, and opportunity to assume other community roles.

• **Create or reinforce community identity and commitment:**   It is often through some form of organization that people develop awareness of common interest and mutuality of circumstance. An organization can offer an arena—a space, a structure, a safe vehicle—through which residents can come in contact with each other around mutual needs or interests and through which they can generate a common experience, a sense of belonging, and a shared history. Each community organization has stakeholders—people who have an interest in the success of the organization or in the goals it is trying to accomplish, people who are leaders, volunteers, and consumers. Organizations can channel and reinforce the time, energy, and commitment that stakeholders invest in promoting shared efforts to advance the well-being of the community.

• **Support community advocacy and exertion of power:**   Organizations are vehicles through which commitment to the community is often translated into action and problems are solved, directly or indirectly. Organizations can create a power base in the community and garner political support from outside the community. They can be positioned to mobilize residents and other stakeholders to demand the community's "fair share" of a public resource, to block a development plan that is not perceived to be in the community's interests, or to attract a special initiative or resource to the community. People may speak up and fight back individually. But it is often when they join with others in some organizational context that their voices are strongest and most likely to be heard.

The roles played by organizations in the community often overlap or reinforce each other. A school can provide education to children, engage and promote leadership among parents, and contribute to a sense of shared interest and community identity among diverse groups of families. Similarly, a church can provide a place to worship, deliver social services, and help get out the vote in an important election. Moreover, organizations can form partnerships and coalitions to increase the impact of the roles they play. They can join together to work on particular projects, to create an integrated service system, or to increase their access to resources or their clout in the larger political environment (see Chapter 5).

STRATEGIES TO FOSTER ORGANIZATIONAL DEVELOPMENT

Organizations are not distributed evenly across communities. Some communities have strong organizations in a wide range of sectors—social, economic, political, educational, and so forth. Others have a large number of organizations, but few that are functioning at their full potential, owing to lack of funds or leadership or lack of connection or responsiveness to their constituencies. Still other communities have few well-functioning organizations or have entire organizational sectors, such as banking or child care, that are severely underdeveloped.

A common starting point for many capacity-building initiatives is some form of organizational audit to assess the community's organizational assets and needs. Such an audit may rely on a review of existing materials about the community, or it may supplement such a review with additional information from, for example, formal surveys of residents and organizations or a "snowball" reconnaissance that takes advantage of the connections among people and organizations in the community. The information is intended to help initiative participants design a revitalization strategy that builds on the talents and resources of existing community organizations while it strengthens and supplements these assets. In some initiatives, planners have mapped the distribution of public, commercial, and nonprofit organizations across the community to create a visual representation of the community's organizational resources and needs.

The challenge for initiative planners is to learn enough from the organizational audit to allow them to adopt some strategic combination of the three primary approaches to building organizational strength in a community. First, they can help organizations perform their current roles better or more efficiently. Second, they can help organizations take on new functions or play new roles in the community. Finally, they can build new community organizations. Each of these approaches aims to inject new kinds of organizational capacity into the community. The three approaches are not always distinct. An initiative to strengthen a community's CDCs may lead some of these organizations to take on new advocacy or service provision functions. Or an organization that decides to expand the role it plays in the community may find that it eventually wants to spin off the new role into a new organization. What these three approaches to organizational development all share, however, is an assumption—sometimes explicit, sometimes not—that the strength of a community's organizations is directly related to the overall capacity of the community. We shall consider this assumption following a discussion of the approaches themselves.

Before proceeding, however, we should note the special case of public-sector organizations in a community. These are organizations such as the local public school, welfare office, county health clinic, or police precinct station that are located in the community but whose mandate, authority, and resources come from decisions and policies made to varying degrees outside the community. Community efforts to change these public organizations may lead to incremental improvements, for example, in how police or school personnel relate to residents. But fundamental change in public organizations generally requires system reform that goes beyond the community, including changes in the ways these organizations are linked to each other within the community, the ways they relate to the larger systems in which they are embedded, and the level and use of the resources they receive. Although there are some exceptions, most community capacity–building initiatives have not been well positioned, on their own, to provide the leverage needed for significant reform of public-sector systems. Thus, most of the following discussion on strategies to build organizational strength focuses on nonprofit, and to a lesser extent, private organizations in the community.

Strengthening Existing Organizations

This approach focuses on helping organizations in the community fulfill their missions and perform their roles more effectively. We need to distinguish, however, between strategies to strengthen organizations that want to change (or at least say they do) and strategies to strengthen organizations that do not profess—or actually resist—a change agenda. The primary vehicles for strengthening organizations in the first case are technical assistance (TA) and other forms of support, such as training and peer learning, small grants or core operating funds, and help in gaining access to new relationships and financing sources. In the second case, when organizations are less amenable to change, the more common approaches are advocacy and other forms of pressure that stimulate organizational change, combined with the organizing efforts that will be described in Chapter 4.

Technical Assistance, Grants, and Other Forms of Support

Technical assistance (TA) is probably the strategy employed most often for strengthening organizations. Traditional organizational development assistance has focused on such areas as fund-raising, strategic planning, staff and board development, and financial and management systems. (Staff and board development is largely addressed in Chapter 2.) Other forms of assistance can strengthen organizations: providing training, facilitating peer learning, and contributing space, loaned staff, equipment, or other resources. Finally, TA is often linked with other forms of concrete help, such as small grants or core operating support. If provided in ways that build sustainable skills, knowledge, and systems, TA and other forms of support can improve organizational effectiveness over time. The following sections describe some of the issues involved in trying to do so.

Finding and Structuring Appropriate TA

Some localities have TA organizations that provide generic assistance to the nonprofit sector. Nonprofits in these places may operate in different fields but share a need for help with similar kinds of organizational development tasks that will help them better fulfill their missions. In many areas, however, strong local sources of TA do not exist because of insufficient demand or lack of public or philanthropic investment in TA infrastructure. Initiatives aimed at building organizational strength in such localities often turn to out-of-town TA providers, who may not have a complete understanding of the local context and are generally unable to have the kind of ongoing presence that might be most helpful in supporting the organization's development. Although they aspired to using local TA providers, all three of our core cases[2] ended up relying heavily on national rather than local providers, especially in their early years. The Glades Community Development Corporation (GCDC) in western Palm Beach County used a variety of national experts; the four sites of the Neighborhood and Family Initiative (NFI) were supported initially by one national provider, the Center for Community Change; and the Consensus Organizing Demonstration Program's (CODP) plan to transition out of a TA role and replace itself with local providers ran into problems in two of its three sites owing to local shortages of appropriate providers.

Finding appropriate TA that aims to transfer skills and build long-term organizational capacity can be a challenge (Wahl, Cahill, and Fruchter, 1998). Not all providers who have the relevant technical skills are well suited for work in a community capacity–building context. The provider must understand the difference between providing expert knowledge and building an organization's capacity to apply new knowledge effectively, between performing a particular service or activity ("doing it") and helping an organization learn how to provide that service or activity itself ("teaching the client to do it"). TA providers with a capacity-building orientation are committed to the latter type of TA, even though it can mean working themselves out of a job. This orientation often requires patience, particularly if the assisted organization is committed to working in a participatory fashion and if participants have very different levels of experience and skill. In CODP, all of these issues came into play. New Orleans, for example, certainly has many attorneys with the technical skills to incorporate nonprofit organizations, but it was difficult for the CODP effort there to identify individuals with those skills who also had the desire and commitment to help resident volunteers (who generally met in their neighborhood, either for breakfast or in the evening) work through questions about structure, bylaws, and organizational mission. The CODP effort in eastern Palm Beach County found only one such attorney, but she was committed enough to agree to work with all six of the initiative's CDCs. In contrast, the fast-growing county's numerous real estate professionals were largely uninterested in helping to foster the growth of nonprofit development groups. Once it became clear that the new CDCs were serious about doing development rather than being a source of deals for other developers, these professionals fell by the wayside.

Once appropriate providers are identified, the challenge becomes one of structuring the relationship between them and the organization to maximize productive exchange and build long-term capacity. This involves addressing such questions as who defines the TA task, who (i.e., staff, director, or board of the organization) is the focus of the TA effort, who pays the provider, to whom the provider is accountable, how different providers coordinate their work, how much of the TA is mandated, and how much of it is driven by demand. In many community initiatives, these issues were not resolved effectively and have seriously undermined the value of TA for the organization leading the change effort (Brown and Garg, 1997; Pitcoff, 1997; Brown, Branch, and Lee, 1999). More recently, however, foundations and organizations appear to have recognized that reaching some understanding on these issues is important for the success of their partnerships. Concurrently, the organizational development field has devoted increasing attention to strategies to promote "learning organizations" that are characterized by "the continuous testing of experience and the transformation of that experience into knowledge—accessible to the whole organization and relevant to its core purpose" (Senge et al., 1994:49; see also Schon, 1983). Use of this approach in TA efforts focuses on creating the processes and structures needed for continuous learning in an organization and on the shifts in organizational culture required to support ongoing reflection and honest dialogue. The idea is that as an organization adopts these processes and values, it is much better positioned to use expert TA, both programmatic and organizational, effectively. Although the community capacity–building field has yet to embrace this approach on any significant scale, interest has been generated and translated into the start of implementation (Brown, Pitt, and Hirota, 1999).

Combining TA and Grants

Some funders have found ways to link TA with other forms of concrete help, such as small one-time grants or multiyear operating support. The grants may be directed toward particular organizational-development needs, such as creating a management information system, or they may provide general operating support.

The Charles Stewart Mott Foundation's Intermediary Support Program, for example, links grantmaking and TA. The program aims to "incubate and strengthen emerging community-based groups that evidence creative efforts to deal with significant local issues" (Toney, 1997:7). Each of the six participating Intermediary Support Organizations (ISOs) provides TA and small grants to a diverse mix of groups in low-income communities around the country.

An assessment of the program in 1995–96 revealed that the primary forms of TA provided to the 101 emerging organizations focused on fund-raising, management skills, strategic planning, leadership development, and board and staff development. Groups also received assistance with member recruitment, media coverage, campaign development, coalition building, and strategy and issue development. The small grants that accompanied this assistance generally ranged from $5,000 to $12,000, allowing groups to "pay for phones, print flyers, reimburse volunteer costs, and cover other costs that go into bringing people together to work on a collective project" (Toney 1997:6). An assessment of this approach reported its effectiveness for organizations targeted by the Mott program: emerging groups that tended to be young (most were three years old or less), small (with median budgets of $45,000), and often reliant on part-time or volunteer staff. The report notes that the ISOs' technical assistance "shortens the time necessary for groups to make a significant difference in their communities" (ibid.). This finding is consistent with other grants programs in which small organizations receive both funds and TA to move to the next level of development.[3]

The six ISOs in the Mott program are national, regional, or citywide intermediaries, as opposed to intermediaries based in one particular community. GCDC and the four NFI collaboratives, on the other hand, are local intermediaries that shared the explicit charge of strengthening the community's organizational infrastructure by assisting individual organizations and by creating connections among them. Because local intermediaries are, at least in theory, embedded in the community, they are often well positioned to identify opportunities for targeting resources and providing TA in ways that are consistent with practices and values of the community. Although this was often the case for the GCDC and NFI collaboratives, the fact that they were new organizations limited their ability to provide sufficiently sustained, sufficiently intensive support to a number of struggling groups. Thus, we need more experience with well-established local intermediaries to assess the relative benefits of local versus broader-based intermediaries in delivering effective combinations of TA and funding resources to support a community's organizational infrastructure.

Supporting Sectoral TA

Sectoral TA is provided to like-minded organizations—CDCs, day care centers, block clubs—that are presumed to share similar tasks and problems. Although this type of TA may address some of the same needs addressed by generic types, it can also be tailored to the particular characteristics and technical needs of the sector (e.g., how to finance affordable housing, meet state regulations for day care, or organize and sustain active block clubs). Best practices can be introduced, peer learning and support networks can be fostered, and joint enterprises can be developed more easily if organizations share similar goals and challenges. By targeting organizations in a single sector rather than in a single community, this approach can be used to strengthen multiple communities.

The Neighborhood Development Support Collaborative (NDSC) represents a sectoral approach that combines TA and grants to build the capacity of organizations working in the community development field. Supported by a consortium of local and national funders that joined together in 1986, NDSC is designed to provide support to CDCs in the greater Boston area. From 1986 to 1993, NDSC I provided strategic-planning assistance and operating-support grants to fifteen CDCs. NDSC II, which is still under way, broadened the range and number of groups served and the types of support provided, including capitalization, training and TA, strategic-planning and management assistance, and several kinds of program development grants. Since 1993, twenty CDCs have been awarded grants, and twenty-five have received training.

An ongoing evaluation of NDSC notes that the initiative has built the capacity of the participating CDCs to carry out housing production and management and to play a catalytic role in the development process in their neighborhoods (Clay, 1990, 1993, 1997). The multiyear funding enabled the CDCs to "build their core operation to a new level, add program elements, test development ideas for feasibility, expand services to a larger area, and address tenant needs" (Clay, 1993:ii). NDSC also played an important role in increasing the support for housing and community development among funders, including the United Way. United Way did not fund housing development groups until NDSC demonstrated that these groups could meet United Way's organizational standards. Thus, the NDSC built stronger community development organizations and contributed to a more supportive funding environment for those organizations.

Several other national initiatives have been structured to produce similar impacts among CDCs, most significantly the National Community Development Initiative (NCDI) (Walker and Weinheimer, 1998), a $250-million, ten-year effort in twenty-three cities and the Ford Foundation's Community Development Partnership Strategy (Ford Foundation, 1996) in seventeen cities. The notion is that community development capacity is enhanced through funds that are obtained from multiple sources and granted directly to CDCs but are administered through an intermediary, which often provides TA and training along with the grant support. As in NDSC, the implicit assumption in these efforts is that helping CDCs helps the neighborhood.

NCDI evaluators are beginning to test this assumption by studying the neighborhood effects of the approach beyond its direct benefits to the CDCs and the residents of their housing. The evaluation measures of CDC capacity include: ability to plan effectively, ability to secure resources, program delivery capacity, strong internal management and governance, and ability to network with other entities.[4] Neighborhood effects resulting from increased CDC capacity that may be explored in the next phase of the evaluation include: public safety, property values, and the neighborhood's physical conditions; the social and economic conditions of its residents; and the vitality of the local retail and commercial sectors (C. Walker, personal communication, 1998). Although the methodological challenges generated by trying to link CDC capacity and community conditions are significant (see Briggs, Mueller, and Sullivan, 1997), this research should provide an initial assessment of the contribution of an organizational development strategy (in this case, focused on CDCs) to community capacity.

Advocacy

Some organizations resist efforts to "strengthen" them, or simply do not share the organizational-change agendas that may be developed by community residents or by other constituencies or organizations in the community. In this case, efforts to build community capacity through organizational development tend to adopt advocacy or other forms of pressure that aim to stimulate organizational change from outside the target organizations. Although organizing (addressed in Chapter 4) represents the most common strategy for exerting outside pressure (especially vis-à-vis public agencies), other ways to stimulate change in "resistant" organizations have also proven useful.

GCDC employed two potentially far-reaching strategies to improve the functioning of existing Glades organizations that were perceived to resist efforts to make them more responsive to community needs. These strategies combined research, training, and advocacy to change organizations through outside pressure. One strategy involved Empowerment Evaluation Workshops (cosponsored with the National Civic League), which trained citizens to assess and monitor organizations that serve Glades residents (Wallis, 1998). The idea behind these workshops was to promote the community's capacity to hold local organizations accountable for their use of resources received or administered on behalf of the community. GCDC put together a diverse group of about twenty people who participated in the year-long process of learning a methodology to assess an organization's effectiveness within the context of the community's needs and priorities. By using a standard set of questions and a framework for analyzing responses to determine how well organizations were actually carrying out their missions, this group played a significant role in making the issue of accountability a critical aspect of the community dialogue about how to improve services and programs for Glades residents.

The other GCDC strategy stemmed from a 1994 survey, which found that ninety-one public or private health and human service agencies existed in the Glades. People who lived outside the Glades and commuted in on a daily basis held the majority of the management and administrative positions in these agencies. GCDC staff began working with educational institutions in the area and with the personnel officers at schools and other public agencies to determine what skills or credentials were necessary to obtain the various positions and how best to initiate that preparatory training or course work for Glades residents. When an institution seemed unresponsive to providing these courses, even when it was charged to do so by its public mandate and funding, GCDC was able to mobilize its "friends" (board members, county or state officials, media representatives) and exert informal pressures to promote the institution's cooperation. GCDC's rationale for this approach was that placing more Glades residents in management positions in health and human service organizations would not only provide important opportunities to these residents but would also make it more likely that these organizations would develop programs that are increasingly responsive to local needs and priorities.

Helping Existing Organizations Take
on New Roles or Functions

The goal of this approach is to help organizations expand their missions—or implement their missions in an expanded way—by taking on new roles or functions that would address unmet community needs. As with the previous strategy, the aim is to build on the organizational assets that exist in a community. This approach differs from the previous one, however, in that its focus is less on helping an organization improve what it does than on helping it do something new, such as assume new responsibilities, sponsor new activities, or serve new target groups. The strategy assumes that the organization is already fulfilling some functions effectively, so it could reasonably be expected to do the same with an expanded role.

In efforts to promote community capacity, the form that this strategy takes often involves broadening the organization's services to be more comprehensive. For example:

• **The Community Building Initiative (CBI),** a CCI sponsored by the Local Initiatives Support Corporation, challenged roughly forty CDCs in eleven cities to compete in adding to their physical bricks-and-mortar development activities program initiatives intended to "rebuild the social infrastructure of communities" in such areas as health care, employment, children and youth, crime and safety, and public services (Community Building Initiative, 1994).

• **The Edna McConnell Clark Foundation's Neighborhood Partners Initiative (NPI)** challenged five lead organizations (a diverse group of CDCs, multiservice organizations, and an organizing group) to function more comprehensively in their neighborhoods, either by adding new services and programs or by working in partnerships with other organizations inside and outside the neighborhood (Brown, Branch, and Lee, 1999).

• **Seedco,** a national intermediary that facilitates partnerships between large institutions and surrounding low-income communities, designed a Historically Black Colleges and Universities (HBCU) initiative to help these institutions revitalize their neighborhoods through a range of community development strategies that had not been part of their traditional educational mission.

Churches and other religious institutions constitute another kind of organization through which change initiatives often aim to build community capacity. In many distressed communities, churches are among the few viable, indigenous social organizations committed to fostering the development of individuals, families, and the community as a whole (Metro Denver Black Church Initiative, 1994). They are good places to hold meetings, they can assemble a group of people who share mutual interests, and they often have significant local credibility (Center for Community Change, 1993). Numerous faith-based initiatives, sponsored by such national organizations as the Congress of National Black Churches or by community foundations working with networks of local churches, have provided financial and TA to churches to develop and implement new programs in their communities, adding social services or economic development activities to their more traditional religious functions (Scheie et al., 1991).

In each of the initiatives described above, as well as in a range of faith-based initiatives, well-established community organizations receive assistance to take on new roles or functions on behalf of the communities in which they are embedded. Using existing organizations to increase community capacity has many advantages. These organizations have successful track records, relationships with residents and local organizations, and an active stake in the well-being of the community. Having established credibility and legitimacy within the community, they are often well positioned to take on new roles or to assume leadership for new community improvement efforts. Working with existing organizations requires, in most cases, less time and fewer resources than starting from scratch. In addition, other organizations in the community are less likely to perceive the expansion of an existing organization, as opposed to the creation of a new one, as a potential competitor for funds.

This approach to building community capacity is not without its potential obstacles and challenges, however. Two potential barriers in asking community organizations to expand their roles or functions are particularly important. The first involves how the organization is selected. The second stems from barriers to change within the targeted organization.

Selecting Organizations to Take on New Roles or Functions

When an organization expands its roles or functions in response to an articulated community need, there may be few external obstacles to its development. What often happens in initiatives designed to build community capacity, however, is that the sponsor—generally a foundation, an arm of government, or an intermediary outside the community—selects or anoints an organization to participate. Even if the selection takes place through a competitive process involving the review of multiple organizations, sponsors may be tempted to turn to an organization that is well connected politically or with which they are familiar or comfortable. Or they may select a less-than-optimal organization because it is viewed from outside as the only viable one in the community.

An organization selected in this manner, however, may not be well positioned in the community to carry out the new tasks. Although it may welcome the additional resources, it can be hampered by not yet having gone through a process of building the necessary community support for the enterprise. Without the cooperation of other key community organizations, the organization funded to take on new roles or functions in the community can face substantial barriers to implementation. For example, in the Neighborhood Strategies Project, a three-site community initiative in New York City, there was so much competition for funds and such a long history of divisions within one of the target neighborhoods that the organization selected to bring groups together in support of an economic development agenda simply did not have the political leverage or capacity to bring others to the table to move that agenda along (Hirota, Brown, and Butler, 1998). In another case, when the grant funds for an expanded mission arrived, one of the lead organizations experienced a great deal of pressure to regrant some of these funds to another nonprofit in the neighborhood and to hire individuals referred by that organization. Although it was able to find a compromise whereby it helped the nonprofit raise its own funds, the lead organization spent significant time and energy managing the fallout from this conflict (Brown, Branch, and Lee, 1999).

A somewhat different example of the challenges created by the selection process comes from one of our core case studies. In New Orleans, the CODP team did not initially designate the Central City neighborhood as one of its six target areas; the team felt that the base of capable volunteers was too small to sustain a CDC board. All Congregations Together (ACT), a successful citywide organizing group that included the neighborhood's Catholic church in its network, staged a protest to challenge this decision. Given strong turnout at the event, the team reversed its decision. The problem it had seen, however, was real: the resulting board was small and weak, and the group accomplished little. After several years, the CDC finally regrouped when a dynamic new priest was assigned to the parish and mobilized a base of volunteers.

Sponsors are increasingly recognizing the significance of the ways in which they select organizations to play expanded community roles and are exploring how the selection process can enhance, rather than endanger, a capacity-building initiative's chances of success. In some cases, sponsors require the lead organization to solicit input and support from other organizations in the community as part of the application, or they fund a planning process during which these relationships are supposed to be forged. In the North Lawndale neighborhood in Chicago, for example, the Steans Family Foundation decided not to start its initiative with a large grant to a lead organization. Rather, the foundation chose to first spend several years in the community investing in community organizing and in organizational and leadership development. The aim of this type of approach is to develop effective working relationships with different parts of the community, to be responsive to a wide range of capacity-building needs, and to generate learning and trust on all sides (Brown and Garg, 1997; Brown, Butler, and Hamilton, in press).

Addressing Organizational Barriers to Change

The second challenge in assisting existing community organizations take on new roles or functions is internal and stems from the organizational demands that are created by the new role or function. Adding new services often challenges an organization to establish new capacities to plan and deliver the services in a timely, coordinated, responsive manner. If the new service is to benefit from the organization's existing resources, which is one of the main rationales for working with an existing organization rather than starting a new one, it must be integrated into the organization, both operationally and philosophically. Staff with the requisite skills and experience must be recruited and supported. New divisions of labor and power relations within the organization may need to be negotiated (Pitcoff, 1998).

Further, taking on new roles or functions, especially those that involve an explicit commitment to community building, often challenges the organization to develop new relationships with residents and other stakeholders, relationships that involve an altered balance of power and responsibility. To continue with examples cited earlier, both CBI and NPI charged the participating organizations with undertaking an inclusive planning process involving residents and other stakeholders. Similarly, churches delivering new secular services and participants in the HBCU initiative had to develop new relationships with community residents and organizations and new ways of working together. Staff in all four of these examples needed new skills in organizing and in involving residents in planning and decision-making.

Frequently these new relationships have important implications for such issues as organizational culture, policy, and governance. Without significant outside resources, training, and support or coaching, organizations have a natural tendency to resist change or to implement change in ways that do not threaten the organization's basic modus operandi. For example,

• An organizing group that tries to establish a community partnership may find itself in uncomfortable relationships with organizations that have been the target of its advocacy efforts in the past.

• A newly hired organizer at a CDC may feel isolated from other staff who resist or resent taking the time needed for a participatory community planning process in light of the CDC's need to deliver concrete outcomes to its sponsors.

• A housing organization may find it difficult to both manage housing and foster the development of tenants' associations, because its perceived role as a landlord limits its ability to engage residents. Or, alternatively, it may succeed in mobilizing residents, who then press demands for improvements and services that the organization is unprepared to meet.

• The board of a social services agency may be challenged to modify its governance structure when staff's leadership development efforts result in a group of residents who demand a larger decision-making role in the organization.

• A church involved for the first time with the creation of affordable housing may run into significant tensions with its housing development partner over timelines, style, language, and priorities.

NPI, described earlier, presents two "mirror image" examples of internal challenges faced by an organization taking on new functions. Bronx ACORN, a local arm of the national network of organizers working under the umbrella of the Association of Community Organizations for Reform Now (ACORN), accepted the invitation of the Edna McConnell Clark Foundation to become one of five participating sites in NPI. A key requirement of participation was broadening its organizing approach to encompass other community-building strategies, in particular, the development and provision of social services. Participation in this experiment in "organizational cross-dressing" (Johnson, 1999) has forced Bronx ACORN to address concerns, both from the community and from within the organization, that its identity as an organizer and advocate, its culture of direct action, and its basic organizing mandate would be undermined by providing social services. Two of the several strategies Bronx ACORN has used to address these concerns are to look for opportunities to link individual service needs with its broader social and political agenda and to partner with other organizations in the community that offer services not provided by ACORN (Brown, Branch, and Lee, 1999). Other organizations—CDCs and family service agencies—were also challenged by their participation in NPI to develop new capacities and to reconcile their own organizational philosophies with NPI's more comprehensive vision. Their particular challenges were quite different from ACORN's, however, requiring a shift away from a professionally driven, services-dominated approach to a more collaborative model that emphasized resident engagement and community organizing.

A common thread through the discussion of barriers to change is the issue of organizational ownership. To what extent does the organization being improved or expanded want to change, understand the implications of change (or that there may be implications), and assume ownership and manage the change process? And to what extent do funders try to cultivate this ownership, and with what degree of success? Clearly, the more an organizational development or change strategy is internalized rather than imposed from outside, the more likely it is to yield positive sustained organizational change. The following three cases illustrate different degrees of ownership of the changes required when an organization takes on new roles in the community. They also illustrate strategies for promoting that ownership.

CODP.   In Palm Beach County, the CODP team elected, despite the acknowledged risks, to work with existing (but newly formed) groups in two of the six target neighborhoods. In both instances, the existing group was given the option of working with CODP if it would agree to (1) adopt the program's basic strategy of focusing initial activities on real estate development, and (2) reconstitute itself as a more inclusive group (one group consisted entirely of members of a neighborhood church coalition led by a pastor; the other consisted mainly of white home owners). Both agreed. The home owners' group, however, consistently resisted the community organizer's efforts to add renters and people of color to its board: some individuals nominated by the organizer were rejected outright; others joined but quickly (and accurately) felt isolated and dropped out. CODP considered dropping this group on several occasions, but allowed it to continue even though it had not met its commitment. (The organization's narrow membership base subsequently jeopardized its funding stream).

The church-linked group took its commitment to diversity much more seriously and was initially very successful; it was, in fact, the first of the six local CDCs to reach each of the early program milestones. The energy of the founders, however, centered on a broader community improvement agenda. When progress on their development project slowed for technical reasons, some members turned their attention to other activities, and participation gradually withered. These two examples illustrate the limitations of externally stimulated organizational-change efforts: even when the groups professed desire to make internal changes in order to participate in the initiative, the promised changes were not forthcoming in the long run. The groups had neither the capacity nor the commitment to actually implement and sustain the changes over time.

Oak Hill CDC.   William Traynor, an experienced training and TA provider, reports the following case (see Pitcoff, 1998:7). Oak Hill CDC in Massachusetts determined that it needed to involve residents and other constituents in planning and decision-making but, like many community organizations, struggled with how to do so. Its first step was to hold monthly "involvement mapping" staff meetings:

> At these meetings the whole staff would discuss individuals on the CDC board or committees or those involved in volunteer activities—what they were doing . . . , did they have leadership development needs, and so forth. By the end of the meeting, the group would have prepared a "hot sheet" of eight to twelve action steps to be carried out over the next month. Each staff member was required to take at least one action step. . . . This singular change in monthly staff operations produced, in a very short time, a range of impacts on the organization's culture:

• It involved the whole staff—not just the organizers and outreach staff—in an analysis of the organization's human resources needs and the importance of leadership development.

• It raised issues about accountability: of the staff to the leaders, of the leaders to the community, and of staff to each other. As a result, it raised a long-dormant question about whether the CDC should have a formal membership structure.

• It taught the staff, including the executive director, some lessons about the work of the organizers and outreach staff members. Their work came to be seen as more valuable and complex and therefore more appreciated.

• It raised issues related to decision-making, to the relationship between the board and the committees, to the role of non–board members who sit on committees, to the need for having a range of community forums to introduce people to the organization, and to the need for using the annual meeting as a genuine opportunity to set organizational priorities.

• It raised the profile of leadership development to an entirely different level, as an activity that needed to be funded and staffed.

Traynor concludes that "small operational changes that become part of an organization's normal functioning can often create 'cognitive shifts' in thinking" that, in turn, reinforce organizational ownership of the change goal.

United Neighborhood Houses (UNH).   Historically, settlement houses functioned as neighborhood intermediaries that had a mission to provide comprehensive and integrated services, address community problems, and carry out a broad social reform agenda. Over the last fifty years, however, the professionalization of social work and the increasing dependence of the settlement on publicly funded programs that tend to target categorical "problem" populations or people who fit into rigidly defined entitlement programs have undermined the settlement's community-building role. Individuals may be "serviced," but settlement directors report that "too often staff and time limitations allow community strengths and resources to be overlooked; connections to other resources and networks to unravel; opportunities for participation and leadership to go unexploited; and a family's sense of belonging to and responsibility for the neighborhood to go unsupported" (Brown, 1995:6). In other words, settlements' contribution to community capacity has been seriously eroded over time.

In the early 1990s, UNH, a membership organization of thirty-eight settlement houses in New York City, demonstrated a renewed interest in community building and in taking on some of the community-building functions for which the settlement traditionally has been known.[5] They took the following initiatives:

•   **Establishing a systemwide UNH community-building committee:**
The committee was created to provide a forum to support, develop, and
implement community-building activity across settlement houses. Several settlements have created their own internal committees in a parallel effort to heighten the awareness among staff, board members, residents, and
program participants of their role as stakeholders in their communities.

•   **Revising strategic planning processes:**   Settlements endeavored to
be explicit about the development of community-building approaches
within their strategic plans. One settlement, for example, launched a self-
assessment process through which participants examined how the work,
mission, and role of the settlement specifically included and reflected community-building goals, values, and strategies.

•   **Promoting the ideas behind community building:**   This included
raising them in such venues as board meetings, newsletters, and meetings
of member agency board presidents. It also included offering various forums—workshops, training sessions, brown-bag discussions, structured
mentoring—for learning and creating networks among staff, and supporting ongoing documentation of and reflection about the organizational-change effort.

•   **Fostering community-building projects:**   Such projects were developed both by individual settlements and groups of settlements. One example is the Bronx Cluster's Community-Building Project, in which ten
settlement houses share three community organizers who work to "help
develop and support an overall community-building framework through
such activities as cross-settlement staff workshops and production of a
cluster newsletter and calendar of events" (Hirota and Ferroussier-Davis,
1998:7). Project staff also help each settlement to create and execute specific activities such as local organizing projects and leadership training for
community residents.

The result of this deliberate effort to create and support within and
among settlement houses and at UNH an organizational environment that
fosters community-building practice has been a range of new settlement
roles and activities. Although some settlements have always had community organizers on staff, additional houses have created such positions or
have restructured programs and job titles to highlight community-building approaches. One settlement, for example, transformed the title of its
Department of Housing and Family Programs into the Department of Or-
ganizing/Community Services. Changes in language, if new organizational rewards and behaviors accompany them, have turned out to provide
important support for organizational change, helping staff move beyond
their bureaucratically defined job roles and find new ways of working with
residents. As part of this shift, many settlements now refer to "program

participants" rather than "clients" to avoid the implications of a clinical model and to promote the active engagement of residents in program planning and implementation. The documentation of this change effort concludes that there is a "growing shift away from the service provider-client paradigm. . . . Settlements are developing and supporting expanded roles for [community] stakeholders, who are participating in strategic planning and implementation of settlement and community efforts, taking part in civic action and advocacy, raising, promoting, and responding to critical issues, and taking greater responsibility for the life of their community" (Hirota and Ferroussier-Davis, 1998:17).

Taking on (or returning to) a community-building role has involved many challenges for UNH and its membership. Some of these challenges are structural: Requirements attached to funding (particularly from public sources) constrain a flexible definition of staff roles and tasks, and time constraints can lead to treating community building as a project or as one staff person's job rather than as a way for all staff to approach settlement work. Other challenges are simply a function of the difficulty of organizational change. Still others relate to new questions and tasks that the organizational-change goal has generated. For example, What is the best way to build individual and community capacity simultaneously? How can the settlement be most useful in a community that is very divided? Or, how can the settlement play an advocacy role with and on behalf of the community around such policy issues as housing and welfare reform without jeopardizing its public funding?

Clearly, the effort to expand the settlement's community-building role is still very much a work in process. The links to community capacity are encouraging, however. Communities with settlements that have embraced this new (or old) role are now more likely to offer leadership development, services that incorporate participants' views and preferences, and community-wide cultural events that reach deep into different groups of residents, as well as places where public forums can be held or people can meet to address common problems. Community capacity is thus being enhanced by building on organizations that are already embedded to some degree in the community and by deliberately trying to add to or strengthen their community-building role.

Building New Organizations

Some community-building initiatives focus on creating new organizations when there is a significant gap in the number or kind of organizations in a community or when working through an existing organization is perceived as ill advised—politically or otherwise. In a community that has been long polarized by ethnic strife, for example, it may be that no existing organization has a chance of generating a new, inclusive community-building process. Or the only viable organization in the community may be so embedded in organizational and political relationships that it is unrealistic to expect it to be able to take on new community-building roles or functions that might threaten business as usual. In communities that have experienced significant disinvestment, there may simply be no organization with which to work.

Electing to establish a new organization does not necessarily resolve the underlying community issues that make it difficult to find a promising existing organization to work with in the community. For example, in attempting to establish new CDCs in two neighborhoods, the CODP team in New Orleans considered potential groups to collaborate on the projects and form the bases for a new CDC. In one sharply divided neighborhood, it concluded that the animosity between two candidate groups would make it impossible to build a viable, inclusive new organization. In the other neighborhood, the sharply segregated African-American and white communities were both interested in the CDC concept, and both felt it would be inappropriate to create a CDC that did not include the entire neighborhood. The program team decided to support their effort to work together despite the difficulties this would—and did—entail. In each of several other neighborhoods, the team found an existing CDC with strong political ties to its local city council delegate; each had a history of receiving city-allocated funds without producing a discernible impact in the community. This political and ethical track record was one with which CODP ultimately decided not to engage; instead, the team looked to other neighborhoods in which to target its efforts.

Building a new organization can take place *de novo* or as a process of incubation within an existing organization, in which case the new entity is eventually spun off as an independent organization. CODP, for example, focused on establishing new CDCs and on building coalitions among them. NFI created new community collaboratives that were housed independently from but supported by a local community foundation; three of the four collaboratives ultimately incorporated as independent organizations. GCDC was established as a new intermediary in the community but, until it incorporated five years later, was a project of the local community foundation. GCDC and two of the NFI collaboratives incubated and spun off new organizations to fill particular service gaps in their respective communities. For example, NFI in Memphis created and spun off a CDC to address its housing agenda; in Milwaukee, NFI developed or helped establish two new organizations—a collaborative organization of five existing CBOs (discussed in Chapter 5) and a community financial institution founded to encourage investment in businesses and housing in the neighborhood. Similarly, GCDC helped to create and spin off a business incubator, a medical mobile van, and a community theater.

Incubating New Organizations

Using a host organization to incubate a new one can allow the new organization to develop at a quicker pace and with fewer risks than it would on its own. However, this approach presents its own challenges. The timing and process of assuming independence can become tricky, resembling what some have likened to the struggles a parent and adolescent experience as the child matures. In addition, the ongoing relationship between the new organization and its former host is sometimes complex. The Glades case provides several good examples of these dynamics. As described earlier, the process through which GCDC established itself as an organization independent of its parent community foundation was fraught with tensions over several years; it is a testament to the commitment and leadership of both GCDC and the community foundation that they emerged from the transition with mutual support and respect intact. When GCDC went on to incubate several other organizations, its board had to address the same issues that the community foundation faced several years earlier—how to balance its support and control during the transition; how to deal with quality-control issues; when to stop serving as a fiscal agent for the new organization, and so forth. If such issues can be resolved productively, a new organization can have an important source of ongoing support that is likely to be invaluable in its early years.

On the other hand, tensions around control, credit, and ownership may evolve when spin-off organizations are created as a strategy for institutionalizing particular kinds of productive capacities in the community. In NFI, for example, some such tensions arose with regard to new organizations created by the collaboratives in Milwaukee and Memphis. In each case, the initial funding and development of the new organizations' missions were supplied by the collaboratives, and interlocking board memberships were put in place as a way to maintain some oversight and facilitate communication between the new organizations and the collaboratives. As the organizations found their feet, they began to operate increasingly independently, raising money from other sources and identifying their own priorities and trajectories. In the Memphis case, which involved a new CDC, the relationship sometimes became hostile, with the collaborative at times disowning the new organization's problems and at other times wanting some credit for supporting its successes. In Milwaukee, having transferred implementation responsibility for the bulk of NFI's community-change agenda to two, now-independent nonprofits, the collaborative found itself in a quandary about its own role. Despite wanting to protect its survival, the collaborative had increasingly "worked itself out of a job" by creating or helping to found other organizations that represented NFI's principal contribution to community capacity in that site. Eventually, the collaborative in Milwaukee embraced this role, recognizing that indeed at the organizational level, the capacity it had helped build resided in these new, formal organizations and in some organizations that had existed prior to NFI's development and had been invigorated and increasingly connected to one another over the course of the initiative. In the end, the collaborative allocated the remainder of its funding under NFI to four separate organizations to continue their work in community and economic development, leadership, and youth programming, and has allocated money to support TA to selected Harambee nonprofits through the Nonprofit Management Fund, a pool of philanthropic funds available to nonprofits and administered by the Milwaukee Foundation.

Sometimes an internal organizational tension that threatens to undermine the group's core mission or basic culture sparks a spin-off organization. For example, the Northwest Bronx Community and Clergy Coalition (NWBCCC) organized tenants in a cluster of Bronx neighborhoods in an effort to stop the northward spread of arson and housing disinvestment that was rapidly sweeping the South Bronx in the 1970s. The coalition's primary strategy was to educate tenants to resist and report landlord activities that could lay the groundwork for arson. However, it also saw the need to rehabilitate deteriorated buildings that landlords could not (or would not) repair or maintain—in essence, to build a fire wall against further deterioration and disinvestment. However, NWBCCC's board did not want to assume an ongoing development and landlord role in the community. It was concerned that such a role could potentially interfere both with its organizing and advocacy role and with residents' understanding of the central purpose of the organization. So staff and board members from the NWBCCC created new community development nonprofits to pursue this housing development strategy. These organizations, such as the Fordham Bedford Housing Corporation and the University Neighborhood Housing Program, partner with the NWBCCC on many specific projects but are managed and operate independently of the NWBCCC. Similarly, GCDC faced a conflict between its role as a community intermediary and pressure to develop particular services that were much needed in the community. It resolved this conflict in some cases by starting services—such as a mobile medical unit—but spinning them off as early as possible to avoid the perception among other community organizations that its primary function was providing services and, as a consequence, that it was a potential competitor for funds. In both the NWBCCC and GCDC cases, spinning off the new functions or activities was critical to maintaining each organization's core identity and operational integrity.

Challenges Facing New Organizations

Although building new organizations avoids some of the potential problems in working with existing organizations that are described earlier, it poses other challenges. Three of the most significant revolve around time and resources, organizational turf, and goals and expectations.

Time and Resources. It takes an enormous amount of time and resources to launch a new organization and to help it move through its initial stages of development. Even with outside TA and a group of supportive funders, GCDC took five years to become an independent nonprofit with an operative strategic plan. The NFI collaboratives spent about three years mainly in addressing governance issues, learning to work together, and developing a broad strategic plan. When the three collaboratives that decided to do so incorporated as independent nonprofits, they began another stage of foundational organizational development—reviewing and revising bylaws, recruiting and training board members, revisiting their mission, marketing themselves, and seeking funds. Although they had been in operation for some time as collaboratives, at the point of incorporation they were almost required to start again as new organizations. CODP worked out detailed plans for supporting the formation and development of the newly organized CDCs over a two-year period. In contrast, its failure to recognize the need for such a supported gestation period for the *coalitions* that these CDCs attempted to form clearly contributed to ultimate collapse of the coalitions.

Organizations in their early developmental stages tend to spend a great deal of energy on building internal infrastructure and finding effective ways of doing business before they are ready to function productively and at full scale in the community. Despite the fact that funders may recognize that they cannot responsibly provide start-up funds for an organization and then expect it to become independent overnight, they are often wary of the long-term investment that a new organization can require. If they are accustomed to a fairly arms-length relationship with their grantees, funders may be quite surprised by the extent of hands-on involvement that assuring the success of a new organization might require, and they may or may not be prepared, themselves, to adapt to this unanticipated new role.

In some cases, urgent community needs pressure new organizations to deliver programmatically before they have achieved sufficient organizational strength. In NFI in Memphis, for example, the collaborative and community foundation supported the creation of the Orange Mound De-

velopment Corporation (OMDC), a new CDC in the neighborhood to implement NFI's housing and home ownership agenda. In part because of
the paucity of CDCs in the area and the clear need for housing development, OMDC was able to leverage substantial project funding to purchase,
renovate, and sell several properties in the neighborhood. At the time,
however, the organization was poorly staffed, had an unstable board, and
had not yet developed the internal administrative and financial systems to
allow it to operate independently and to accomplish both its organizational development tasks and the project requirements it had agreed to fulfill. In-depth TA was provided to help see the organization through these
challenges. But because of time pressure and issues of staff competence
and support, the TA provider acted essentially as surrogate staff and was
not able to build the capacity of the organization itself. It took several more
years for a stable staff, board, and administrative systems to be put in place
so that the organization was able to operate independently in pursuing its
housing agenda.

Organizational Turf.   A second challenge involved in building new organizations stems from competition over turf. Designers of both the CODP
and the GCDC initiatives selected communities with relatively underdeveloped organizational infrastructures—the new organizations did not
have to compete for "space" in order to establish themselves. This is especially important in communities that have experienced chronic disinvestment: if a new organization is perceived as siphoning off resources that
would otherwise have gone to existing organizations, that organization is
likely to experience significant barriers to community acceptance. Competition for scarce resources makes it hard for other organizations to support
a new organization, even if the services it intends to provide are valued by
the community.

Goals and Expectations for the New Organization.   In capacity-building efforts, funders outside the community often play a central role in the
creation of new community organizations. Multiple and sometimes conflicting expectations for how these organizations should develop, however, are not uncommon, because funders bring their own goals and
expectations for (not to mention varying degrees of control over) the agendas and timetables of the new entities. Often the conflict stems from a tension between process and product goals, or between building long-term
organizational capacity and producing shorter-term program outcomes.
This process / product tension is characteristic of many community initiatives whose approach posits that sustainable development depends in part
on the way in which that development takes place, generally requiring resident participation and ownership while building leadership and long-
term capacity (Kubisch et al., 1997; Rubin, 1995). These goals are not

necessarily inconsistent with the production of outcomes in such areas as housing, employment, child welfare, and economic development. But it has proven difficult, in most cases, to integrate process and product goals effectively.

The new CDCs that were created through CODP organizing had both product and process goals. They had a clearly articulated goal of developing housing and other community-improvement projects, but they were also seen as a vehicle for creating strong and diverse resident boards that could begin to exert a broader influence inside and outside the community. In two of the three cities, CODP teams did not effectively develop and convey to funders and the new boards "softer" milestones involving various indicators of organizational and leadership development to complement "harder" measures of housing and other project outcomes. After three years in New Orleans, none of the seven CDCs had broken ground on a project. In Palm Beach County, only two CDCs were active in housing production, and that accomplishment came at the expense of organizational growth and development. Only in Little Rock were the CDCs able in the early years to make progress toward both the process and product goals of the initiative.

GCDC and NFI ran into similar tensions. Although GCDC aimed to carry out a very ambitious social and economic-development agenda, the pace and ambition of this agenda had to be consistent with the requirement to build common ground with and investment by different sectors of the community. This meant that GCDC's staff felt that they could not get "too far in front of the community," but GCDC's funders worried about the effects of delayed, concrete development action, organizational drift, and a lack of visible community impacts. Similar tensions about expectations for the pace of development characterized the NFI collaboratives. One source of this tension was the need to reconcile long-term goals with short-term grant periods. Another was differences between some collaborative members—often residents—who voiced a need to produce visible projects in the short run and others who placed a high priority on projects that would take more time to develop but would, in their view, have more lasting and significant community impacts. In many cases, the collaboratives ended up focusing primarily on either the short or the long term, finding it difficult to reconcile both perspectives operationally.

Identifying and supporting grassroots groups that are in the process of becoming formal organizations is another way in which funders support the creation of new organizations in a community. Like the case of starting new organizations from scratch, this approach can generate tensions between the funder and the organization about how and at what pace to grow, as well as how to deal with unexpected circumstances along the way. When grassroots groups evolve into larger and more bureaucratic organizations with commitments to produce specific goods and services (e.g., housing units, publicly funded units of social service), they can experience multiple pressures that weaken their ties to the immediate community. As they grow, these organizations tend to become more staff-driven; more professional, formal, and bureaucratic in their practices and culture; less reliant on community volunteers and less embedded in informal community networks; and less flexible and possibly less responsive to community needs (see Knoke and Wood, 1981; Milofsky, 1988; Powell and Friedkin, 1987). Funders can be more comfortable dealing with professional staff, who may look and speak more like them than do volunteer community members. This can serve to reinforce the power differences between paid staff and volunteers and further weaken a sense of community ownership. In these cases, both the funders and the new organizations need to recognize the pressures that are likely to accompany growth, and they need to build in the time and resources required to maintain the organization's connections to the community. These connections often represent one of the organization's greatest strengths, as well as an important factor in the funder's decision to make a grant to the organization in the first place. Thus, it is critically important that plans for growth be accompanied by explicit strategies for supporting the key processes and structures—for example, an inclusive board, ongoing outreach and community organizing, community members on key committees, good information about neighborhood circumstances and priorities—that can continue to promote and deepen the organization's capacity to be responsive to its constituents.

RELATIONSHIP BETWEEN ORGANIZATIONAL DEVELOPMENT AND COMMUNITY CAPACITY

We have examined three different approaches to building organizational strength in a community. Although each of these approaches has its benefits and challenges, we have seen how investments in organizational development can result in new and stronger organizations playing important roles in communities. What is less clear, however, is the precise relationship between the strength of the organizations in a community and the community's overall capacity. Building organizational capacity is not exactly the same as building community capacity, although there may be conditions under which these two capacities are likely to be highly aligned. According to our framework (see Figure 1), this alignment will be greatest if organizations in a community actively reinforce a sense of community and commitment to that community among residents, and provide vehicles for addressing the community's problems and gaining access to resources, both within and outside the community.

To maximize the impact of organizational development strategies on community capacity, it may be important to exploit the connections between this strategy and the other three described in this volume. In other words, building or strengthening organizations may only have modest implications for the overall capacity of the community if this strategy does not at the same time build leadership, social capital, and ties among organizations. If that is the case, the ways in which community initiatives build organizational capacity should be shaped, in part, by asking how they can contribute to the development of leadership, effective networks and social capital, and organizational collaboration in the process. For example, does the organizational development effort somehow nurture, enhance, or multiply individual skills and talents? Does it provide a forum for bringing people together to identify and act upon common goals? Does it contribute to an organizational infrastructure in the community that is collaborative, inclusive, and responsive to a range of key local needs? To the extent that these questions can be answered positively, the link between organizational development and community capacity is likely to be close.

Another way of thinking about the connection between organizational development and community capacity is suggested by current conceptions of organizational effectiveness, which emphasize the creation of organizations that are both mission- and constituent-driven, and capable of flexibility and rapid response. According to prevailing theory, this is accomplished by making mission and vision the standard against which all organizational activities are reflected and evaluated, increasing the participation of constituents and staff in decision-making, and developing the organization's capacity to respond to a rapidly changing environment (Ackoff, 1994; Knauft, Berger, and Gray, 1994; Kanter, 1997). These three elements of organizational effectiveness seem particularly relevant for community capacity as described in our framework. Organizations striving to be mission-driven have to work hard to resist inevitable tendencies to focus inward toward organizational maintenance and survival. If guided by a mission that involves serving the community in one way or another, organizations should, according to current theory about effectiveness, establish a set of mission-generated community outcome goals to which they hold themselves accountable. And as "learning organizations," they should have built-in mechanisms for ongoing assessment of their practice as community concerns and conditions evolve (see, e.g., Ellerman, 1998).

Establishing accountability is important in low-income communities into which substantial resources flow "on behalf of the community," often through government agencies for which few accountability mechanisms exist. This is one of the reasons why having a strong connection to its con-stituency(ies) is an important indicator of organizational effectiveness. A well-informed and active constituency can provide ongoing feedback about how well the organization is fulfilling its mission and how emerg-ing needs and changes in the environment might require changes in the or-ganization's policies and practice. A strong community base also helps an organization to make a credible case for more funding and to have a voice in policy debates on issues, such as welfare reform or affordable housing, that are likely to have significant effects on the neighborhood. Thus, an ac-tive and engaged constituency is related to both organizational and com-munity capacity: It can enhance an organization's power and voice, and it can increase the community's role in shaping organizational agendas to be more responsive to the needs of the community. This is why organizations, like churches, with a voluntary broad-based membership and built-in ac-countability have a special contribution to make to overall community capacity.

Although responsiveness to community constituencies often takes more time on the part of the organization's staff and board, especially if decision-making is truly participatory, the rationale for this expenditure of resources is its contribution to organizational effectiveness and sus-tainability. Throughout the chapter we have noted the kinds of tensions that exist in organizations that strive to establish and maintain connec-tions to their constituencies: tensions about organizational ownership and change and about balancing expectations for process and instrumental goals. Although there are many mechanisms through which an organiza-tion can be responsive to its constituencies, we know little about their rel-ative benefits in actual operation. Our limited reconnaissance suggests that these mechanisms do not have to be limited to, or even necessarily have to include, involving residents and other neighborhood stakeholders in the organization's board. Indeed, organizations may identify other approach-es that are equally or more efficient and effective in engaging particular groups. Such approaches might include supporting residents' initiatives; engaging service recipients or consumers in ongoing feedback; and in-volving people as volunteers, members of committees or advisory groups, or participants in periodic self-evaluation and strategic-planning sessions for the organization (Nonprofit Sector Research Fund, 1999). Many com-munity-based organizations consider hiring local residents an important way to reduce their distance from the community. Although it often re-quires an organization to develop innovative recruitment and selection strategies, as well as ongoing supervision and opportunities for training and advancement, hiring community residents can help an organization gain legitimacy and operate more responsively in the community (Bruner, 1998). In sum, we have begun to identify ways in which organizations create links to the community that can both increase organizational effectiveness and contribute to community capacity. But there is much more to learn about how these linkages work operationally and how they influence the ways a community actually functions.

The connection between strengthening community-based organizations and building community capacity provides the rationale for a number of foundation investments in organizations as the vehicles through which residents can identify and act on their concerns to improve neighborhood conditions. The assumption is that people can gain a stronger voice and exercise more power through involvement in community-based organizations than they would if they acted individually (Charles Stewart Mott Foundation, 1984). Thus, the organization works directly to improve community conditions (e.g., improve schools, stimulate housing development, protect the rights of immigrants) and indirectly to produce an engaged citizenry and leadership, "which when tapped, can create stability and security in the most troubled and impoverished community" (ibid.:15). Kretzman and McKnight (1993) note that every community organization is a potential "treasure chest" for the community if it can connect with and mobilize the capacities of local citizens. The more an organization can develop relationships that are authentic rather than token, mutual rather than one-sided, and flexible rather than rigid, the more an organization is likely to be able to connect effectively to its constituency and, through this connection, contribute to community capacity.

NOTES

1. Funders are increasingly recognizing the symbiotic relationship they have with organizations: "Funders need partners or we'll be like one hand clapping. Supporting organizational effectiveness is a 'win-win' situation," *Foundation News,* January/February, 1999, p. 15.
2. See Introduction for a brief explanation of the three initiatives—Neighborhood and Family Initiative, Glades Community Development Corporation, and Consensus Organizing Demonstration Program—used for the core case studies of this book. See Appendices for full explanations.
3. One such example is described in Mayer (1994).
4. These measures are similar though not identical to the five measures of organizational capacity (resource, organizational, network, programmatic, and political capacity) that Norman Glickman and Lisa Servon (1998) suggest.
5. The many organizational supports UNH and its settlement house members have used to foster, implement, and sustain community-building efforts, including those summarized here, are described in Hirota and Ferroussier-Davis, 1998).

4

Community Organizing

Beyond developing the individual components of community (people and organizations), capacity-building efforts often focus on developing relationships among these components and on collective action. Community organizing is one approach to doing so. We define community organizing broadly as the process of bringing people together to solve community problems and address collective goals. The objectives of a community-organizing effort vary, ranging from the procurement of resources and the acquisition of power to the redefinition of group identity. They may seek to overturn a set of institutions entirely, or they may wish to improve the institutions' efficiency, responsiveness, and relationship with clients.

Community organizing may involve not only individuals, but also organizations and networks mobilized to reach a common goal. In most initiatives, organizing will probably occur to some degree on all of these levels. In our framework for understanding community capacity building (Figure 1), organizing can promote different kinds of community capacity. Bringing residents together for collective action may produce normative outcomes, such as a sense of community or more effective socialization of young people. Organizing may enhance the social capital of individuals by increasing and strengthening relations among neighbors and by developing trust and recognition of mutual interests. Residents may be organized to seek improvement in the delivery of goods and services, such as policing or sanitation, and this may entail gaining greater influence and access to resources outside the community—what we have called a fundamental characteristic of capacity. Community-organizing efforts may also be used to reform governance mechanisms and improve decision-making among a set of actors that are already working together, or help to create new alliances.

Although "community capacity building" is a relatively newly defined area of policy and practice, community organizing is an established activity with a long and illustrious history.[1] There are philosophical schools of community organizing grounded in political ideology and theories of practice. These are *actual* schools and training centers that provide training for organizers, sending them back to their communities fitted with techniques, tactics, and knowledge. There are courses in social work schools and other study programs that expose students to the history, methods, and intent of organizing for social change. And there are active debates, such as the contemporary one between those who emphasize conflict and direct action as a principal tool versus those who espouse consensus-based approaches. We use a very broad definition of community organizing, recognizing that it goes far beyond the set of strategies historically associated with traditional organizing. We do so because our interest lies in exploring the ways people come together to solve common problems and pursue collective goals. The question that guides our inquiry is: How do community capacity–building efforts engage in community organizing, and toward what end? This chapter first discusses the types of strategies that are employed for effecting particular kinds of change, then considers some of the cross-cutting issues and challenges that face the majority of community capacity–building initiatives with an organizing component.

COMMUNITY-ORGANIZING STRATEGIES

Community organizing offers numerous avenues for developing community capacity. It increases residents' exposure to new people and organizations, both inside and outside their community, and enables them to acquire new knowledge and skills. It fosters network development among participants, who may then use the momentum and new relationships to take on other activities. It can enhance a community's access to resources and increase feelings of community and belonging among residents.

Community capacity–building initiatives use a range of community organizing strategies to achieve these ends. Since the aim of the chapter is to look at the relationship between community organizing and capacity building, we begin by looking at dimensions of organizing strategies currently used in community-based initiatives, the tactics they use, and the kinds of capacity they engender (or fail to engender). As with the leadership strategies described in Chapter 2, each strategy here has the following three basic dimensions that reflect a choice along a continuum: (1) whether to use a strategy based on conflict or consensus; (2) whether to focus on a single issue or multiple issues; and (3) whether to recruit individuals directly or through existing organizations.

Conflict versus Consensus

Community capacity–building efforts seek to change existing conditions, whether to bring about increased self-efficacy or to reach a practical goal, such as clean streets. The appropriate strategic choice between con-flict and consensus building hinges on an assessment of how important stakeholders are likely to react to change efforts and on assumptions about the most effective ways to respond to their reactions. No matter how laud-able, the proposed intervention can be expected to encounter resistance at some points. Some individuals or organizations may benefit directly from the status quo; for example, city sanitation workers may not be cleaning the streets in neighborhoods with high crime rates and may resist assign-ments to do so. Other stakeholders may simply see no reason to change, assuming that change would require some effort while providing little benefit to them. Such inertia is especially common in large bureaucratic or-ganizations. The strategy chosen by a community capacity–building effort is usually selected to deal effectively with anticipated resistance. That choice will also affect how others react to the desire for change and will de-termine the types of steps that an initiative can take to mobilize residents. It will also have important consequences for the types of capacity initia-tives build.

Conflict-Based Strategies.   Conflict-based organizing approaches to building community capacity, which have a long history, employ opposi-tional tactics to bring about desired ends. Marches at city hall, sit-ins at a university administration building, and mass street-based protests (com-monly referred to as *actions*) are some of the most public and well-known tactics. The decision to employ this strategy is sometimes motivated sim-ply by a frustration with the status quo. But the rationale for using conflict is the presumption that powerful individuals and institutions will not change their ways—so that a perceived inequity or injustice can be changed—unless direct pressure is used. The initial objective may be to publicize and raise awareness of a perceived disparity or injustice, but the effort will have a more concrete ultimate goal—such as dismantling a mu-nicipal job queue under the sway of racist unions or forcing changes in the practices of a discriminatory homeowners' association. One of the most popular and successful examples of the conflict-style approach is the In-dustrial Areas Foundation (IAF) organizing model, developed by Saul Alinsky in the mid–twentieth century. From its beginnings in one neigh-borhood in Chicago, the IAF engages in parish-based organizing through working with local churches, and now supports a network of organizing efforts working through about forty local organizations in eight states and the United Kingdom. The presence of such an external facilitator or spon-sor can enhance capacity building by providing a local effort with the nec-essary resources, and enabling it to learn from others who share similar circumstances. It has been employed effectively, for example, by Balti-moreans United in Leadership Development (BUILD), an IAF-affiliated or-ganizing intermediary that works through churches to organize citizen

direct action campaigns.[2] BUILD's success in mobilizing people to participate in public protests has on occasion enabled it to act in a representa-
tional role, with smaller protests seen as having the backing of several
thousand additional people. Similarly, People United for a Better Oakland
Organization (PUEBLO) is an organizing intermediary associated with the
Center for Third World Organizing (CTWO). PUEBLO, which provides
support and engages in organizing campaigns with affiliates in Oakland,
Denver, and Portland, Oregon, spearheaded a campaign to challenge police abuse and to reform the civilian review board, which monitors police
response to allegations of abuse. The campaign centered on providing a
hotline and assistance in filing complaints and culminated in a city hall
hearing at which about two hundred people gathered to challenge the
city's handling of the issue.

Consensus-Based Strategies. In contrast to conflict-based strategies,
consensus-based approaches to organizing do not presume that conflict is
required to stimulate change. Rather, organizers taking this approach seek
to identify and work with people in influential positions who would welcome change or at least be open to it. They tend to eschew or downplay oppositional tactics. Instead, they work to produce change by promoting
mutual respect and productive interaction among community residents,
organizations, and external actors in ways that are expected to alter their
relative influence and ability to get things done. Emphasis is placed on
identifying and cultivating opportunities for mutual benefit. The Consensus Organizing Institute has been a leader in developing consensus-based
approaches to creating community capacity. Its founder, Michael Eichler,
describes the consensus approach this way:

> Instead of taking power from those who have it, consensus organizers build
> relationships in which power is shared for mutual benefit. . . . Cooperation,
> rather than confrontation, [becomes] the modus operandi for solving a
> neighborhood problem. (Eichler, 1998:26)

The Consensus Organizing Demonstration Project (CODP), one of our
core case studies,[3] provides an example of the approach. The project began
by identifying localities in which local philanthropies and a cadre of influential bankers and other corporate leaders were willing to support the
organization of CDCs as a way to improve conditions in low-income
communities—starting with the development of affordable housing. The
philanthropies were already focused on assisting those communities; the
bankers and corporate leaders typically had the twin motives of civic concern and self-interest, believing that strengthening poor neighborhoods
would be good for business. The bankers, in particular, saw the potential
of a new stream of Community Reinvestment Act (CRA) lending.

CODP then used a technique called *parallel organizing*, in which CODP staff mobilized residents of low-income communities, as well as "movers and shakers" outside those communities who could help and support the residents. In six target neighborhoods in each locality, organizers identified a representative group of residents and other local stakeholders (e.g., business owners, service providers) who agreed with this approach to improving their community and were willing to volunteer to implement the new CDCs. Thus, both the local stakeholders and their external supporters agreed on the objective and the strategy. The CODP organizers provided various kinds of organizational development and technical support to the CDC volunteers to enable them to select and pursue their initial projects. At the same time, they sought to educate the financial supporters about community development and to keep them aware of the volunteers' growing skills and accomplishments—laying the foundation for mutually respectful and beneficial relationships.

Relative Advantages and Disadvantages. Conflict- and consensus-based approaches will be more or less suitable to different types of circumstances. There are cases in which individuals in positions of influence are, in fact, genuinely opposed to the types of change communities would like to see happen. In such circumstances, a conflict-based approach may not only be preferable, it may be the only realistic alternative. In a traditional conflict-based strategy, an action—a mass mobilization of community residents—would be the tactic of choice. This approach can also be attractive when the issue at hand is pressing and seems to necessitate an immediate collective response, for example, to force the immediate end to dumping toxic waste in a residential neighborhood. A history of such conflict-filled situations, however, is likely to impede collaborative efforts to effectively address the problem.

The use of conflict can also generate public exposure more readily because the initiative's oppositional techniques are intentionally quite visible and because conflict tends to draw media attention. This publicity facilitates mobilization of public awareness and sympathy that can force change, for example, in city policy or the allocation of certain public funds. In contrast, in consensus organizing, dialogue and collaboration involve fewer people and usually take place in private—in a church meeting hall or a conference room rather than city hall plaza. Public attention is deliberately avoided until the expected gains have been achieved, when credit for the accomplishments is typically shared broadly.

Conflict approaches often provide a clear, simple statement of the problem. However, the solution, if articulated at all, may only be implicit. Community-based protests that seek to eliminate police brutality, for example, may use strongly charged wording that attracts residents and garners widespread support, but the organizing effort itself may not provide the actual alternatives that police and community representatives can use to improve the situation. In the short run, the organizing action may even heighten tension. Indeed, the provision of reform guidelines is often not a conflict-based effort; the action simply seeks to state the problem and mobilize support for change. Even when specific demands are made, they are likely to be broad. Protesters might demand, for example, that the city commit to providing a certain number of new beds and shelters for homeless individuals, without suggesting where the shelters should be built or which other funded activities should be canceled or postponed to pay for them—issues that might fragment the protesting group.

In contrast, consensus approaches tend to accommodate more nuanced discussion of complex problems, and they typically seek both to identify remedial programs that enjoy broad support and to assume some responsibility for implementing them. Because conflict-based approaches rely on the power of numbers, they mobilize greater numbers of people, but many of these, especially those who participate only for large public actions, have limited involvement. Consensus approaches tend to engage smaller numbers of people, but to keep them engaged over a sustained period of time, to build strong ties among them, and to build their individual and collective skills.

More broadly, the two types of approaches appear to develop different kinds of skills and networks. Conflict-based efforts typically focus on issues of accountability. Adherents of conflict tactics draw on the language of rights and justice, and participants learn to challenge authority collectively in an effort to hold influential people, such as elected officials or corporate board members, accountable for their actions. In this sense, the approach is fundamentally political. Conflict-based approaches, however, are less useful in building the capacity of individuals and communities to reconstruct programs, foundations, organizations, and the like. Participants in consensus organizing are more likely to learn to seek common ground, to compromise, and to develop solutions that are perceived as broadly beneficial to all parties. They also learn different ways to interact with those who are in power—actors who may not necessarily share the participants' views, but who have the resources that they are seeking or the capacity to bring about the changes they desire.

Combining Strategies.   Over the past fifty years, community organizing has gradually moved from an emphasis on confrontation toward a greater focus on consensus building. The shift has been stimulated partly by national social and political trends and partly by the internal dynamics of sustained capacity-building efforts. In the contemporary era of "collaboration" and "partnerships," the use of conflict is seen as less politically acceptable and hence as less effective than in years past. At the same time, changes within communities have altered the nature of community-organizing work. Consider the comments of an activist associated with conflict-based strategies:

> The assumptions that communities organized around twenty, thirty, and forty years ago are no longer valid. When the [IAF] began organizing during the fifties and sixties, its goal was to balance asymmetric power relationships within existing intermediary institutions. Today's organizers and leaders face dual challenges of restoring the civic culture that traditionally gave strength to intermediary institutions. . . . The work of IAF is best conceptualized as strengthening democratic culture through the development of civil society and citizenship—through conversation and negotiation.

This national shift is mirrored at the local level in a variety of circumstances—for example, in the experience of the elected tenant management boards in the public housing complexes administered by the Chicago Housing Authority (CHA). The boards once relied on the use of protests, rent strikes, door-to-door campaigns, and other confrontational and highly public demonstrations against inadequate CHA management policies. The use of conflict strategies was immensely useful in the 1960s and early 1970s, when the national tenor of grassroots organizing was based in such direct, confrontational challenges. However by the 1980s, as the national mood of protest subsided and blacks moved from "rebellion to reform" (Manning, 1984), the tenant leaders also entered the fray of bureaucratic policymaking. They began to rely on private meetings and closed-door negotiations with CHA officials (as opposed to highly publicized challenges) to voice the concerns of their constituents and to gain resources or win changes in public policy. Currently, tenant leaders have a strong voice in some of the city-federal collaborative planning sessions aimed at redeveloping the land tracts on which some of the largest public housing developments in Chicago are located.

This shift away from conflict-based approaches does not mean that they are obsolete, however. A proponent of conflict-based community organizing warns that the move toward collaborative principles may compromise the work of grassroots organizing:

> There is this feeling that the optimum relationship that CDCs need to have with the community is love-ins with mayors, corporations, and banks. And, therefore anything that might disturb that love-in is counterproductive. Well, the point is that that's not the way to win a war. And that love-ins, I think, are sometimes a prescription for mediocrity. You never want a love-in with a government. You want tension. You want to be able to beat the hell out of them and them knowing that you can do that, as well as showing that you want to cooperate where it is possible.

Establishing a position of power and then cooperating when possible aptly describes the internal dynamics of some conflict-based capacity-building efforts that are sustained over time. One example is the Communities Organized for Public Service (COPS) effort in San Antonio, a network of locally based coalitions of residents and other stakeholders initially brought together through faith-based organizing under the auspices of IAF. During its early years, when COPS was marginalized, its strategy was confrontational, involving, for example, sustained, disruptive actions at major banks. As it gained influence, however, COPS's approach shifted. Its "living wage" campaign grew out of local neighborhood-based meetings with residents who wanted to address the difficulties experienced by households whose income from work was insufficient to support its members. COPS staffers brought members of these households together to confront state legislators and businesspeople with demands to improve wages, training, and other factors tied to self-sustenance. At the same time, COPS developed Project Quest, funded by city and state governments, to initiate training and wage supports for workers. Although their work to sustain the program involves lobbying legislative leaders, COPS staffers argue that their capacity to mobilize large numbers of residents at neighborhood meetings or at the doorsteps of the state capitol forms the basis of their political clout and their ability to garner attention from external elites.

The experience of the Dudley Street Neighborhood Initiative (DSNI) in Boston illustrates an even sharper shift in the orientation and mission of an intervention over time. DSNI began by organizing public demonstrations against illegal dumping; they, in turn, catalyzed not only further actions but also an overall change in the organization. It has evolved into a major agency focusing on a range of development issues that it addresses collaboratively with the private sector and city government, in part, through the use of eminent domain powers (conferred to it by the city), which allow DSNI to redirect the use of property within a portion of the neighborhood. Today, its efforts are invested less in protest and more in conversations and collaborations with residents, city officials, corporate actors, and other CBOs (Medoff and Sklar, 1984). In both the DSNI and COPS example, the shift has been part of a move from simply trying to hold others accountable and get them to address a problem, toward assuming some active responsibility for identifying and implementing improvement efforts.

More difficult to manage than such gradual shifts is the simultaneous use of both approaches. For instance, many efforts in the recent wave of comprehensive community initiatives (CCIs)—often strongly inclined toward collaboration—have shown a willingness to turn to protest and confrontation in particular cases. In one, the Neighborhood Partners Initiative (NPI) in New York City, some sites organized mass demonstrations for better postal service, and others organized tenants' associations that "fought" bad landlords while at the same time trying to find some common ground with officials from the city's housing department about changing policies that were detrimental to the neighborhood.

Capacity-building initiatives reliant on external funding may lose support if they are perceived to shift from one tactic to another. The use of both strategies can also challenge an initiative's identity and its public image, thereby threatening its ability to recruit residents or retain allies who might have been drawn to the initiative because of its use of conflict (or consensus).

Single versus Multiple Issues

The second strategic dimension of choice for an organizing intervention is whether to focus on a single issue or multiple issues. In some cases, community-organizing efforts may choose to focus on a single issue (or a small set of interrelated issues) through targeted organizing strategies. In other cases, an organizing campaign may take on a wide range of concerns, either addressing them in concert or moving from one issue to another over time. Although it is not always the case, single-issue campaigns often tend to be highly targeted and therefore short-lived, such that their collective energy does not persist beyond the resolution of the issue at hand. In contrast, multiple-issue campaigns tend to institutionalize their collective energy by creating a mechanism to sponsor future organizing activities.

Single-Issue Strategies.   Efforts that build community capacity by focusing on a single issue (e.g., toxic waste) or a set of intimately linked issues (e.g., environmental quality) are *targeted organizing strategies.* Typically, such initiatives cast their membership net widely, welcoming anyone who shares their concerns. However, they may also engage in strategic recruitment by screening participants in terms of their interest, commitment, qualifications, or knowledge of the issues involved. By bringing people together and promoting unified action around a focal set of concerns, targeted organizing efforts hope to enhance the problem-solving capacities of communities, as well as to serve as a vehicle for strengthening community bonds and commitment. Although they sometimes recruit organizations, these initiatives focus most often on individual residents and other stakeholders. For example, early in its existence, the Neighborhood and Family Initiative (NFI) collaborative in the north end of Hartford organized a series of forums to protest a board of education proposal to restructure the curriculum of a neighborhood middle school. The proposal was part of a citywide plan to transform a set of middle schools to provide specialized instruction in different substantive areas, such as science, mathematics, and the arts. The collaborative spearheaded the effort to oppose the plan, which would have designated the north-end school to have a concentrated arts curriculum (while providing "hard science" concentrations for south-end schools), and mobilized neighborhood residents and organizations to protest. Eventually, the plan was withdrawn.

Targeted organizing is a particularly useful strategy for resolving issues in low-income communities because fewer resources are required; the single issue provides a focal point for resident recruitment, and the issue enables the initiative to make efficient use of limited resident involvement.

Multiple-Issues Strategies.   Capacity-building efforts also use multiple issues to recruit and mobilize actors. PUEBLO, mentioned above as employing conflict-based approaches, is also a prominent, fairly well-known example of multiple-issue organizing. PUEBLO staff use multiple methods to recruit large numbers of residents, typically bringing them together by soliciting their concerns and then leading a demonstration or protest to act on those concerns. Residents list their problems and needs, and the staff help them organize in a manner that increases social bonds, develops their commitment to the community, and tries to enable them to solve their problems. Staff members attempt to maintain continuous contact with a local pool of residents through phone calls, mailings, door-to-door visits, and invitations to join particular organizing campaigns. They also convene on a regular basis with a smaller "core membership," to whom they assign part of the responsibility for helping bring out more of the "general membership" for the bigger actions. Thus, the staff makes strategic use of residents' energies, drawing on their resources to different degrees, depending on the individual. The issue receiving focus can change over time, and change usually is driven by the expressed will of residents.

This type of multiple-issue organizing approach is similar to strategies used by other organizations, such as the Association of Community Organizations for Reform Now (ACORN), that enter a community and promote direct action on the part of residents. PUEBLO, however, distinguishes its approach from that of ACORN and others by its explicit search for issues that it can politicize to highlight the existence of racial inequities, as well as power asymmetries based on race and class. In the words of the PUEBLO director, by expressing a preference for issues that allow it to advance a particular ideological agenda, PUEBLO tries "to make a fairly strong statement about racism in general and to explicate what we think are cases of racial oppression and exploitation, in particular, and to also model multiracial ways of responding to the issues that we want to address."

Relative Advantages and Disadvantages.   Targeted organizing is an effective way to generate community capacity because residents are asked to play defined roles and to address a single concern. In this way, demands on their time are kept to a minimum. Given the significant constraints on residents' time, this is an important factor, whether the initiative is seeking to organize large numbers of residents or is searching for the commitment of only a few. There is always the risk, however, that such capacity is tied to the status of the problem or concern in question and that, once the issue is resolved, the capacity generated may dissipate, although it may remain available in a latent state possibly to be activated again. Collaborations of residents that have successfully addressed an issue may generate ties and mutual trust among participants and collaborating organizations. Block clubs, for example, often are loose-knit assemblages of residents who come together to address a problem, only to go their separate ways (or remain connected in other ways) until another issue arises.

Another risk of targeted organizing efforts is the possible lack of interest within the community over one particular issue. As a means to cater to the diversity that exists in a community, an organization may therefore seek to organize around multiple issues. This approach has the particular advantage of continually renewing collective capacity, at least among those constituencies that are involved or affected. PUEBLO's approach is illustrative. It has chosen multiple issues in order to connect with Oakland's many different racial and ethnic populations, each of which has its particular concerns. PUEBLO's multiple-issue strategy not only ensures that some constituency will be working on behalf of the community at any given time, but it also reflects the fact that different members of the community will feel passionate about different issues, and their motives to become involved will depend on the issue in question. Moreover, for any single issue, there may be multiple opinions. PUEBLO feels that its own efforts increase collective capacity, not by forcing people to agree on an issue, but by providing a forum for typically unrepresented opinions to reach the light of day:

> I think we actually challenge the notion that there is—that in any of our communities—there is a kind of single voice on the issues, and I think crime and public safety is a prime example where there certainly is a vocal, maybe numerical majority which at this point is calling for more punishment, more arrests, more swift and direct police action. Does that mean that this community unambivalently and unanimously believes that? I don't think so. I think there's also an active group of folks that want to see another approach, and so the extent that we organize and kind of represent that sentiment, that's what our role [is].

The recent wave of community policing initiatives is an excellent example of the diversity of community opinion that can manifest along a single issue. In Chicago, community policing has involved residents and local organizations. Law enforcement personnel work with residents, block clubs, and community organizations to increase resident safety. The intent is to draw on resident awareness of happenings in the community to help police conduct surveillance and investigation, to create productive relations between residents and police officers, and to strengthen the level of involvement of residents in their community. An important obstacle that has arisen is the different opinions residents have of the police. Those who feel alienated from law enforcement have advocated a "self-help" strategy to address problems such as gang activity and narcotics trafficking. In many instances, they have taken matters into their own hands, eschewing the community-policing effort entirely by approaching gang members on their own and by establishing relationships with them or challenging them with threats or protests. They have formed "community watches" to monitor drug selling and gang recruitment, and they have charged some residents with the task of approaching gang leaders to relay their concerns. Other residents feel that this is a dangerous strategy and prefer to enlist police officers as the neighborhood's primary liaison with gangs and criminals (see Venkatesh, 1999). Interestingly, the self-help advocates have used their collective labors to expand their work beyond the issue of policing. Some have joined together to oppose city proposals for redevelopment that would eliminate low-income housing in their neighborhoods.[4]

Both targeted and multiple-issue organizing have shown promise for the development of community capacity. Targeted organizing campaigns provide a clear catalyst for resident mobilization and can be effective in providing short-term victories, as well as providing a foundation for positive and renewable resident interactions and network development. A well-funded and well-planned multiple-issue campaign can be suited to the development of community capacity by acknowledging various interest groups and gathering them around the table to engage in sustained dialogue and collaboration. Multiple-issue campaigns (assuming the organizational infrastructure exists to support them) may have more flexibility to respond to demographic and political changes in the residential base, dedicating their resources accordingly as issues and concerns arise.

Another advantage of the multiple-issue strategy is that it uses any organizing effort as a pedagogic device to make a client pool aware of hidden, abstract, or underlying dimensions of particular issues. The aim is to expose power structures that reproduce inequities in different contexts. By focusing on structural matters, this tactic lays the groundwork for future mobilization by moving the focus of the effort away from the concrete issue at hand, to a larger institutional apparatus—for example, city administration or corporate-government ties—that residents can identify, even if they cannot directly affect it. However, moving from the practical issue at-hand to an ideological or political level risks alienating residents who do not share the political beliefs of the organizing effort. For example, persons who wish to join a PUEBLO campaign that targets industrial polluters may be motivated by an interest in bettering their community, but they may have no interest in the larger political goals of PUEBLO, and their decision on whether to participate could ultimately reflect their personal degree of opposition to PUEBLO's political views. PUEBLO is cognizant of this problem: As a PUEBLO organizer states, the organization is interested in representing a political voice in the community, not the community per se.

Combining Strategies.   Single-issue campaigns can sometimes become a starting point for capacity-building initiatives to develop into more comprehensive efforts. This change may accompany a change in the level of formality of the organization. For example, neighborhood block clubs commonly focus on crime prevention and security matters but may turn their attention to infrastructure and social issues when they arise. Block clubs are exemplary mechanisms through which resident commitment, connection, and associational action can be fostered. "Tenant patrol" associations in public housing complexes play a similar role, recruiting residents into round-the-clock observation of social behavior—gang activity, the play of children, the movement of strangers—in the housing development. Block clubs and tenant patrol associations tend to have informal organizational structures. In fact, they will often disband or remain dormant after their initial work is completed until a new issue arises and motivates residents to act again in a unified effort.

The organizational structure of block clubs is generally quite casual; they typically lack a title of incorporation, officers, and formal committees. Rather, they are informal associations of residents whose principal shared attribute is geographic propinquity. In this way, and in their potential to endure over time (even through periods of inactivity), they are distinct from many traditional organizing campaigns. Block clubs are also distinct because they often have a fluid and informal leadership structure, their membership ebbs and flows, and they depart from a central tenet of traditional single-issue mobilization; in the words of CTWO's Gary Delgado, a veteran organizer, "They opt not to develop an ongoing powerful organization that can generally advocate the interests of a constituency but to make specific demands from one institution at a specific point in time" (Delgado, 1994:47).

The shift by block clubs from a single focus to a broader one can occur in at least two ways. In some cases, existing clubs that are dormant or have a limited focus can be mobilized by an external agent. For example, Blocks Together in Chicago began as a loose network of several block clubs in the racially mixed and ethnically diverse neighborhood of Humboldt Park. A community organizer from the National Training and Information Center, a Chicago-based organizing intermediary, approached the clubs and recruited them into a network, using a vision of building a grassroots organization and a larger structure that could more effectively gain access to funding and city resources. As participation increased, residents identified a wider array of concerns, from safety and policing to ecological and physical infrastructure problems, to schools and the allocation of city services. Some of these issues transcended neighborhood boundaries to address metropolitan matters. For example, a movement to assist a local elementary school evolved into a campaign that addressed the nature of school funding for the city as a whole. In the words of the organization's director:

> After a couple of years as we were growing [we were] able to take on bigger issues, communitywide issues, such as education. Like school overcrowding, or school repairs. The viaduct was one of those big issues of Blocks Together where they said we have all those crumbling viaducts and residents were hit by rocks falling and pieces falling from the viaducts, so there was a campaign where Blocks Together went after the railroad company and held them accountable.

In other cases, block residents can come together around a broad community improvement goal but begin with a single, actionable issue. In Hartford, for example, the Upper Albany Neighborhood Collaborative (UANC), part of the NFI initiative, has worked with block clubs on an expanding array of community projects, including participation in farming cooperatives that produce food for lower-income and elderly residents, advocating for improved neighborhood lighting, installing smoke detectors in homes, and campaigning for the placement of a police substation in a neighborhood.

As block clubs increase the formality of their organizational structure, they may move away from the specific set of issues that catalyzed their formation to a wider range of resident concerns. In this manner, targeted organizing may evolve into the recruitment of residents concerned with multiple issues, although at any one time one particular concern may stand at the forefront of the block club's efforts to mobilize residents and effect change.

Direct versus Organization-Based Recruitment

The third strategic dimension of choice concerns the extent to which organizing efforts to create community capacity recruit individuals directly or work through existing organizations and associations in the neighborhood. Both strategies are prevalent in community capacity–building initiatives, and sometimes they coexist.

Direct Recruitment Strategies.   A number of methods are used to engender broad involvement in an effort, including mass mailings, door-to-door canvassing, and telephone solicitation. When the recruits assemble, the organizer typically interacts with them to choose a set of concerns that will guide their collective efforts. The organizer also tries to develop indigenous leaders from the pool of participants. In low-income neighborhoods, direct recruitment strategies typically employ protest and strategic-pressure tactics, and are therefore usually oriented toward conflict rather than consensus.

ACORN, founded in 1970, was the first "group to develop a replicable organizing model for a direct-membership community organization" (Delgado, 1994:28). ACORN is present in twenty-seven cities and employs direct-recruitment mobilization strategies—from informal networking and door-to-door canvassing to organizing house meetings and holding neighborhoodwide meetings—for a diverse array of issues, which are identified and developed through the organizing process and range from bank lending to campaign reform.

Capacity-building initiatives that use an intermediary organization to lend structure to the initiative typically use some form of direct recruitment. Often this is done through the use of a core group of residents who are trained to go back into the community to recruit other residents and learn about common concerns. The NFI collaborative in Milwaukee, for example, hired an outreach worker to conduct door-to-door visits and recruitment efforts, and engaged collaborative members living in the neighborhood in an "each one reach one" campaign. These tactics were meant to provide information and gather feedback from residents on their priorities and needs, as well as to recruit resident volunteers to serve on collaborative committees and engage in collaborative-sponsored activities. Although an outside organizer may be used, a trained resident may often have an identifiable, more intimate connection with other low-income residents.

One localized form of direct recruitment to increase community capacity is the creation and use of local block clubs. Because they often include individuals with a property investment in the neighborhood, block club members display great concern and commitment to local issues. Participants may already be familiar with one another before the club is formed. This is not a necessary condition, however, and persons recruited into the block club may have had no previous ties to their neighbors, especially in urban and renter communities. The founder of a block club in the Washington Park neighborhood of Chicago makes precisely this point:

> I passed by these people every day, a lot of us had houses on the same street, it's just that we never got out and said hi, and now, we got meetings and we know each other, our families do things together. If the [Neighborhood Club] didn't get going, we probably would still pass by each other, never say hi.

Organization-Based Recruitment. An alternative approach to mobilizing individuals is to work through existing organizations in communities. Here, individuals are recruited by virtue of being members, patrons, or clients of an organization such as a church, CBO, or neighborhood association. The strategic emphasis in this mode of recruitment is to use an organization (or set of organizations) as the vehicle for locating, screening, and recruiting residents into the capacity-building effort. This mediator may be a single organization or a federation of existing organizations.

Perhaps the most common empirical example of this strategy is faith-based communities. In this case, churches are the principal organizations through which resident recruitment is conducted. This strategy is most widely used by IAF, which has organizers in cities across the country that bring together churchgoers to address a variety of neighborhood issues identified by residents or organizational leaders but that differ by community. In Texas, for example, COPS draws on IAF strategies through the use of "house meetings" that take place in homes, churches, schools, or other meeting places, where residents and organizations discuss and identify relevant community concerns. In each community, this basic framework—with the church at the center—is replicated. Community capacity here is partly evident in the community's ability to solve local problems by engaging these local associational networks, but it also draws strength from its participation in a network of other communities organized in similar fashion.

Relative Advantages and Disadvantages.   The principal disadvantage of direct-recruitment strategies is that they do not directly build on the networks and access to individuals that some organizations provide, and they therefore often require more effort and time to mobilize large numbers of residents for any given action. However, direct-recruitment strategies are often well suited to targeting neglected or marginalized constituencies typically found in poor communities where residents do not have much involvement with local organizations. For example, No More Wars, a Chicago-based organization specializing in dispute resolution among the city's street gangs, wanted to increase youth voter registration in Chicago's principally African-American South Side communities as part of its larger interest in developing a base of residents whom they could mobilize to participate in public demonstrations. The organization enlisted the support of ex–gang members who had intimate knowledge about at-risk youths. These ex-members walked the streets, visited dens where drugs where sold, and sponsored educational campaigns to register alienated youths to vote. The organization then used the enlisted youths in boycotts against local merchants who did not hire African Americans and in marches against school funding inequities. The ex–gang members also recruited individuals in their communities who, based on the legitimacy they had built because of their work as conflict mediators, had access to youth at the margins (Venkatesh, 1999). Other service providers in the South Side communities had been conducting similar efforts, but their success was less because they were using more-mainstream organizations to locate and attract at-risk youths. Since these youths have limited contact with schools, service providers, libraries, churches, and so forth, these mainstream organizations were not able to reach this youth population.

In those instances when direct recruitment successfully engages large numbers of residents in public lobbying, their actions effectively advertise community capacity both to other community residents and to the wider world. In some low-income areas, such advertising helps gain community-wide support. For example, for many reasons, public housing tenants have particularly low rates of involvement in political efforts. Part of their hesitation is based on their perception that participation may endanger their receipt of government subsidies or their ability to remain in public housing (see Venkatesh, 2000). Consequently, tenant leaders face great difficulty enlisting support for their programs and initiatives, especially if these challenge the status quo. As one leader who wanted to organize a grocery store boycott in her public housing community explained:

> These folks think that if they sign the petition, the [Housing Authority] is gonna kick them out. They don't understand their rights, they're afraid. You can't blame them: They're poor, they got nowhere to go, if they start yelling, they think they're gonna lose their apartment.

The same leader found that her ability to bring community residents together gradually increased once residents saw that peers and neighbors who participated in the boycott did not lose their leases or government benefits.

In contrast to direct recruitment, one limitation of the organization-based approach is that the networks for resident recruitment will be related to the particular characteristics of the organizations. Faith-based networks, for example, will likely not include individuals with no ties to a church. This dynamic can hold for any effort, not simply those working within religious networks and associations. This does not necessarily imply that all sectors of the community need to be represented in each capacity-building effort. As noted above, in some cases, community capacity may be generated through the involvement of small numbers of residents. The more important point is that care must be taken not to assume that collective capacity for the overall community will follow when recruitment is grounded in the work and constituencies of existing organizations.

Another potential disadvantage of relying on organizations to spearhead organizing in a community is that community organizations may vary widely in their knowledge of and access to community residents, particularly in communities with extreme institutional evisceration and poverty. Daily social interaction may proceed largely on an informal basis, and people may not actively patronize local organizations when in need. Or they may seek the assistance of grassroots organizations that are "under the radar" of prominent capacity-building efforts.

This strategy does provide advantages, however. Local organizations can facilitate resident recruitment because they have access to constituents, are perceived as already invested in the health and welfare of the community, and are in touch, at least from one perspective, with community needs and assets. Certain existing organizations may also have a history of advocacy (lobbying as well as community organizing) and so will understand the levels of interest and commitment of their constituents and can add legitimacy, speed up the implementation process, and attract residents who may not be responsive to direct outreach.

This recruitment strategy is also used to screen for residents who will be suitable for the capacity-building process. Suitability may differ by initiative and can be assessed with criteria such as knowledge of the issues involved, level of interest in the initiative, or commitment to the community. The Partnership for Neighborhood Initiatives (PNI), a project supported by a consortium of public and private funders and service providers in West Palm Beach, Florida, wanted "genuine residents" who had "some sense of who they were and what they wanted to accomplish." In COPS, different levels of resident involvement are sought, ranging from a "local leader" to people who will simply attend meetings. In fact, most initiatives that focus on mobilizing organizations seek to cultivate leadership, not just resident participation. Churches and other community-based organizations can facilitate the selection process because pastors, principals, social service agency directors, and others are aware of the capacities of their members (or clients or congregations) and can suggest appropriate individuals.

CODP is an example of the costs entailed when not using organizations to screen for resident participants. Here, initiative organizers chose to develop their own "chains" of connections to residents, based mainly on referrals from people that they interviewed. As a result, each organizer spent about three months identifying a core group of twelve to eighteen members for each of two CDCs. At the same time, this initiative illustrates the potential benefits that can accompany those costs: the CDC members demonstrated intense commitment over a long period of time, and they enjoyed sustained credibility as community representatives because they so clearly reflected the diversity of their respective neighborhoods.

The potential advantages of using existing organizations, however, are not always realized in practice. Local organizations come with their own "baggage" and may not be easy to work with in all communities. They may have ongoing turf battles with one another, may compete for the same funding pools, or may be seen as having their interests aligned with particular subpopulations. Neighborhood associations, for example, are widely seen as aligned with the interests of home owners, and CDCs with those of low-income residents (Chaskin, 2000). Existing interorganizational relationships may seriously affect the ability to forge a collective community-wide effort. In NFI's Milwaukee site, tension arose between the collaborative and existing organizations in the community, as well between the NFI collaborative and some of the new organizations spawned by the effort. The creation of the collaborative highlighted many of the established differences among these organizations. Such relations may not be easily discoverable, and in some cases, they may only surface after the initiative has been developed and implemented. For example, the Chicago Community Trust's Children, Youth, and Families Initiative created a collaborative (the Grand Boulevard Federation) in a large South Side Chicago community to reform service provision for youth. The federation was dominated by the largest providers—those with a large staff, experience in grant procurement, or political clout in larger government and philanthropic circles. This made the engagement of smaller service providers difficult, since many of them had felt alienated from the larger providers in the past.

Combining Strategies. Although the use of block clubs for direct action via direct recruitment has traditionally been cited as an example of a small group of residents acting together in local matters, there have been creative uses of block club networks as organizations through which individuals are recruited into programs and kept abreast of resources available to them. In NFI's Hartford site, UANC has attempted to build a network of block clubs formally linked to it through a standing committee. This arrangement, in theory, would foster relationships among neighbors and connect them to resources available through NFI. As one resident suggests:

> [It's] one way to make sure that the residents here can take advantage of the training that they say they were going to offer or the buying of houses that they say they were going to offer. And the people come to something on a regular basis. It's better than just putting out sporadic calls, you know, "Come, we want to talk to you." But if there are regular meetings and regular gatherings and people get to know one another. I lived here for twenty years, I didn't know anybody until I got involved in this. You know, people on my street, I used to see them, but now I know their names, you know, you have smiles and nods and all of the contact that goes on. I know people far better, and people are more interactive than they ever were.

In this case, the individual block clubs in Hartford began through the use of direct recruitment. But once incorporated into the NFI collaborative, they became examples of existing organizations through which residents could be recruited and engaged.

A somewhat contrasting use of block clubs in a larger network to promote community capacity comes from Blocks Together in Chicago. Its founder used the block club strategically:

> Basically, what happened was I would go out, I would door knock, I would identify issues, I would identify residents that would be willing to work together, and we started out on a block level where we just get like thirty, forty residents from one particular block who would meet and basically identify a number of issues.

Blocks Together began by developing a "core group of residents" who were committed to canvassing, contacting city officials, researching information, attending public meetings, and so forth. After starting with a single club that organized around small but important quality-of-life issues, the organization eventually expanded to cover 150 blocks and began to take on bigger, communitywide issues. Even when part of the network, the block club was always focused on specific issues—to fix a broken light, to protest school funding—and the direct recruitment of residents has always remained at the core of Blocks Together's organizing efforts to address local issues. Here (as with UANC in the Hartford NFI site), the club is the building block for a larger network or for other community-organizing efforts that seek to capitalize on the existence of localized resident groups. Unlike UANC, however, the creation of Blocks Together did not involve a shift from direct-recruitment organizing to organization-based recruitment. That is, the formation of a network of block clubs by Blocks Together was not intended to replace the direct-recruitment strategy.

There are, however, other examples of community capacity building in which direct recruitment and organization-based recruitment have been combined. PNI used both strategies, albeit at different stages of the initiative, to enhance the likelihood of promoting and sustaining resident participation. PNI staff first identified a core, or "catalytic," group by mailing out letters to over six hundred nonprofit organizations and local associations, including civic groups and churches. They identified a small number of residents and other stakeholders who displayed enough commitment to the community to help with a large-scale membership drive. A trained organizer then helped this small group of leaders conduct door-to-door canvassing, mass mailings, town hall meetings, and other direct-recruitment activities to bring community members into the initiative.

CROSS-CUTTING ISSUES

Regardless of their preferred organizing strategy, capacity-building initiatives will all face a generic set of challenges when they organize community residents. We highlight several particularly pressing issues because of their bearing on the broader effort to create community capacity. These include outreach and communication activities aimed at the target population, the representation and diversity of the neighborhoods where these people live, and sustaining the involvement of residents from these neighborhoods.

Outreach and Communication

Many contemporary community capacity–building initiatives operate as though the process of reaching out to residents is instrumental in creating community capacity and is, in itself, an important and necessary task. This belief differs significantly from the attitude of many traditional community organizers, who view outreach as a step toward a more "practical" goal, such as reforming institutions or publicizing injustices. Other organizers may avoid highly publicized outreach entirely in their work to avoid giving advance notice to their opposition. Our survey of what is taking place within community capacity–building initiatives today suggests that outreach and communication may indeed be critical for building capacity in impoverished neighborhoods, but is unlikely to be sufficient for fully developing that capacity.

In some cases, outreach may be accompanied by efforts focusing on the organizing strategies discussed above. In other cases, however, outreach campaigns and limited organizing for information sharing and the recruitment of small cadres of volunteers are the extent of the organizing component of the capacity-building effort. In NFI, for example, the collaboratives employed a number of outreach means, but only rarely went beyond such outreach to mobilize the community in the way one would expect of more traditional organizing efforts. The most central strategy was an informal and almost unspoken one to operate through the networks of association provided by collaborative members. Milwaukee went furthest in institutionalizing this notion through its Each One Reach One campaign. It also used more-targeted strategies, including a "skills inventory" survey of about 230 households, which introduced NFI to residents and gathered information on their priorities, skills, and work experience. Hartford sponsored a number of issue-based community forums, and both Hartford and Memphis fielded household surveys on resident perceptions and concerns. In these instances, community outreach becomes a substitute for community organizing, and initiatives may stop at striving to create mechanisms to communicate with the community about community priorities or, more likely, initiative activities, rather than striving to mobilize the community to action.

To some degree, all initiatives that seek to build capacity in a community will have to make their existence known to residents of that community. In some instances, an indigenous effort such as a block club may conduct a relatively thorough canvassing and assessment of community needs. Similarly, an external sponsor of a CCI might advertise its program to organizations and residents. In the cases of NFI and many other contemporary CCIs, such advertising has been an integral part of attracting resident interest and gaining local legitimacy. In other cases, a community-organizing effort may initially be more discreet in order to avoid raising expectations that cannot quickly be met. Efforts that seek to build capacity by mass enlistment of residents will obviously have to devote much time and energy to marketing and information dissemination.

Many capacity-building efforts have framed outreach and communication as community-organizing endeavors, activities that can enhance individual and collective capacities. They aim to provide for a flow of information between the initiative and a large proportion of community residents, as well as to begin to seed interactions among residents toward the creation of broader and denser interpersonal networks. In NFI, for example, the use of outreach and support of community forums was seen as a possible mechanism for enhancing interpersonal interaction among neighbors, as well as sharing critical information. Even the door-to-door canvassing and Each One Reach One campaigns in Milwaukee were fundamentally about information sharing, and, to some extent, soliciting potential volunteer interest. But these efforts were not generally connected to mobilizing the community at large for a particular end.

PNI engaged in outreach and communication activities and provides an example of the benefits that outreach and communication can potentially have for an initiative seeking to promote capacity at the community level. Here, initial contact with residents and stakeholders was made through knocking on doors, attending community meetings, sponsoring community events, informing local government representatives and politicians about the initiative, mobilizing informal community networks through the agency of involved residents, and gathering and sharing neighborhood data. The functions served by each activity in the overall initiative varied. For example, by gathering and sharing neighborhood data, initiative staff could work with residents to develop a vision for the neighborhood, based on a relatively accurate portrait of the residents' needs and priorities. Mobilizing informal networks helped broaden the initiative's reach into the community. Door-to-door canvassing and attending community meetings were helpful for promoting the change effort among diverse constituencies and acquainting the initiative staff with local stakeholders. In this manner, PNI shares with NFI sites the use of outreach as a means to develop social capital and rejuvenate the networks of associations among residents and organizations, not simply to publicize their own initiative. Although critical, these activities stop short of the kind of intentional mobilization and collective action generally referred to as community organizing.

Although outreach and communication, by themselves, do not constitute community organizing as we have defined it, they are often vital to capacity-building efforts in neighborhoods where the populace is alienated from institutions and lacks self-efficacy. Thus, it is not surprising that many community capacity–building efforts in impoverished neighborhoods emphasize the importance of systematic, sustained outreach and communication as a key strategy. In the words of one CCI director: "[Our goal] is to help residents who heretofore had never been involved, had never taken responsibility or any collective action to change the conditions in which they lived."

Capacity-building efforts may also place weight on outreach and communication in order to serve neglected or difficult-to-reach segments of a community. The gang intervention programs in Chicago sponsored by the Boys and Girls Clubs in America (BGCA), for example, hired outreach workers—typically ex–gang members—whose sole responsibility was to disseminate information to gang members regarding the availability of BGCA services and programs. The use of ex–gang members was seen as a means of gaining legitimacy in the eyes of alienated, at-risk youths. As one staff member stated:

> The OGs [ex–gang members] are the ones these kids will listen to. . . . It's a way for us to show we're for real, to show that we ain't trying to put something over them. You know, you see one of your brothers telling you about what we're doing, then you may listen to what he says.

Many of the recent community capacity–building initiatives have argued that the ability to engage in continuous communication with segments of the residential population is itself a sign of capacity. Thus, these initiatives place great weight on outreach and communication. The notion that sharing information is an organizing strategy—irrespective of whether the population receiving the information is then motivated toward practical action in the short run—may hold some merit when considered in institutionally depleted communities that are not well integrated into larger social institutions and spaces (another important characteristic of capacity). In these situations, resources are depleted, and people cannot always rely on institutions and formal public arenas as places to solicit information and express opinions and concerns. Instead, they turn to informal methods to communicate and share with one another. The community's capacity is not always easily discernible because it may be embedded in social networks and associations that are not easily transferable to a visible arena and a formal institutionalized initiative. The challenge for capacity-building initiatives, then, is to identify these forms of embedded knowledge, and it is reasonable to expect that many capacity-building efforts would emphasize outreach to capitalize on that knowledge. Moreover, these early steps to increase contact with the population may themselves promote a sense of belonging by creating a common knowledge about community-related issues. The use of outreach and communication, however, does not equate with the full development of community capacity. Outreach may help to create a sense of community and identify committed individuals, but it must be joined with other strategies if it is to help residents solve problems and gain access to resources in the wider world.

Representation and Diversity

Many capacity-building initiatives are based in low-income communities of color, and some are in areas where multiple ethnic cultures, languages, and constituencies coexist. These initiatives offer an extreme example of the need to be aware of problems of representation and diversity when recruiting residents into capacity-building efforts. Community-organizing techniques bring this issue into sharp relief, since they are typically designed to come directly into contact with an array of individuals, groups, and organizations. In communities where such diversity exists, the success of the initiative may depend on its success in mobilizing people from each constituent group.

Explicit attention to diversity is important because people from different ethnic groups will often feel differential attachment to particular issues. Thus, mobilizing individuals may become a particular challenge, to say nothing of forging consensus among them. This is likely to become increasingly true in cities across the nation as our population becomes increasingly diverse, with Latino and Asian populations—each coming from many different nations—playing larger and larger roles. In Oakland, for example, PUEBLO's target population is about 40 percent African-American, 30 percent white non-Latino, and 15 percent each Latino and Asian—both of which include people from several different countries. As one organizer suggests, this presents particular challenges for engaging these populations, both in terms of language and culture and because the groups become involved in different issues. Thus, building community capacity involves developing multiple capacities:

> Certainly language is a big thing. With the Asian community in particular, we don't have the capacity to speak—it's kind of now almost equally divided among Cambodian, Cantonese, and Vietnamese speaking, and there's also Hmong. So that's a kind of central one and I think, to some extent, [it affects] the issues you choose. I think the police brutality, the police accountability issues tend to attract more African Americans unless you do more deliberate things to get other folks in.

Recruiting members of numerous social groups is only the beginning of the challenges faced in working with diverse communities; sustaining their participation often requires quiet but persistent effort. In the two NFI communities (Milwaukee and Hartford) with somewhat ethnically diverse populations, efforts to engage members of the Latino communities met with only limited early success, and ultimately even modest participation could not be sustained. When participation can be engaged, particular efforts to promote communication and understanding need to be supported. For example, DSNI provides its written materials in English, Spanish, and Cape Verdian and does simultaneous translation of meeting deliberations into these languages. PUEBLO has conducted various culture-specific activities for its general membership to publicize cultural differences and create mutual understanding. In the words of one PUEBLO organizer:

> We have certain things about doing cultural work that looks to expand people's notion of what a developing, multicultural [community] kind of looks like. So we do membership meetings that focus on Black History month, on Day of the Dead, we do something for Lunar New Year, so we at least try to model a kind of multicultural ethos within the organization, kind of the organizational culture. And then we do try to really have folks closely examine some of the racial dimensions of the different campaigns that we look at.

Issues of diversity arise not only around race and ethnicity. Groups with divergent interests may be identified by a wide variety of attributes, including class, income, religion, sexual orientation, house-owner status, or residence in particular geographic subareas of the community. PNI, for example, faced divisions between high-income homeowners and low-income renters; not only did each group feel threatened by the other, but the renters were long-time residents whereas the homeowners were new to the area.

Various groups in the community may have a history of comfortable interaction, of quiet but separate coexistence, or of conflict (such as the struggles between public housing residents and local home owners in an area undergoing gentrification). Such differences need to be identified early, and common ground established, in order for an organizing effort to succeed; hence, the nature of differences and the effort required to bridge them should influence the choice of neighborhoods to target for community capacity building, as well as the resources and tactics that are brought to bear.

CODP dealt with this issue directly in its program design. In addition to building CDC boards that were racially and ethnically diverse, organizers were required to recruit members of six major interest groups (renters, home owners, business owners, religious leaders, representatives of service agencies, and representatives of major institutions such as hospitals and schools) to the board of every new CDC. This was done to ensure that the projects chosen would actually be in the interests of the community and that no major segment of the community could claim to be (or be perceived to be) left out of the process. By building legitimacy this way, the initiative reduced the likelihood of opposition to its projects and maintained its consensus orientation. Differences of opinion based on differing interests (e.g., renters versus property owners) had to be resolved within the board before projects were launched.

The need for sensitivity to representation and diversity often gives community organizing an advantage over other capacity-building strategies that do not pay as much attention to these issues. The NFI experience, as one participant notes, illustrates a problem that can arise when leadership in an initiative is assumed by well-meaning but nonrepresentative volunteers:

> They're residents, true, but they don't have to deal with the day-to-day struggle that a lot of the residents have to deal with. And since they don't have to deal with it they might miss some of the struggle. Although their intentions are good, the programs that they are designing and that they are writing for the resident [are] good in concept [but] they missed that little thing that would make it work.

Good organizers, however, routinely seek a mandate for their work from representatives of a broad cross section of the community. Other strategies could do this, too, but it is not intrinsic to their approaches. Hence, community organizing is less vulnerable to dependence on a few (not necessarily representative) people for information about the community.

Sustaining Involvement

Building and exercising community capacity is time-consuming and labor intensive. As a result, sustaining the involvement of resident volunteers is an ongoing challenge. It is not necessary for large numbers of residents to remain continuously involved in order for an initiative to generate community capacity, but any successful effort will require a modest number of residents who are committed to the process and who remain actively engaged for "the long haul." Achieving this involvement requires consistent attention to two distinct but related tasks. The first is to maintain the active participation of the "core" group of residents once they have been identified and recruited. The second is to maintain contact with adequate numbers of community residents so that the actions of the effort are seen as legitimately grounded in community priorities and so that people who leave the core group can be replaced. Community-organizing efforts typically employ two approaches to accomplish each of these tasks.

The first approach to sustaining engagement of the core group is leadership development. This motivates participants because they can perceive that they are gaining new competencies and because those competencies enhance their ability to make contributions and assume responsibility. The CODP experience illustrates this approach clearly. From the outset, the initiative declared that the resident volunteers would be responsible for doing the work of the initiative. Periodic training sessions gave them access to new information and tools that enabled them to take on new tasks as their projects progressed. Practice and coaching reinforced the lessons and skills between training sessions. Residents could see that their participation was part of a personal development trajectory, and program staff consistently reinforced the idea that successful completion of the initiative's projects would position the volunteers to make a real difference for their communities.

Maintaining residents' confidence that their efforts will lead to meaningful change in the community is the second way to sustain their engagement. It is related to leadership development in the sense that acquisition of new skills is one tangible form of progress. Staff affirmation that the initiative's activities will lead to important community improvements is essential, but it can only sustain energetic engagement for so long. Participants need to see positive outcomes. Organizers achieve this by structuring processes that enable participants to experience periodic victories (e.g., a demonstration at city hall that wins an agreement to improve city services to the neighborhood). Sometimes these periodic successes are directly related to the stated goal. When this is not possible, process accomplishments, such as finally forging consensus on an issue with which the group has struggled, provide a comparable sense of forward motion.

Over time, some turnover in the core group, no matter how committed, is inevitable. People move or acquire new responsibilities at home or simply burn out. A good community capacity–building effort needs a reliable approach to replacing and acculturating new leadership. One approach, appropriate when an organizing effort already has a broad base, is to reconnect regularly with residents already familiar with the initiative. PUEBLO uses this approach, conducting periodic outreach efforts to maintain contact with households that have participated in previous activities or have expressed interest in doing so. Its goal is to be in touch with each household at least once a year. In addition, the cultural events PUEBLO sponsors help to maintain resident awareness of and contact with the group. This approach is simplified in efforts that have elected to work through existing organizations, since those organizations likely have in place norms and mechanisms that keep members connected to the group.

An alternative approach is continuous work to involve new residents in the initiative's activities, steadily bringing new individuals into the effort. COPS uses house meetings, through which local leaders not only keep in touch with constituents but also identify new people interested, willing, and able to work in a collective effort. The Glades Community Development Corporation (GCDC) in western Palm Beach County, Florida, has also used this approach, but in a rather different way. The core group recruited to participate in GCDC's Vision to Action program used a series of retreats to develop a community revitalization strategy. Having done so, the group then spent months reaching out to the community to solicit input and build support for the agenda. Various members of this group became engaged in efforts to implement individual elements of the agenda, recruiting other residents to help them.

Although bringing in new blood can energize an ongoing effort, it can also be disruptive if not managed well. New participants may need to acquire certain skills and information before they can engage effectively with those who are already involved. Hartford NFI illustrates the kinds of problems that can ensue when integrative mechanisms are not in place. The collaborative wanted to increase the level of resident involvement and did, in fact, periodically generate increases in resident participation at its meetings. The collaborative, however, had difficulty managing this periodic community input, which often complicated organizational functioning. The problem was exacerbated by high levels of turnover on the collaborative board, which not only signaled other unresolved issues, but also left fewer people to acculturate and respond to new participants.

On the other hand, failure to be proactive in renewing the ranks leads to its own problems. Many of the CODP sites, for example, sustained resident involvement over an extended period. Eventually, however, the CDC boards began to experience attrition. CODP organizers were trained to be attentive to race, ethnicity, and other social distinctions in their work. But at two of the three CODP sites, their time was diverted to nonorganizing activities. At some CDCs, the board simply got smaller, leaving those who remained to take on additional work. At other CDCs, those who remained on the board tended to fill vacancies with people they already knew and trusted—which meant that they tended to recruit from their existing networks, either formal or informal. Both responses resulted in boards that no longer fully represented the diversity of the community.

THE ROLE OF COMMUNITY ORGANIZING

This chapter has presented an overview of the role that community organizing plays in contemporary initiatives to build community capacity. Three strategic choices were identified: that between conflict or consensus, between a focus on single or multiple issues, and between direct-recruitment or organization-based mobilization. Initiatives display extraordinary diversity and creativity in the ways they bring people together for collective action, and the types of community capacity that can be engendered have some relationship to the strategic choices that are made. Some general points can be stated.

The often-heard comment that community capacity depends in some fundamental way on "resident involvement" is a truism that is not always helpful in understanding how resident involvement can assist in the development of capacity. As pointed out in the introduction, many communities with demonstrable capacity do not have large segments of the residential populace working on behalf of the collective good. Indeed, as people's networks increasingly go beyond neighborhood boundaries, fewer people have a deep-seated connection to their local territory. Communities often rely on the active engagement of a small cadre of residents who are willing to become involved in the community's affairs, monitor its needs, and act accordingly to address concerns. At times, these residents may enlist the support of broader segments of the community (for example, through a petition drive or a town hall meeting), but they may also prefer to use more informal, associational tactics to address common problems. As we noted in our analytic framework (Figure 1), the existence of such commitment, enacted as a problem-solving mechanism by individuals, organizations, and the networks of association among them is one of the fundamental characteristics of a community with capacity.

We should not expect the situation to be much different in disadvantaged communities that host formal capacity-building efforts. Based on our examination of current initiatives, the likelihood of success in such efforts appears to be based on the ability of initiative staff to recruit, train, and sustain the involvement of a group—not necessarily large—of residents who will be so committed. (The exceptional case, of course, is the initiative geared toward large-scale mobilization of residents for a protest, demonstration, or other social action. In these cases, numbers matter, but perhaps not sustained engagement.) This is not easy in any community. But in disadvantaged areas, these generic problems are exacerbated by crime, poverty, residential mobility, and other factors.

These particular problems make it imperative for capacity-building efforts to develop a core group of active participants while simultaneously reaching into the wider population to connect with other potential volunteers. In other words, initiatives must identify stakeholders who are ready and willing to translate their commitment to the neighborhood into participation in a capacity-building effort. And they must develop means to locate other individuals with the potential to play equally important roles in the capacity-building process. These individuals can substitute for people who leave the core group. They can also mobilize for large mass actions, engage in midrange involvement (ranging from fully involved to

tangentially related), and offer targeted assistance, such as gathering petition signatures or door-to-door canvassing. Finally, their involvement in
such activities may ultimately strengthen informal social connections
among neighbors who become so involved, and increase the availability of
instrumental network relations among them. These may in turn be used to
exchange information, favors, and aid and contribute to local mechanisms
of informal social control and problem solving, which are characteristics of
a community with capacity.

NOTES

1. For a historical view of early organizing in America, see Fisher (1994).
2. For one treatment of BUILD's work in Baltimore, see McDougall (1993).
3. See Introduction for a brief explanation of the three initiatives—NFI, GCDC,
    and CODP—used for the core case studies of this book. See Appendix for
    full explanations.
4. Understanding the community-level impact of targeted organizing efforts
    is difficult, especially since many are not directly interested in promoting
    the general capacity of communities. The benefits of unified action may
    manifest years after the campaign or effort is over, and the effects of partic-
    ipation may never be clearly articulated by those involved. Notwithstand-
    ing these concerns, collective action for any purpose, however short-lived,
    may generate associations and networks among residents that can be im-
    portant forms of social capital that residents may draw on to address issues
    in the future.

5

Collaborations, Partnerships, and Organizational Networks

Efforts to build community capacity often focus on the organizational infrastructure of a community, seeking to change the ways individual organizations relate to one another and to organizations and actors beyond the neighborhood. We think of this approach as building *social capital* among organizations; fostering networks of positive relations among organizations gives them better access to resources and to a socially defined context that informs decision-making within organizations and structures relations among them.[1] In terms of our framework (Figure 1), the strategy of fostering interorganizational relations operates through organizations and organizational networks to foster a collective capacity for problem solving, resource allocation, and connection to resources beyond the community, as well as particular outcome goals.

Efforts that take this approach may pursue a variety of goals. They may seek to increase the influence of the community on policy decisions that affect it. They may attempt to create a new, expanded, or more effective capacity for producing public goods and services. They may try to strengthen and institutionalize an ongoing community problem-solving or decision-making capacity. And they may seek to create the means for providing increased access to external resources.[2]

Efforts to promote effective relations among organizations may also take many forms. They may employ such formal organizational strategies as creating new, collaborative, or umbrella organizations; extending instrumental relations among existing community-based organizations (CBOs) through joint-venture agreements; or establishing integrated service delivery systems in selected sectors, such as the human services sector. Alternatively, these strategies can be much more informal: They may involve organizing processes of communication, deliberation, and action among neighborhood actors, as well as between them and actors in the larger community; or they may focus on building networks of affinity organizations such as neighborhood churches, businesses, or youth-serving organizations. Depending on their purpose, such network-building strategies may seek to link organizations that are similar (e.g., CDCs), or those that differ in ways that make them complementary (e.g., churches, labor unions, and welfare rights groups). Some of these efforts will focus exclusively on relationships among community organizations; others will include outside agencies that bring (or have the potential to bring) important resources (money, political influence, prestige, scarce skills, etc.) to the relationship.

This chapter explores approaches to building community capacity through strategies focusing on organizational collaborations, partnerships, and networks of interorganizational relations. We outline the impetus and rationale for engaging in interorganizational relationships, describe the principal strategies through which such relations have been built in the context of community capacity-building efforts, and highlight core issues and emerging lessons about attempts to develop community capacity through such strategies.

IMPETUS AND RATIONALE

Focus on interorganizational relations and the development of organizational collaborations has increased over the last few decades.[3] Stimulating such relations has been the intent of numerous efforts supported by philanthropy and the public sector. At a local level, they aim to foster instrumental links among particular organizations operating in the neighborhood to encourage more effective and responsive provision of services and development activities. Connecting a youth service organization with a local school and creating a network of local services for the homeless are examples of this approach. At a wider level, such efforts seek broad "systems reform" in the funding, development, and delivery of services. The Partnership for Neighborhood Initiative (PNI) in Palm Beach County, Florida, exemplifies such an effort; it pools the resources of a range of public-sector service agencies, taxing districts, and local philanthropies to provide more flexible and responsive funding and service provision to local communities. In this case, interagency collaboration at the systems level is connected to a community-level planning and coordinating function through neighborhood "collaboratives" composed of residents, business owners, and representatives of CBOs and area nonprofit organizations. Through these collaboratives, neighborhoods are charged with developing comprehensive health and human service plans for the neighborhoods, and they gain access to the steering committees of county agencies and local funders to negotiate for financial support to implement these plans.

The impetus for focusing on interorganizational relations as a strategy for creating community capacity stems from a combination of circumstances. First, the "problem" of community revitalization and the goal of creating an ongoing community capacity to address it generally lies beyond the ability of any single organization to address. Most organizations confine their work to one or two sectors of community activity (e.g., housing, advocacy, human service provision), and each by itself has relatively limited access to external resources and political influence.

Second, organizations work in an environment characterized by considerable complexity and uncertainty.[4] Reaching out to develop positive interorganizational relations is one way of attempting to control some of the uncertainty in the environment that can significantly affect an organization's ability to survive and function. In addition to its potential benefit for the individual CBO, it provides the possibility of building a broader *community* capacity by combining organizational resources toward greater community impact and by combining organizational agendas toward greater community influence.

Finally, in formal interventions, the impetus to collaborate is often driven by financial incentives or the explicit requirements of funders. Funder mandates to collaborate derive from the recognition that individual organizations are incapable, by themselves, of addressing the range of issues required for community revitalization, as well as from the belief by funders that the activity they support is more likely to succeed if it enjoys broad-based support. Such mandates also reflect the belief that a collaborative effort is likely to have greater political legitimacy than any single organization can muster and therefore is more likely to attract other resources. Efforts to strengthen the institutional infrastructure of a community through interorganizational relationship-building strategies are thus the products of the combined influence of the complexity of the problem, environmental uncertainty, and an increasing perception of interdependence among organizations, and are often catalyzed by an external funder.

STRATEGIES FOR BUILDING
ORGANIZATIONAL COLLABORATION

Strategies for building organizational collaboration in a community fall into three broad categories: (1) establishing or supporting broker organizations that can foster and convene partnerships and networks among existing organizations; (2) creating mechanisms of direct, ongoing communication and collective planning and action among organizations; and (3) supporting or engaging in particular partnerships focused on specific goals and activities.

These strategies are ideal types. Although they may exist in pure forms, they will in many cases coexist, or a strategy to build one type of interorganizational collaboration may provide a foundation for building other types. In addition, for each of these strategies, both funders and participating organizations in the community are likely to have more than one goal, and may or may not prioritize those goals in the same way.

Creating Broker Organizations

Creating a broker organization represents an attempt to provide a mediating institution embedded in the community that can act as an ongoing mechanism for problem solving, resource development and acquisition, and, possibly, a degree of governance and decision-making at the community level. Fundamentally, broker organizations serve as organizational mechanisms through which relations may be created, fostered, or negotiated.

We use the term *broker organization* here to define a particular kind of intermediary organization that is specifically engaged in mediating, promoting, and nurturing instrumental relationships among organizations in a community, or between them and organizations outside the community. Although they may perform the other roles that characterize the work of intermediary organizations in general (e.g., providing technical assistance to other organizations, monitoring their activities and accomplishments, or acting as a pass-through for funding), the principal defining role of broker organizations is to *mediate and foster relations*. As instruments of an ongoing community capacity, we also define them as necessarily *in* the community, operating as a kind of bridge to information and resources within and beyond the boundaries of the community, but fundamentally seen as part of it.[5]

In some cases, an existing CBO evolves (or is specifically supported by funding efforts) to expand its mission and build its organizational capacity to play this brokering role. In the South Bronx, for example, the Comprehensive Community Revitalization Program (CCRP supported several CDCs to act as local intermediaries, expanding their missions by becoming broker organizations for their neighborhoods. The principal advantage of this strategy is that it builds on existing organizational advantages—staff, facilities, existing relationships—and avoids the lengthy and complex process of creating a new organization to perform this role. This was a significant advantage for CCRP, which was able to add to and mobilize CDC resources in relatively short order (Burns and Spilka, 1984).

In other cases, especially in environments where no viable candidate organization exists to take on this role, new formal organizations have been created to fulfill this purpose. The Glades Community Development Corporation (GCDC) in Florida is an excellent example[6] of a broker organization created to build community capacity by developing an institutional infrastructure and connecting it to resources outside the community. Viewed from one perspective, the task of developing GCDC was an organizational development task (see Chapter 3); a new organization was created to perform a set of functions not being performed by existing organizations working on behalf of the community. Seen from another perspective, the principal function of this organization is as a broker, charged with the task of helping to build and integrate an organizational infrastructure in the community—a collective resource that represents a broader, more powerful, and potentially more sustainable local capacity for solving problems, capturing and developing resources, and influencing policy and practice.

In yet other cases, less formal entities such as unincorporated councils or collaboratives are created to act as broker organizations in a community. The Neighborhood and Family Initiative (NFI) provides an example of this approach. NFI created new neighborhood collaboratives—initially unincorporated and operating under the auspices of community foundations in each of four cities—to serve as the principal mechanism for building relationships among neighborhood stakeholders and external resources. Relations among collaborative members affiliated with an organization (which also includes neighborhood residents unaffiliated with any organization) largely reflect the kinds of interorganizational relations the collaborative seeks to foster. But since the individuals from these organizations do not represent, in a formal sense, the organizations from which they come, the collaboratives tend not to be *in themselves* institutionalized mechanisms of interorganizational action (as a coalition or federation of member organizations, working together to better coordinate their particular roles and resources, might be). Rather, the collaboratives represent a gathering of people with skills, perspectives, and access to knowledge and resources who operate as a single entity. This entity seeks to plan and facilitate the implementation of comprehensive strategies for neighborhood development; develop networks of relationships among institutions within a broad, shared frame of reference; and strategically link these networks within a general, comprehensive plan. The development of new broker organizations that incorporate participation from existing organizational interests makes some sense in organizationally complex environments (where, for example, anointing a single organization is likely to lead to resistance from others). However, the process of establishing them and the complexities of running them, are daunting.

Broker organizations are necessarily at the center of the desired set of new relationships, a position that makes the broker organization of great potential value to the community. For actors outside the community, an organization in such a position can provide a clear and ongoing point of contact through which information, feedback, funding, and policy positions can be exchanged or negotiated. For actors within the community, it can provide an accessible clearinghouse for information, a mechanism for coordinating activities, and a tool to strengthen community influence by aggregating many community voices into one. In this way a successful broker organization will bring together several components of community capacity and, in the process, develop effective networks by connecting organizations to one another, residents to organizations, and both groups to outside resources. Developing a broker organization in a community is an attractive strategy because of the broker's potential to perform these functions effectively and with relative efficiency. It accomplishes these functions in a number of ways.

Often, broker organizations act as *matchmakers*, bringing separate organizations together for particular purposes. For example, GCDC brought together the three Glades municipalities to help them develop an effective tourism strategy for the region. Instead of continuing to compete for resources, the three cities and their chambers of commerce worked, with GCDC's help, to create the Western Communities Tourism Alliance, a joint vehicle through which a regional strategy for tourism could be funded and implemented. An advantage of supporting broker organizations to play this type of role is that it is relatively uncontentious and potentially fruitful in concrete ways. To the extent that the broker can serve as a neutral third party in pulling complementary organizations together to pursue a common interest, it can provide the impetus for a limited (and therefore manageable) partnership to do a particular thing—share space or staff, draft a joint proposal, mutually provide information and referrals, pool resources for joint provision of a service—that would not have occurred without the broker's catalyzing it. Further, successfully fostering such coupling lays the groundwork for evolving relations among these organizations, as well as for tapping into the networks provided by each. It also develops trust in the broker's intentions and capacity, which, in turn, enhances the broker's ability to catalyze similar relations among other organizations.

A broker organization may also act as a *conduit and clearing house for information and resources*. The CDCs in CCRP, for example, working with the Federation of Employment and Guidance Services, linked their job resource centers to allow each CDC to provide comprehensive information on jobs and support services within and beyond the Bronx (Burns and Spilka, 1984). Similarly, the NFI collaboratives in Detroit and Milwaukee operated as a conduit for program-related investment (PRI) funds from the Ford Foundation, channeled through Seedco, a national nonprofit intermediary. The collaboratives in these cases helped identify development projects (in some cases working to bring several organizations together to develop a proposal), made decisions on which project proposals to submit to Seedco, and helped the grantee organization and Seedco negotiate issues concerning financing and technical assistance. GCDC performed a similar function, helping identify resources for such new programs as the Med-Mobile and the Home Instruction Program for Preschool Youngsters (HIPPY) and providing technical assistance to these emerging programs once they received initial funding.

The principal advantage here is efficiency. The existence of a broker organization—recognized both by internal actors (CBOs and residents) and by external actors (foundations, government agencies, etc.) as a point of contact and clearinghouse through which they can access and channel information and resources—streamlines communications, enhances neighborhood-level access, and simplifies distribution. It is important to note, however, that a broker organization is unlikely to be successful in this role if it is perceived as competing with local organizations for resources and acting as a gatekeeper through which others must pass to obtain resources. To be successful, the broker must both act *and* be perceived as acting to facilitate access, not control it.

Finally and most ambitious, broker organizations may assume varying degrees of a *community "governance"* function, structuring deliberation and decision-making processes and, based on them, speaking for and acting on behalf of the entire community. In response to a request by the city of Milwaukee, for example, the NFI collaborative convened a series of planning sessions among neighborhood organizations and some residents to identify strategic priorities for the whole neighborhood and to determine the programmatic role that each organization would play in implementing them. The resulting plan is being used to inform the allocation of Community Development Block Grant (CDBG) funds by the city. Similarly, the coalition organization formed by the CDCs that were organized by the Consensus Development Demonstration Program (CODP) in Little Rock was invited by Pulaski County to prepare its application to the EZ/EC program and to administer the county's EZ/EC effort if it received funding. Coalition staff, with help from volunteer CDC board members and the CODP program officer, convened an inclusive planning process and prepared an application that won EC designation for the county.

Many different kinds of organizations may play a governance role. In some cases, particularly where their status is informal, several organizations may vie for recognition as a representative of the neighborhood that can make decisions on its behalf or represent its interests to actors (funders, developers, service agencies, local government) beyond the neighborhood. In some cases, local government may formally identify a particular neighborhood organization as the official representative of the neighborhood; in other cases there is a de facto recognition of a particular organization with which local government will interact and other actors (such as developers) will be expected to negotiate. In areas where city government has developed operational relations with neighborhoods through such organizations citywide, brokers often play a much larger governance role.

One example is the Historic East Baltimore Community Action Coalition (HEBCAC), one of several umbrella organizations in the city organized around neighborhood areas. As in the NFI collaboratives, membership on HEBCAC's board is drawn from a range of organizations, including businesses, local government, major local institutions, and neighborhood and tenants' associations. Unlike the NFI collaboratives, HEBCAC was from the beginning created as an independent nonprofit organization, its members *officially* represent their organizations, and there is significantly more involvement of local government and major institutions on its board. HEBCAC provides a forum for broad planning, develops and implements a range of projects in the neighborhood through its own staff, seeks to develop collaborative arrangements among service providers, and operates as a neighborhood-representing organization for a cluster of neighborhoods on the East Side of Baltimore. It also serves as the governance entity for one of Baltimore's "village centers" under the city's Empowerment Zone (EZ) program.

The principal advantages here concern mobilization and influence. Because of its structural position and organizational resources, a broker organization is a potentially effective catalyst for organizing participation of community organizations for collective deliberation, decision-making, and action. To the extent that it does so successfully, is able to mobilize its constituency effectively, and is viewed as a broadly supported, legitimate representative for the participating organizations and the entire community, a broker organization will have heightened access to and influence on other actors, such as local government, private developers, and large institutions operating in (or making decisions that have an impact on) the community. Such legitimacy and support, however, is often contested. So to be effective in this role, broker organizations need to relieve concerns about competition for power and control.

Negotiating Issues of Power and Control.   The same roles that make a broker organization of significant potential value to the community also place the organization in a position of potentially significant power—one that other organizations may or may not be willing to support. The broker organization, by virtue of its central position, can to a certain extent control access to information, opportunity, and resources; it can also make choices that may not redound equally to the well-being of all members of an interorganizational network (Burt, 1992; Knoke, 1990). In the case of HEBCAC, for example, all funds provided to Baltimore's East Side through the federal EZ/EC program are channeled through the organization, as are a range of negotiations with developers, city government, and powerful institutions such as the Johns Hopkins Medical Center. Similarly, GCDC and the NFI collaboratives have, in particular instances, operated as gate-keepers for resources, information, and technical assistance, which were then targeted to particular organizations in the community rather than to others. Not all broker organizations need to be gatekeepers in this way, and it is a position that some may seek and others (such as GCDC) may seek to avoid. Those brokers that constitute official channels for the distribution of resources, however, by necessity take on this role.

The fact that broker organizations in the context of community capaci-ty building are constituent based, operating in many ways in the name and on behalf of the community, raises a number of issues regarding the extent to which they are able to do so with sufficient knowledge and approval of the community as a whole. Indeed, in some cases, the very process of iden-tifying (or developing) such an organization can set in motion very com-plex political dynamics.

In Chicago, for example, the prospect of receiving significantly more federal funds through the EZ/EC program set in motion intensive politi-cal maneuvering, which led to a challenge of the mayor's choice of orga-nizations to come together as the local EC/EZ governance entity and to a shift in the center of political influence to include particular CBOs not pre-viously involved. Initially, the mayor selected thirty-two people (repre-senting businesses, community agencies, and state and local governments) to serve as members of the Empowerment Zone Coordinating Council (EZCC), which was charged with selecting the geographic zone, suggest-ing initial strategies, soliciting resident support for planning the effort, and identifying resources. Following a series of town hall meetings, the EZCC announced the selection of three noncontiguous areas, or neighborhood clusters, as the proposed zone, and began the formal application planning process. At a public meeting to launch the planning process, several lead-ers of CBOs not represented on the EZCC commandeered the podium and asked city staff to leave so that community representatives could decide how to proceed with a new agenda of their own. To counterbalance the mayor's EZCC, the group of participants who led the confrontation formed the Empowerment Zone Governance Council (EZGC), with repre-sentatives from each of the three neighborhood clusters. The EZGC became the link between EZCC and the neighborhoods, providing input to EZCC and disseminating information to the three neighborhood clusters. Shortly before it submitted the EC/EZ application, EZCC was restructured to formally include representatives from EZGC.

Similarly in Minneapolis, when the city designated lead neighborhood agencies in particular for its Neighborhood Revitalization Program (NRP), the availability of new funds altered the power base and focus of some community organizations. In one instance, a group of primarily white homeowners took control of the designated agency's board and opposed the organization's plan to develop leasehold cooperatives for (primarily black) lower-income families and to renovate and expand a park and playground (Briggs, Mueller, and Sullivan, 1997). In another instance, the lead organization working in the poor southern part of the black community, which saw itself as speaking for this community, encountered an influx of working- and middle-class black homeowners attracted by the availability of NRP funds. Again, conflict over spending priorities and the relative power of the homeowners made it difficult for the organization to be both a convener for NRP and an advocate for the poor.

The ability of a broker organization to mediate successfully among community organizations and between them and actors beyond the community relies on the extent to which both internal and external actors perceive the broker as having legitimacy within the community, the ability to act as a neutral convener, and the organizational capacity to build relationships and maintain them over time. Legitimacy concerns both participants and process; it requires assembling the appropriate range of stakeholders and structuring procedures through which these stakeholders perceive the opportunity to present their concerns and influence decisions that will affect the community. It may also depend on the broker's definition of its role and its approach to engaging stakeholders. For example, legitimacy will likely increase if the broker helps position different sectors of the community to speak for themselves, rather than arrogating to itself the role of speaking on their behalf. A staff member of one such organization described the staff's role this way:

> We are sort of like the interpreter for any one of the partners dealing with the other. I think the word interpreter is a pretty good one because each part of our world has a different language, and it is our job to be able to decipher, reassemble, and be able to communicate to the other entities in a way that creates proactivity rather than reactivity.

Fundamental to the perception of neutrality and recognition of legitimacy is the extent to which a broker organization can establish a level of *trust* in its intentions, abilities, likely contributions, and respect for other organizations' roles and importance.[7] Such trust is built over time and influenced by both individual and organizational factors.

At the individual level, the ability of a broker organization to build trust among other organizations relies on the personal skills, attributes, and relationships of organizational leaders and representatives. Informal relationships among individuals are often the catalyst for broader organizational relations and are the principal mechanisms through which such relations are maintained and ultimately become institutionalized (Granovetter, 1985). Staff capacity and competence (staff skills, time, inclination, configuration), the nature of board membership, and the role played by board members are all critical components at this level.

At the organizational level, the ability of a broker organization to build trust requires having an agenda broad enough to incorporate and work on behalf of (rather than subsume, dominate, or ignore) the agendas of other community organizations, as well as to have an independent source of funding so that its support is not seen to be in competition with that of other organizations.

Issues of trust and legitimacy have much to do with the state of the existing organizational environment. In organizationally dense contexts, or where there is a history of contentious relations among organizations, the work of a broker organization is likely to be more difficult, and acceptance of its role may be problematic. Under NFI in Milwaukee, for example, the relationship between the Harambee Ombudsman Project Inc. (HOPI), a long-standing CBO in the target neighborhood and the NFI collaborative has been a continuing source of tension, in large part because HOPI saw the collaborative as attempting to usurp that organization's historical role and position. Although HOPI was invited by the NFI collaborative to participate in its work, this gesture was not viewed as an appropriate solution. In the words of a HOPI board member:

> [NFI's creation] has given the illusion or impression that there is a new Harambee organization apart from the Ombudsman. There's this Harambee collaborative, and they've got money and they've got this and they've got that. And that's not good, although it's true. It has created a schism. Harambee collaborative will be meeting upstairs in the same building and people don't know which meeting to attend, where to go, this type of thing.

Although HOPI has retained representation on the NFI collaborative, competition between the two brokers is constantly being negotiated. For instance, in the example given earlier, after convening local organizations in response to the city request and leading them through the planning process, the collaborative declined to take on the implementation role, and the city turned to HOPI to act as the official neighborhood-representing organization for the allocation of CDBG funds. In this role, HOPI convenes residents and local organizations on a periodic basis to review priorities to be used by the city in determining CDBG allocations. By reconciling roles in this particular case, an aspect of the community's capacity to influence policy and resource allocation through the work of a broker organization was preserved.

Ongoing Mechanisms of Interorganizational Connection

Ongoing mechanisms of interorganizational connection exhibit great variety. They may be formal or informal, time limited or enduring, and may include many organizations or only a few. They may provide a forum for addressing a broad range of circumstances facing the community, or be more narrowly defined, focusing on a particular part of the neighborhood or a particular issue, such as services or jobs. They may be the product of processes set in motion by a broker organization, but need not be. And although they might also serve a brokering function, their distinctive feature is that, rather than principally mediating between sets of organizations, the mechanism is *itself* the instrument of relational interaction.

Broadly Focused Coalitions. Broadly focused organizational coalitions come in different forms. Some draw together organizations within a single community. These coalitions may include organizations of just one type, such as churches or block clubs, or they may encompass various types, perhaps including churches, businesses, service providers, neighborhood associations, and development organizations. Others are made up of similar organizations from different neighborhoods, intended both to enhance the organizational capacity of member organizations and to increase their ability to capture resources (financial, technical, informational) or their influence with local government or other actors in the broader community. In CODP, for example, one purpose of the new coalition organizations formed by the CDCs in Palm Beach County and Little Rock was to gain access to more and higher-quality staff than the individual CDCs could afford on their own and to ensure that all the CDCs would receive the services of those staff. Corporate and philanthropic funders found this arrangement very attractive because it would require less general operating support to sustain than staffing individual CDCs and would increase technical quality as well. Another purpose of the coalition organizations was to increase the CDCs' influence with county government, a role similar to that played by membership organizations of CDCs in other cities and states.

Some broadly focused organizational coalitions focus on promoting relationships among different kinds of organizations in areas that incorporate, but are larger than individual neighborhoods. These coalitions attempt to enhance community capacity by allowing the communities to accomplish things they could not accomplish alone. An example is the North Hartford Initiative (NHI), in which the NFI collaborative has played varying roles. NHI began as an informal council of CBOs in the predominantly black neighborhoods of Hartford's North End; it initially served as a vehicle to create a comprehensive development plan and oversee ongoing comprehensive planning for that area. NHI later incorporated as a congress of member organizations; it aims to develop consensus among organizations with an investment in the North End and to assure that neighborhood planning incorporates their priorities. Its members include the major CBOs from all five of north Hartford's neighborhoods, as well as representatives from several city agencies. The member CBOs view NHI not only as a way to leverage resources and partnerships to accomplish specific projects (ranging from housing and economic development to education and health services), but also as a way to increase the political influence of their neighborhoods on city policy and thereby match the role and influence of a long-established organization that operates in and represents several predominantly white and Latino neighborhoods in the South End. NHI is in the early stages of its development and has largely focused on formalizing its organization, creating bylaws and procedures, and establishing relations among its members and between it and the city. The initiative has little funding and has not yet sponsored any significant programmatic activity, so whether it will ultimately achieve its aims is unclear.

A far more established and broadly inclusive example is the Local Investment Commission (LINC) in Kansas City. LINC describes itself as a *process* (rather than a structured program or organization) that brings together consumers, business and civic leaders, and community and neighborhood activists. Originally founded as an advisory board to help direct reform of the Missouri Department of Social Services in Jackson County, LINC quickly expanded its mission. It now operates as a decision-making body charged with the program design, funding, and oversight of systems-reform activities, and is the governance entity responsible for Missouri's Comprehensive Neighborhood Services (Caring Communities) Initiative.

LINC is governed by three tiers of committees. A *commission* of thirty-six voting members—all private citizens (ranging from business leaders to neighborhood activists) rather than representatives of particular organizations or constituencies—sets the broad agenda, makes funding decisions, and negotiates with state agencies to institute particular policy changes. A *professional cabinet* of public and private service providers advises the commission. *Working committees* are responsible for planning and implementing initiatives under the LINC umbrella. Working committees include representatives of schools, businesses, local government, and service-providing agencies, as well as citizens—especially residents of defined neighborhoods that are the units of planning for LINC's comprehensive neighborhood services. Particularly in the second and third tiers, LINC serves as a mechanism of direct interorganizational interaction.[8] LINC has significant financial resources and has supported a range of programmatic activity, including a welfare-to-work wage supplement project, several efforts to increase and improve child-care provision, and the provision of "comprehensive neighborhood services" delivered by service providers linked to local schools. Both its access to resources and its support from government have been significant factors in its progress.

A principal advantage of broadly focused coalitions is their reach and flexibility. When a wide range of organizations establishes a forum for ongoing communication and possible collaboration, they create the potential to mobilize different kinds of resources around issues as they arise. And, to the extent that network members can be organized to speak and act in concert at moments of crisis, such coalitions are likely to develop greater influence on policy and practice that can affect their constituents.

Issue-Focused Coalitions.   Other mechanisms of interorganizational relations include coalitions that limit their agendas to specific issues or sectors. These mechanisms include community coalitions that focus on sectoral concerns (e.g., housing or economic development) within particular neighborhoods, as well as efforts to connect neighborhoods to broad systems-reform initiatives aimed at specific issues. Much of the systems-reform work has focused on health and human services. For example, a number of efforts have sought to bring together neighborhood residents, community-based service providers, and government agencies responsible for funding or delivering services in a particular service sector. The Edna McConnell Clark Foundation is supporting such activity in several cities around the issue of child protection, seeking to connect local service providers and neighborhood residents with child protective services to reduce the incidence of child abuse and neglect. Around the issue of child mental health, the Annie E. Casey Foundation has supported partnerships among state agencies (child welfare, mental health, juvenile justice) and has tried to connect them to neighborhood-level governance structures that plan for and provide oversight to the initiative.

Other efforts to create or support coalitions around specific sectors have focused more narrowly on particular neighborhoods, seeking to develop interorganizational mechanisms for local problem solving. GCDC, for example, helped foster a range of ongoing, targeted community coalitions, including a youth council composed of representatives from eighteen different youth groups and a coalition of organizations and individuals concerned about the problem of AIDS in the Glades. Similarly, NFI has fostered or participated in two such entities beyond its collaboratives: the Back to

the Basics Partnership in Detroit and the North Milwaukee Industrial Development Corporation (NMIDC), each of which represents a different approach and focus for ongoing interorganizational collaboration.

The Back to the Basics Partnership in Detroit is an informal but ongoing
network of social service providers operating in the Lower Woodward
Corridor, NFI's target neighborhood. Its goal is to increase the effectiveness of neighborhood services for children, youth, and families by strengthening the working relations among participating organizations, fostering
joint planning, and avoiding duplication of services in the neighborhood.
Many of the service providers (from social service agencies and job-training centers to churches and health care providers) that work in the corridor
participate, although at different levels of consistency and effort. Members
meet once a month to share information about existing programs and resources and to consider priorities and possible collective responses to the
needs of the corridor's residents. In addition, the partnership operates a
small (about $50,000 annually) minigrant program, which provides fund-
ing to nonprofit organizations based in the corridor.[9]

NMIDC is a more formal effort. It was created to plan and manage the
industrial revitalization of the northeast corridor (Riverworks), which lies
adjacent to the Harambee neighborhood; it thus has both a geographic and
a substantive focus. NMIDC is a nonprofit organization formed by five
partner organizations, including HOPI, two CDCs, the NFI collaborative,
and an organization of manufacturers. Although these organizations have
come together formally to create NMIDC (their participation on its board
is mandated by the organization's bylaws), relations among them extend
beyond this, since there is also interlocking board membership among four
of the five partner organizations.

Relationships among the NMIDC partners facilitate two primary ends.
The first is joint planning: the NMIDC board sets priorities and develops
strategies to achieve its mission most effectively. The second is implementation: partner organizations each take on responsibility for particular
components of NMIDC's strategic plan. For example, NMIDC established
an employment service operated by one of its member organizations that
in three years of operation placed 260 residents of Harambee or River West
(an adjacent neighborhood) in jobs throughout the Milwaukee area.[10] Organizing these components under the formal auspices of a nonprofit organization provides for staff and an organizational infrastructure that
formalizes relationships among its partners and provides the means to
support both planning and implementation over time. Under these auspices, NMIDC has created a number of support services for Riverworks's
businesses and neighborhood residents, including a security patrol, a
learning center to train Riverworks employees, and an industrial council
of member companies that has focused on human resource issues. NMIDC

also developed (and later spun off) the Teaching Factory, an independent, nonprofit organization committed to upgrading the technical capacities of Wisconsin's metalworking firms and retaining workers in advanced technologies. Because of its explicit focus on program development and administration, its higher level of financial support, and the formal arrangements provided by its organizational structure, NMIDC has produced more in the way of outputs—buildings, training, employment, services, infrastructure—than has the informal networking strategy of the Back to the Basics Partnership.

Whereas broad-based coalitions have the advantage of reach and flexibility, issue-focused coalitions are able to target the knowledge and resources of members to the particular set of tasks for which they are best suited. Issue-focused coalitions will not be able to respond as broadly to emerging circumstances, but are likely to have a greater impact on their area of focus. In both kinds of coalitions, however, maintaining interorganizational relations and mobilizing member contribution is sometimes difficult. Whether these coalitions are formal or informal, their ability to endure and their potential to act rely on the availability of dedicated resources to provide staff, maintain structured communication among participants, and support the activities that arise out of collective planning processes.

Roles, Functioning, and Challenges of Implementation.   Several of the roles played by coalitions and other ongoing means of linking organizations are similar to those played by broker organizations, but they are particularly focused on convening organizations for collective deliberation and joint action. Compared to broker organizations, however, these mechanisms provide for somewhat more flexible relations among organizations and do not necessarily imbue the coalition organization (whether formal or informal) with the structural autonomy of a broker organization.[11] That is, although the coalition organization may frequently speak for its member organizations and use the weight of its collective resources and influence to pursue shared goals, it is not necessarily in the position of brokering relations among members or using its structural position among networks to control or direct relations or the flow of resources and information. Except perhaps in cases like LINC, in which the governance body is largely responsible for resource allocation among participating organizations for particular initiatives, the issue of power takes on a somewhat different cast than in the case of broker organizations. Members of coalitions and other institutionalized organizational networks remain independent and pool their efforts within an interorganizational framework that does not raise one organization to a position of power with regard to managing relations and access; there is no one overarching authority structure to which all organizations are bound. Instead, issues of power arise within the context of the relative influence and connections that particular member organizations have, and issues of control and impact may arise in connection with what such coalitions and networks are able to *do* by virtue of their coming together.

For example, the principal outcomes of the Back to the Basics Partnership have been the forum of interaction itself and the provision of small grants to support discrete projects undertaken by local service providers. In the words of one member:

> I think support is the best word. On that level the partnership is proving that it can support its members both financially [through the small grants] and through information sharing. That's one of the added values of the coming together. While individual relationships may have existed, with people sitting around the table there's a lot more information exchange and the potential for conflict resolution.

Although these activities reflect the stated goals of the partnership, there has been some frustration among members that more is not being accomplished and that the relationships developing among them are not being leveraged to support more in the way of joint projects or other activities. This is in large part a question of design; the partnership was structured not to sustain instrumental action but to be a forum for informal exchange. Although this exchange can potentially support community capacity by strengthening associational links among members—which may over time lead to increased exposure to opportunity and the development of joint action—the partnership's lack of formal organizational structure and resources preclude it from launching significant programmatic activity without an infusion of additional support from outside or significantly increased contributions from member organizations.

One challenge in stimulating interorganizational relationships is a possible tension between creating organizational capacity on the one hand and a broader *community* capacity on the other. That is, to what extent is fostering interorganizational relations connected both to the benefit of participant organizations *and* to their ability to identify and act on neighborhood interests? As discussed in another context in the conclusion to Chapter 3, making this link relies on the extent to which the organizational infrastructure developed and the organizations that constitute it are sufficiently connected to—knowledgeable of, recognized by, and operating with reference to—the needs, priorities, and values of the community. This may be an issue of both perception and reality. NMIDC, for example, is essentially an organization of organizations in which "local residents are represented by the community organizations on the Board of Directors"

(NMIDC, 1997). The organization is focused principally on creating employment opportunities for residents, not on neighborhood mobilization or facilitating resident involvement in organizational decision-making. As stated by an NMIDC staff member:

> [The residents] don't know us. The businesses know us, but the business owners don't live here. They live out in Mequon, and they only come here [during the day]. So I don't think the neighborhood knows us. The learning center and the employment program are the two things that link us to the neighborhood. . . . We're in the neighborhood, we're right here. People should be able to come in. We don't have that relationship with the neighborhood. And we need it.

This lack of connection has consequences for the organization's role and stature in the community:

> In the general public, there is a lack of understanding about what NMIDC actually does, and therefore the organization is sometimes unfairly judged for not accomplishing something it never set out to do. . . . NMIDC's role is not to be the first point of contact for community residents. The role of NMIDC is not to mobilize the potential employees. The community groups, especially those represented on the board, should be serving as the feeder organizations, as the link between the community and NMIDC. (ibid.:9)

The community capacity building supported by NMIDC is thus generated largely at the organizational level (by promoting business development and supporting the work of member organizations) and at the individual level (by increasing the skills and opportunities of residents to find and retain jobs). To return to the characteristics of community capacity in our framework, NMIDC is a formal mechanism of problem solving and a tool for connecting the community to outside resources. But NMIDC is not intended necessarily to build a sense of community or commitment among individuals who live there, nor does it focus particularly on aspects of participation and informal exchange that would foster informal associational interaction among individual residents or the social capital that might be generated as a result.

Specialized Partnerships

A third strategy for building community capacity through enhanced ties among organizations is to foster specific partnerships to accomplish particular ends. Such partnerships may be the product of relationships facilitated by a broker organization or may arise out of the processes fostered under a coalition or multiorganizational council. They may also be catalyzed by external funding opportunities, or by an organization that sees the possible benefits of a partnership and seeks out one or more organizations willing to work together in specified ways for some mutual benefit.

Specialized partnerships can vary in scope, formality, and intensity. At one end of the spectrum, two organizations may simply establish an informal agreement to share particular types of information. At the other, several organizations may enter into a formal agreement to collaborate on a joint venture, in which relative roles and resource contributions (of staff time, money, equipment, facilities) are contractually established.

Sometimes these partnerships are developed between public institutions or agencies and CBOs or neighborhood associations to address particular issues. Some approaches to organizing community policing and a number of school-linked service partnerships being developed across the country provide examples. In the latter case, local schools serve as central community resources through which to integrate the delivery of a range of services and to facilitate residents' access to them; the schools also provide a focal point and physical space to promote a broader community-building agenda. For example, New York City's Beacons schools (a model of this strategy that is being replicated in several cities nationwide) combine school resources and the resources and activities of CBOs to improve and expand services and activities, enhance information exchange, and support community interaction. The schools largely provide the building itself—a known, accessible, and underused facility in the neighborhood with space to meet, hold classes, provide services, exchange information—and its access to children and their families. The CBOs provide staff to run programs, provide information about services available elsewhere, and make referrals.

In some cases, school-CBO partnerships can link more directly to the pedagogical mission of schools. In one Chicago neighborhood, for example, the Steans Family Foundation is supporting a partnership between a neighborhood high school and a new CDC whose goal is to train students in construction and housing development by developing a vacant lot adjacent to the school. In addition to its vocational aspect, this partnership is attempting to integrate portions of the academic curriculum into the training program.

Similarly, Kansas City CDC, a mature organization with a significant real estate development track record, is collaborating with a large hospital near the edge of its service area to develop single-family homes adjacent to the hospital. The goal is to provide good-quality affordable housing within walking distance of the hospital for some of its numerous low-wage workers, while strengthening the neighborhood housing market and making the community more attractive. Similar partnerships are being supported nationally, e.g., by Seedco's Historically Black Colleges and

Universities (HBCU) program, which helps selected HBCUs work with new or fledgling CDCs in the low-income black neighborhoods adjacent to the colleges.

As with other kinds of interorganizational relations, issues of trust, relative burden, competing agendas, and how to apportion credit for accomplishment within and between organizations may arise in specialized partnerships. Informal agreements may be easier to forge, and partnerships that require less commitment of resources (particularly money) may be less threatening, but these kinds of collaboration are also less likely to endure or have substantial impact. Shifting opportunities and limited organizational capacity to engage in multiple partnerships simultaneously may lead to postponed or unraveled agreements and may undermine the establishment of trust necessary for future alignments. The opportunity to become the lead agency in developing a program funded under Detroit's EZ/EC program, for example, caused the NFI collaborative to shift its priorities and back away from a prior (still informal) agreement to enter into a joint venture with a local CDC to develop an industrial park.

Because such relationships are defined around particular projects or objectives, these partnerships are often less complicated and may be less problematic than broader attempts at collaboration or interorganizational network development. To the extent that the organizational partners can negotiate clear expectations regarding contributions, benefits, and credit, and to the extent that each of the partners has the capacity to contribute (i.e., to hold up its end of the bargain), specialized partnerships offer an attractive strategy both to produce certain defined outcomes and, potentially, to build toward broader interorganizational networks. Even in cases where particular partnership arrangements are time limited, they may give rise to more enduring relations over time or may perform informal brokering functions among organizations through relationships built among staff or board members that connect one organization to the networks of others. Although often the product of interpersonal relations among individuals operating on behalf of their organizations, such relations can, over time, be institutionalized. GCDC, for example, sponsored an economic summit at which public officials and citizens from the three cities came together to develop solutions to the region's economic problems. Because the Glades communities had been isolated from and had competed with each other for so long, the summit was an important step in building a regional perspective and a sense of common interest. A year later, when the federal EZ/EC program was announced, the three cities prepared a joint application, an accomplishment few participants think would have occurred if the cities had not worked together on the economic summit.

CORE ISSUES AND EMERGING LESSONS

A number of factors influence the likelihood that instrumental interorganizational relations will be usefully engaged and sustained. In the context of community capacity building, these include (1) the extent to which the benefits of interorganizational relations are seen, over time, to outweigh the costs; (2) the degree to which the appropriate stakeholders are selected and participate; and (3) the impact of such contextual influences as community history, racial dynamics, and political power.

Costs and Benefits

All interorganizational relationships entail some sharing of resources (money, influence, information) as the price for accomplishing something the engaged organizations could not do individually (Gray, 1985). Organizations will be inclined to enter into such arrangements when the need to work together becomes clear, when opportunity presents itself, when the organizational capacity exists, when the potential parties are known and trusted (or when there is a recognition of interdependence among them and such trust can be built), and when the notion of collaboration or collective action among organizations is, in itself, valued by potential participants (Schermerhorn, 1975; Whetton, 1981; Trist, 1985; Gray, 1985; Hood, Logsdon, and Thompson, 1993). Not all of these conditions need to prevail in order for interorganizational relations to be engaged. But the more that exist, the more likely a collaborative agenda will be embraced, and the more likely the process of collaborative problem solving will continue to evolve.

Although there are clear incentives to engaging in interorganizational relations, there are also a range of organizational costs that need to be negotiated among participants. These include the specific resources each organization is required to provide, a loss of some autonomy and control, added time and likely delays in negotiating expectations and coordinating with partner organizations, and the potential loss of reputation or influence if the collaboration fails. The potential benefits that might offset these costs include the possibility of sharing costs and risks, gaining greater collective influence, learning and developing new solutions, and leveraging additional resources (money, time, materials, connections, political capital) provided by partner organizations or by outside supporters.[12]

Part of an organization's willingness to enter into such relations depends on the extent to which it has the resources to do so and is willing to expend them; another part relies on an analysis of the extent to which the benefits will outweigh the costs over the long term. The resources needed include sufficient skills and inclination on the part of organizational leadership, sufficient time and flexibility, and sufficient financial and technical support. The analysis of costs and benefits requires organizations to come to terms with partners' specified roles and responsibilities, the creation of new (or the acknowledgment of multiple) mechanisms of accountability, the development of consensus around resource allocation, and consideration of potentially different ways of acknowledging contribution and credit for collaboratively pursued successes (and blame for any failures).

One advantage of specialized partnerships in this regard is the organizations' ability to negotiate these issues within relatively defined parameters and to build interorganizational relationships through concrete tasks and responsibilities. Clarity and agreement about expectations of role and contribution are critical, and partnerships among organizations are likely to work better when they are engaged in (1) a clearly defined project (2) that is central to the work of the participating organizations, (3) that involves work to which each organization can make obvious contributions, and (4) that is undertaken by organizations with the capacity (staff, resources, competence) to contribute. In Milwaukee, for example, the Martin Luther King Economic Development Corporation (created by the NFI collaborative and now operating independently) is working in partnership with two other CBOs and the city's business improvement district on a comprehensive commercial and housing development project being implemented in sixteen blocks of the neighborhood targeted by NFI. Responsibility has been delegated to each of the four partner organizations based on its particular interest or expertise, and each organization has the capacity to meet its particular responsibilities based on this division of labor. In contrast, in cases where there is ambiguity about the product or the relative responsibility of the participating organizations, or when particular partners are unable to deliver because of insufficient capacity, the costs borne by the stronger organizations may be too great, thereby endangering the success of the partnership. Aware of the importance of organizational competence, the Beacons program, for example, is careful to select CBOs that have the staff and infrastructure to manage the administrative and programmatic requirements of their role in the partnership. In some cases, however, the school with which a CBO has been matched has proven less capable. In these cases, the difficulty of partnering—inability to get phone calls returned, delayed decisions about student participation or the use of school facilities—has weakened the partnership commitment of the CBO and fostered its resolve to search for other ways to do its work (Wynn, Meyer, and Richards-Schuster, 1999).

Negotiating the costs and benefits of collaboration within the context of coalitions and other mechanisms of ongoing interorganizational connection can be more complicated. On the one hand, to the extent they are framed around broader goals and with expectations for longer-term relationships, these arrangements tend not to have the concrete reference point of a specific project around which to specify roles and galvanize participation. On the other hand, to the extent that such arrangements are relatively informal, the costs to participating organizations may be relatively low. In addition, they are likely to be kept low by organizations that are able to modulate their commitment and participation over time to match their interest, capacity, and perception of benefit as the focus of coalitional action shifts. This situation provides flexibility to individual organizations but weakens the ability of the coalition to depend on consistent member contributions. This tension may be mitigated by establishing a clearly defined mission; negotiating an agreed-upon governance structure (which defines expectations of contribution, protects organizational autonomy, and equitably distributes influence on decision-making); and providing resources that support the coalition's operation and offer clear resource incentives for organizational participation.

The situation is similar when creating or operating through broker organizations. In addition to the issues of legitimacy and trust discussed earlier, broker organizations will need to have the resources (human, financial, technical, political) to foster interorganizational cooperation without being seen as competing players. In NFI for example, to the extent that the collaboratives were able to succeed in this role, they did so because the initiative provided them with an ongoing, dedicated stream of funding from the Ford Foundation, access to the skills and expertise of cross-site technical assistance providers, and varying levels of access to broader resources through the community foundations. Because of their access to funding, the collaboratives have also been able to channel funds to other organizations or to develop programs that could then be transferred to others for implementation. And because of their affiliation with a national initiative of the Ford Foundation and a local community foundation, each collaborative had a relatively high profile that supported the interest and involvement, over time, of a range of participants. This may be difficult to sustain, however, precisely because outside stimulus and support were so important. With the end of NFI as a funded initiative (collaboratives received their final grants from the Ford Foundation in 1998) and the increasing independence of the collaboratives (now incorporated as nonprofit organizations in three of the four sites), the very conditions that have allowed the collaboratives to develop their role as brokering organizations are now disappearing.

Indeed, an outside sponsor and the availability of funding to support collaboration very often play a significant role in catalyzing interorganizational relations. Through the provision of such support, funders—both foundations and government—attempt to address the cost/benefit calculations of individual organizations to foster the development and collective efficacy of a community's organizational infrastructure.

In our core cases, it is unlikely that the relationships that developed would have done so without a funding catalyst, at least not to the same extent or in the same manner. In these cases, the catalyst was composed of three elements: (1) funding granted explicitly to support collaboration, (2) the activities of a local convener to jump-start the process and provide the auspices under which it would operate, and (3) technical assistance in convening the group of participating organizations, setting ground rules, and guiding the process of collaborative planning. But although the availability of funding and some technical assistance was enough to catalyze interaction among organizations under the umbrella of a particular community capacity–building agenda, it was not always enough to address the capacity needs of individual organizations, let alone *individual residents* and other community stakeholders participating as volunteers. In some instances, the mandate to collaborate provided too few cues about what collaboration might entail, what issues it might engage most successfully, how participating organizations would likely benefit, or how relations would be sustained once dedicated funding to them ended.

Selection and Representation

The selection of the "right" players to participate in collaborative endeavors can be a critical factor shaping the dynamics and ultimate success of interorganizational behavior. Participation is often complicated, particularly in the context of community capacity building, because the organizations that comprise the interorganizational networks or partnerships involved are often not simply "work organizations"; they are organizations that in some way seek to speak for and act on behalf of the community. Further, individual community residents are often sought to participate in the planning and governance of organizational as representatives of the people who live in the neighborhood. Although these residents are sometimes formal representatives of neighborhood associations (as in the case of HEBCAC), often they are unaffiliated, participating as individual citizens (as in the case of many EZ/EC governance entities).

The issue of assembling the appropriate participants has at least two dimensions. The first concerns the selection of people who represent relevant stakeholder groups and who, together, are appropriately diverse in terms of race, socioeconomic status, and other characteristics (see Gray, 1985; Wood and Gray, 1991; Mattessich and Monsey, 1992). The second concerns the ability of these representatives—which depends on their having sufficient levels of legitimacy and authority—to engage in the work of the collaboration on behalf of their constituencies.

Selection of Participants. The definition of *stakeholder* in community-building efforts is, in general, sufficiently broad to include virtually anyone—individual or organization—with some connection to the community. Efforts to select stakeholders tend to organize the process around some set of categories that describe kinds of stakeholders (e.g., home owners, low-income residents, business owners, service providers), and to solicit participation from individuals representing groups of those kinds. In some cases, participation is left open: individuals and organizations representing these stakeholder groups are invited to attend and participate in collective planning and to engage in particular relations with one another as they see fit. This is the case, for example, with the Back to the Basics Partnership in Detroit. Rather than trying to *ensure* the actual participation of relevant constituencies, such approaches focus on creating the *opportunity* to participate as a way to foster broad input and networks of connections (although a core set of organizations that participate consistently over time tend ultimately to dominate). In other cases, membership is set (although meetings may still be open): it is limited to particular organizations that are invited (and that agree) to participate. Sometimes membership also includes resident representatives, who may be selected in different ways. Usually, resident representatives are recruited through networks of association that identify particular (formal or informal) leaders. Occasionally, they are chosen by election. In the Dudley Street Neighborhood Initiative (DSNI) in Boston, for example, which best fits our definition of a broker organization, a defined set of organizations is joined by residents (equal numbers from each of the three major ethnic groups in the neighborhood) chosen by neighborhoodwide elections to serve on the organization's board.

Each of these solutions to the problem of stakeholder selection addresses some concerns while leaving others open to challenge. *Open* membership is often said to offer broader opportunity for participation, but it is likely to be bought at the cost of continuity. Lack of continuity can have serious implications for the ability of the group to act and, in any case, tends ultimately to lead to domination of the collaboration by a core few. *Set* membership, in which there are expectations for long-term participation, is more likely to lead to sustainable collective action, assuming that the nature of contribution and responsibility of members is clear and there is strong, acknowledged leadership and support. Who gets selected in or out of membership may always be open to challenge. But this issue can be addressed to some extent by retaining open meetings, as well as through other forums for exchange with stakeholders beyond the collaborative group. It may also be addressed by the method of selection.

Selecting organizations (or resident representatives) into or out of a collaborative group can be a strategic choice, based on the particular contributions participants can be assumed or required to make. In the Lower Woodward Corridor in Detroit, for example, where small nonprofit organizations distrust many of the large institutions, the NFI collaborative focused initially on bringing large institutions to the table, to the exclusion of most smaller organizations. This was a strategic choice on the part of the convening community foundation, which saw these institutions as the actors most likely to leverage change through collaborative endeavor. However, as the community foundation began to exert less control over the effort and the collaborative incorporated as an independent nonprofit organization, organizational representation on its board shifted to include mainly CBOs, whose interests were more closely aligned with each other's than with those of the larger institutions. Institutional representatives generally found the day-to-day deliberations of the collaborative planning process too slow and too unproductive. Ultimately, the institutions began to withdraw as direct participants in governance, either engaging in more specialized partnerships (such as the collaboration between Detroit Medical Center and New Beginnings) or disconnecting entirely. Where the institutions remained available as "resource partners" for a particular project, this arrangement worked well; they were happy, for the most part, to be called on for specific contributions around specific issues that connected with their interests and expertise.

Participant selection may also be a political choice, based on the perceived necessity of having representation from particular organizations or constituencies regardless of assumptions about their contributions. In NFI in Hartford, for example, which has a large West Indian population as well as an African-American one, the collaborative has emphasized the importance of ensuring balanced representation among individual residents and local organizations and between the two groups. Likewise, the inclusion of HOPI and the Orange Mound Civic Organization as members of the NFI collaboratives in Milwaukee and Memphis, respectively, was based more on political considerations than on specific likely contributions. In CODP, senior program staff selected a local program host in each site, based not on the extent of its financial support for the program but on its ability to position the local CODP effort advantageously vis-à-vis the local corporate and civic community. In fact, two of the three local hosts that were selected made no cash contribution at all (although they provided in-kind support, such as free office space).

On the one hand, inclusion of the broadest possible range of stakeholders in the effort provides the greatest possibility of gaining access to resources, covering political bases (and avoiding opposition, if not always fostering active cooperation), and claiming legitimacy to speak and act on behalf of the community (Gray, 1985). On the other hand, the more diverse the group, the longer it is likely to take to reach agreement. Different participants, whomever they represent, have different goals, assumptions, priorities, bases of knowledge, approaches to problem solving, and pressures to show progress. Further, they often have different prior relationships, which contribute to the differential development of trust among collaboration members. All of these differences tend to slow the work of broadly representative collaborations.

Resolving these differences requires, first, an acknowledgment that they exist. Stakeholders are often brought together on the assumption of equal footing—each coming with different but equally valued contributions to make—and with optimistic expectations for building consensus. In fact, unspoken perceptions of relative power, legitimacy, and community connection often underlie stakeholder interactions, and fundamental differences in these perceptions may remain unexplored. Those less experienced or less familiar with dominant modes of decision-making (often representatives of associational neighborhood organizations and unaffiliated residents), for example, may remain silent as they seek to gain some comfort with the personalities and process. This situation leads to a second requirement for resolving differences: explicit, collective negotiation of rules, expectations, and process, and up-front training and leadership development in order for those less experienced to be able to participate more fully.

Ambiguous Representation and Authority. In many community capacity-building efforts (CCIs in particular), the coming together of a range of organizations in pursuit of a collaborative agenda is complicated by the ambiguity surrounding the nature of representation of both individual and institutional players. In NFI, for example, although participants were selected because of the roles they played in local organizations or as engaged residents, they were not recruited to be formal representatives of an organization or constituency. Rather, they participated as individuals with a particular perspective and (presumably) with access to particular resources, based on their organizational or neighborhood connections. This situation is true of most similarly structured collaborative ventures, such as other foundation-funded CCIs and the governance bodies assembled by many cities under the federal EZ/EC program.[13]

In such situations, where participants are not *formal* representatives, the assumption of representation—of speaking for and acting on behalf of a constituency—is generally felt by all participants. Because of this ambiguity, issues of legitimacy come into play, in which members may vie for recognition as a legitimate representative of a particular constituency. Although neighborhood residence is the principal criterion for legitimacy, others often feel their stake deserves equal recognition. A business owner in one NFI community expressed this sentiment:

> I regard myself as being a resident business [in the neighborhood]. I don't live [there]. I don't sleep there. But I am tied by almost an umbilical cord to the [neighborhood] and my home in [the suburbs]. Because if the alarm goes

off, I have to leave [my home] and come down here immediately. When there's a shooting, I feel it. If there's a fire next door, it touches me too.

As indicated previously, this tension around legitimacy is further complicated by the unequal distribution of power and influence among diverse partners. In community collaborations that mix resident participation with the participation of multiple organizations (CDCs, service agencies), organizational representatives tend to hold relatively greater sway. They tend to be more numerous, more accustomed to operating within an organized strategic-planning context, and more familiar and comfortable with each other and with external institutional players (e.g., government agencies) represented at the table.

In some cases, the ambiguous nature of representation has led to unrealistic expectations about what participants are able to contribute. In these instances, the issue of participant authority comes into play: that is, how much authority representatives have to commit the resources of their organization to the coalition's work. In the NFI collaboratives, for example, the CBO representatives have generally been executive directors with authority to speak on behalf of their organizations, whereas representatives of larger institutions and local government have to a large extent not been able to do so without returning to their host organizations for approval. Though often resolvable, this has sometimes caused delay and sometimes disillusionment regarding unspoken expectations about what such partners might be able to contribute. One city official put it this way:

> I think I have to be very careful in my personal capacity or my official capacity about making commitments that I can't follow through on because invariably when we do that we run into trouble down the line. . . . I know some of [the activities planned] will involve a request for assistance from the city, and the city wants to be a partner, but I'm also real aware that there's limitations to what we can do.

The ambiguity of representation in efforts like NFI provides some useful flexibility and makes it less costly for organizations to participate, since they are not necessarily bound by participants recruited because of their organizational affiliations. However, collaborations can make greater headway on their agendas when there are clear, agreed-upon expectations regarding stakeholder contribution and likely benefit and when organizational stakeholders come from a position of sufficient power and influence to make decisions and commit resources on behalf of their organizations.

Contextual Influences

A large part of the organizational calculus about whether or when to collaborate centers around need, opportunity, and capacity. But this determination is made neither objectively nor in a vacuum. The task of building the organizational infrastructure of a community as a strategy for developing community capacity is influenced by broader issues of context—the history of relations among organizations; the unequal distribution of influence and power; local dynamics concerning race, ethnicity, and class; and the economic and policy context at the metropolitan, state, and national levels—foster or impede interorganizational cooperation.

All transactions are embedded in social relations, and it is largely the nature and history of such relations, as well as the degree to which they can instill trust and cooperation rather than mistrust and competition, that will make meaningful collaboration possible (Granovetter, 1985). In community-based efforts in particular, the social embeddedness of community processes and organizations is a critical conditioning influence that can either support or thwart successful collaboration. The calculation of incentives and costs for engaging in interorganizational relations is often further complicated by the multiple goals, the ambiguity around "bottom line" objectives, and the dynamics of participation and representation in these efforts.

In our core cases, the environmental influence on interorganizational relations differs, owing largely to the extent that the contexts of these cases are characterized by dense or relatively undeveloped institutional infrastructures, by the nature and history of power dynamics (especially informed by issues of race and poverty), and by the emergence of opportunities or constraints generated outside the target community.

Although the communities involved in CODP, for example, differed in the number and range of active community organizations, they had no preexisting CDCs (with the exception of a few nascent organizations). Since the initiative was targeted rather than comprehensive and could therefore focus on a particular aspect of the organizational infrastructure (CDCs), and since there was no complex history of relations among neighborhoods around development issues, the program was able to exert considerable influence over the relationships among the new CDCs as they developed. Local coordinators and community organizers tried to keep the members of each CDC board aware of the progress being made by their peers in other neighborhoods. This flow of information was primarily a tactic to help keep volunteers motivated (e.g., "If you keep this up you could be the first group to buy property"), but it also helped to foster the feeling that the CDCs were all in the same boat—facing similar challenges, having similar needs, and making similar accomplishments—with the unstated implication that they were well suited to work together. Holiday events gave volunteers from different neighborhoods a chance to meet one another under congenial conditions. And when the time came to decide whether to form a coalition, a site visit by members of the CDC that had provided the model for the program's design was a deliberate effort to give volunteers a shared sense of what they might hope to accomplish together.

In contrast, because NFI sought to be comprehensive, it needed to incorporate a broad range of organizations in its work, and in each of the neighborhoods (with the exception of the neighborhood in Memphis) action took place in relatively dense organizational environments. Particularly in the Detroit and Milwaukee neighborhoods, numerous CBOs (and, in Detroit, major locally based institutions) coexist, each performing some set of defined functions, drawing on particular neighborhood assets, focusing on particular aspects of community need, and interacting in different ways with each other and with components of the larger community—local government, regional offices of national service agencies, local and national funders—that influence the organization's functioning and aspects of neighborhood well-being. Despite their coexistence, these organizations have largely worked in isolation, each claiming a particular subpopulation, geographic part of the neighborhood, or substantive area of work as its turf. In some cases, relations among organizations have been characterized historically by a kind of benign avoidance, in some by limited cooperation, and in others by outright conflict and mistrust. How these relations have developed in the past makes a significant difference in terms of the likelihood of productive interorganizational interactions in the future. Conflict and mistrust bred of past interactions or institutionalized expectations are difficult to overcome, and emerging trust and cooperation among rival organizations are likely to be repeatedly challenged and renegotiated.

As outlined in some of the cases mentioned above, the process of interorganizational interaction catalyzed by particular community capacity–building efforts was sometimes sufficient to foster a degree of reconciliation among competing organizations, or it provided an opportunity for building positive relations where, in the past, relations had been neutral or nonexistent. In other cases, organizations that felt threatened by the collaborative endeavor opted out of participation, participated grudgingly, participated but were unable to reconcile historical tensions, or were not asked to participate, based on some strategic choice on the part of the convener.

The nature of interorganizational relations, both historic and contemporary, will play a role in determining the likelihood of engaging in collaborative endeavors and the extent to which such endeavors, when engaged, will prove fruitful or problematic. Hartford, for example, is a small community in which organizational leaders have developed sometimes complicated histories over time. Heads of CBOs know each other from previous interactions serving on the same boards, and often move back and forth from jobs in city agencies to the nonprofit sector. In some cases, these histories have forged bonds of trust and a recognition of common concerns and interests. In others, the recollection of prior opposition endures to hamper future relations, and it has had an impact on collaborative endeavors under NFI. As one respondent recounted:

For example, I was on the board of [a local CBO on which a current member of the collaborative was then on staff]. I resigned from the board because the money was not being used properly. Integrity was lacking. This is remembered by some people—I'm too honest.

Race, resources, and shifts in policy and opportunity generated beyond the local community also play into these dynamics. In NFI, for example, Milwaukee and Hartford are both cities largely divided north and south by race, with African-Americans (and, in Hartford, West Indians) concentrated largely in the poorer, north end of the city. The neighborhoods there (as in similar neighborhoods in other cities) have relatively fewer resources, and the organizations tend to be less well supported than in these better-off, primarily white neighborhoods in other areas. The pressure of competition over these resources, which have become even more critical in some cases because of policy shifts, raises a hurdle to potential interorganizational cooperation. For example, legislation such as welfare reform—which has increased the numbers of former welfare recipients who depend on services provided by CBOs—has catalyzed interorganizational communication and cooperation. But in such cases, as in cases when resources are made available that are *contingent* on such cooperation, the shape of that cooperation is informed by prior relations and expectations. In both of these NFI sites, a growing Latino population has settled at the fringes of the predominantly African-American neighborhoods in which the initiative is taking place and represents an increasingly large proportion of the population of these neighborhoods. Yet efforts to incorporate Latino representation on the collaboratives have proven difficult, and attempts to sustain such representation over time have been unsuccessful. In part, as suggested by both Latino and African-American respondents, this is due to the perception that NFI is a "black" initiative and, in spite of its sometimes concentrated efforts at outreach, is not seen as intended to address or prepared to incorporate Latino constituents.

Historical relationships extend beyond the boundaries of a given neighborhood, and in some cases their embeddedness and resistance to change—that is, the interests that particular stakeholders have in maintaining the status quo—may constrain the ability to use a collaborative strategy to increase community capacity at the individual, organizational, and associational levels. In communities characterized by long-standing divisions based on power differences, it is often very difficult to engage those in power. Such has been the case, for example, in the Glades. As a broker organization, GCDC aims to establish working relationships with and among all the important players in the community. The large sugar companies, however, have for the most part avoided participation in GCDC's public forums, leadership development activities, or economic development efforts. Although they contribute from time to time to particular charitable causes promoted by GCDC, they have not inserted themselves or become invested in GCDC's larger change agenda. This illustrates the limitations of collaboration and the need to identify additional strategies, such as community organizing, to promote engagement of the most powerful sectors of the community.

THE IMPORTANCE OF COLLABORATION

Building community capacity by developing a community's organizational infrastructure draws from and builds on the other major strategies of leadership development, organizational development, and community organizing. Individuals, particularly organizational leaders (staff or board members), are the principal conduits through which relations among organizations develop and are maintained. Organizational capacity, including adequate resources, competent management, and an ability to recognize opportunity and engage in strategic interaction with the organization's environment, is critical for the development of interorganizational relations and for their institutionalization over time. Conversely, these links, when successful, will strengthen the individual capacity of participating organizations by providing them with expanded access to resources, additional opportunities for learning, and greater exposure to knowledge and approaches to problem solving, as well as the potential for a greater constituent voice and greater influence at the policy level. When such activity is well grounded in the needs, priorities, and preferences of community members, community capacity is increased by virtue of these organizations' enhanced influence on behalf of the community, their increased ability to connect to opportunity and resources, and their strengthened capacity to produce particular goods and services redounding to the well-being of community members. The process of connecting organizations to one another is in some ways analogous to the task of supporting the development of interpersonal networks of association, which is the focus of community-organizing strategies. In the context of community capacity building, this process often directly incorporates such organizing strategies as a way to foster the connection between a network of organizations and neighborhood residents.

Successfully engaging in such a strategy therefore relies to a great extent on the degree to which a foundation of active leadership, strong organizations, and (at least some) effective networks of relations between a neighborhood and its organizations exist. As we have seen, there are significant challenges—both operational and political—to this agenda. In particular, organizations need to successfully negotiate issues of differential power, relative contribution, and the establishment of trust among organizations within the community, between them and the residents on whose behalf they work, and between the community and actors in the broader environment. But the potential power of such a strategy is great, particularly to the extent that it provides both an increased internal capacity for planning, organization, and production *and* more effectively connects the community to resources and centers of influence beyond it.

NOTES

1. Organizations are thus treated as "nodes" in relational networks in the same way that individuals might be (Laumann, Galaskiewicz, and Mardsen, 1978), though the most likely mechanism through which such relations operate is individuals connected with the organizations in question. In some cases, these relations may actually consist of building the types of personal relationships (among members of different organizations) that discussions of social capital commonly take as their focus (see, e.g., Granovetter, 1985).

2. These efforts are thus similar, in essence, to particular kinds of interorganizational efforts—*social partnerships*—that tend to be cross-sectoral and focus on problems with a public policy relevance (Waddock, 1991).

3. Analytically, this reflects a shift in perspective from viewing organizations as essentially *closed systems* and focusing on their internal decision-making, administrative, and production processes, to an *open-systems* perspective of organizational structure and behavior in which organizations are seen as imperfectly bounded and engaged in an ongoing interplay with the environments in which they operate. (For review, see especially Scott, 1992.) Operationally, it reflects a recognition on the part of organizations of increased environmental complexity and interconnection, as well as the need to develop strategies to negotiate with one's environment and the organizational actors in it to achieve organizational goals more effectively. The application of this focus to local communities reflects a view of the community as, in part, the nexus of organizational activity and interorganizational linkages within a geographic area. Laumann, Galaskiewicz, and Mardsen (1978) and Knoke (1990), for example, stress the centrality of organizations (as opposed to individuals) as the principal actors in community systems, and the importance of an organization's access to information and resources through associational networks and interorganizational alliances for its influence in the system and its ability to reduce resource dependency.

4. Environmental uncertainty is characterized by a relatively high degree of *heterogeneity* (the degree to which organizations must interact with many different kinds of actors—funders, clients, organizations, etc.), a high level of organizational *change* (e.g., in operations or production), a relatively high level of *threat* to organizational survival (e.g., from the tenuousness of funding support), and the combination of a high degree of *interconnectedness* and low level of *coordination* among organizations (Scott, 1992).

5. The broader label of *intermediary organization,* in contrast, describes organizations that may operate either from within the community or be based outside it, and may play any of a range of roles, including providing technical assistance to other organizations, monitoring their activities and accomplishments, or acting as a pass-through for funding. In the United States, such intermediaries operate at both a national and a local level. National intermediaries, such as the Local Initiative Support Corporation (LISC), the Urban Strategies Council, and Seedco, often play a combination of these roles on behalf of a particular funder, in the same way a community foundation or department of local government might be chosen to act as a local intermediary to provide a formal auspice, funding oversight, and technical assistance for efforts funded by private foundations or higher levels of government. Intermediaries may, but need not, foster relations among community organizations.

6. See the Introduction for a brief explanation of GCDC and the other two initiatives (Neighborhood and Family Initiative and Consensus Organizing Demonstration Program) used for the core case studies of this book. See Appendix for full explanations.

7. Indeed, as Ferguson and Stoutland (1999:44) suggest, trust is critical for the creation of successful alliances of any sort. They suggest four "trust questions" as a diagnostic for whether an alliance is likely to succeed, in which each party to an interorganizational alliance asks itself if its allies have motives compatible to its own, are competent to play their roles, will be dependable, and will act collegially. "If too many actors doubt other's motives, competence, dependability, or collegiality, the alliance is doomed to fail" (ibid.:594).

8. To some extent, umbrella organizations like HEBCAC, discussed as a broker organization above, can also serve as such a mechanism of interorganizational connection by supporting direct interaction and joint action among its member organizations. Similarly, mechanisms like LINC may also play a brokering role, acting as a conduit for information and resources both to the organizations and citizen groups directly related to its programs and to the community at large.

9. The minigrant program is coordinated by the partnership and administered by the Community Foundation of Southeastern Michigan.

10. The employment service was discontinued in 1997 due to insufficient funding.

11. An actor with structural autonomy is positioned to broker and make use of information and resources by maintaining relationships with actors who represent access to other clusters of social actors (beyond the relations maintained by members of the component networks among which he or she is brokering) and to the information, resources, and opportunities they represent (Burt, 1992).

12. Alter and Hage (1993) distill from the organizational literature the costs and benefits of interorganizational collaboration and argue that there is a long-term trend toward interorganizational collaboration because (1) the perception of costs and benefits has changed (regardless of any actual

change in the ratio), especially as organizations consider the calculus within a longer time frame; (2) some new benefits redound to collaborators, particularly the opportunity for organizational learning; and (3) they have learned to engage in communication and negotiation around interorganizational collaboration in ways that reduce the likelihood of noncompliance.

13. HEBCAC is an exception, since each member is a formal representative of a particular organization or neighborhood association, which, in turn, is seen as representing a particular constituency.

6

Conclusion: Possibilities, Limitations, and Next Steps

The community-building agenda that drives many neighborhood-based efforts centers on strengthening each community's capacity so that the efforts can be sustained. The concept of community capacity serves as an evocative banner behind which community-building activities can advance, but references to it are typically quite general. For the concept to be useful, it must be broken down into its constituent elements, which can then be analyzed (individually and in relation to one another) and acted on.

We have attempted to contribute to this task by proposing a definitional framework for community capacity and by exploring attempts to build it. The framework suggests that community capacity is exemplified by a set of core characteristics and operates through the agency of individuals, organizations, and networks to perform particular functions. It also suggests that, although conditioned in part by both micro- and macrolevel contextual influences, community capacity may be built through strategic interventions, which—when successful—may lead not only to increased community capacity but also to other desired community outcomes (see Figure 1). We have analyzed four major strategies that a broad range of interventions have adopted to build capacity, and identified some emerging issues and lessons. This analysis leads to a set of conclusions regarding the possibilities and limitations of the strategies being employed and the community capacity–building agenda as a whole. We discuss these conclusions below. First, we briefly highlight some of the lessons that emerge from our analysis of the four major strategies. We then turn to broader, cross-cutting issues and lessons about community capacity–building efforts as a whole.

STRATEGY-SPECIFIC ISSUES AND LESSONS

Current community-building efforts have adopted four basic strategies to create community capacity: leadership development, organizational development, community organizing, and organizational collaboration. Each focuses on a particular level of social agency (individuals, organizations, networks) and seeks to strengthen certain of the characteristics of communities with capacity—including a sense of community, commitment to community, problem-solving mechanisms, and access to resources. These characteristics are critical to a community's well-being, both as generally available resources and as components of efforts to perform particular functions (e.g., collective planning and advocacy) to achieve particular ends (e.g., greater influence on policy).

Leadership Development

Leadership development strategies vary along two dimensions—process and target. Regarding process, they may provide either formal training or informal "on-the-job" opportunities to learn while engaged in community activities. Regarding target, they may strive either to strengthen individual leaders or to cultivate leadership cadres.

Formal training approaches can suffer if they are unable to connect trained individuals to a broader community improvement agenda. Aware of this potential problem, many leadership training programs build in at least one curriculum element that involves participants in concrete activities undertaken in or on behalf of their community. Conversely, many engagement approaches to leadership development can benefit greatly from targeted, well-timed training programs that build the capacity of individuals to engage in the work effectively and on an equal footing with other participants and community actors. Training can be a particularly effective way to convey technical information and transmit skills. Not surprisingly, the greater the engagement component involved in a leadership development strategy, the more time-consuming it is likely to be, and the more difficult it is to plan and implement.

Training programs designed for groups of prospective leaders have been less common than ones for individuals, but group-focused approaches appear to be gaining favor and to hold considerable promise. The difficulties involved in improving neighborhoods that have deteriorated over a sustained period are considerable, and they can easily overwhelm the efforts of scattered individuals. Cadres of individuals, trained in the process of effecting change and committed to doing so, appear more likely to be able to make a real difference.

Organizational Development

Efforts to build a community's organizational strength focus on some combination of three different strategies: strengthening existing organizations, helping existing organizations take on new functions or roles, and building new organizations. The primary vehicle for strengthening existing organizations is technical assistance (TA), sometimes combined with grants. The success of this approach depends heavily on finding providers who are committed to the often time-consuming role of building long-term organizational capacity, rather than simply providing short-term technical expertise on discrete issues. However, for organizations invested in the status quo that resist pressures to change, technical assistance is not likely to be an effective tool. In these cases, advocacy, community organizing, and other forms of pressure exerted from outside the organizations represent more promising approaches.

Strategies that seek to help existing organizations add new roles or functions require sensitivity both to the process for selecting organizations (to ensure they have community support for the new role) and to the ability of the chosen organizations to successfully shoulder the demands of that role. The more an organizational development strategy is internalized by the selected organizations, rather than imposed from outside, the more likely it is to result in positive and sustained organizational change.

Creating new organizations is the most demanding of the three strategies. Besides requiring a great deal of time and resources, this approach can run into problems if the new organization is seen to infringe on the place and role of existing organizations. And other problems are likely to arise if expectations for producing program outcomes overshadow the need to build organizational capacity. New organizations will falter and fail to contribute to broaden community capacity if they are burdened with unreasonable expectations about the time and effort needed to become well enough established to take on ambitious programmatic responsibility. Similarly, the likelihood of success will be reduced if the task of building the organization's connections to and support of the larger community are not addressed.

Any effort to strengthen a community's organizations as a means to enhance community capacity should promote organizations with strong connections to community residents and other stakeholders. These connections enable organizations to respond flexibly to changing community concerns and conditions. Connected, responsive organizations become the vehicles through which residents can gain a more powerful voice.

Community Organizing

Community-organizing strategies vary along three principal dimensions. Each dimension is defined as a continuum between pairs of opposite approaches: conflict versus consensus, single issue versus multiple issues, direct recruitment versus organization-based recruitment. Regardless of where they fall along each continuum, however, all community organizing strategies share the objective of engaging residents in sustained collective action around issues important to them. In addition, many community-building efforts conduct a variety of outreach and communication activities intended to inform residents about planned or ongoing activities, interest them in those activities, and engage their participation in some way. These activities are often referred to as community organizing, but differ from mainstream community organizing in that they rarely strive for sustained collective action, which is an essential feature of organizing.

Each approach to community organizing has advantages and limitations, and sensible choices must be made in context. Political conflict is a visible, direct tool for change that can be very effective in obtaining commitments from powerful people or institutions to behave differently. It can be a blunt instrument, however, and can alienate (sometimes for a very long time) important local stakeholders from whom the community will want resources and support. This limitation is especially the case in the current environment, with its emphasis on partnerships and collaboration. Consensus-based approaches avoid these problems; on the other hand, they may not push firmly toward developing the political power of residents—surely an important aspect of their ability to achieve greater equality.

Single-issue organizing can be easier than efforts that require participants to understand more multifaceted, complex issues. It is often harder to sustain, however, especially if the problem addressed is at least partially resolved (e.g., block watch efforts decline as a result of reduction in crime) or is overshadowed in the public eye. Multi-issue organizing requires more education of participants and is therefore more time-consuming. But education is, itself, part of the process of building the capacity of residents to take effective action on the community's behalf. To take visible action, the multi-issue approach must begin with a specific issue, such as affordable housing. But this can occur only after the foundation for broadening out or moving on to other issues has been laid.

Existing organizations, especially congregations and block clubs, are commonly mobilized in community-organizing efforts. Use of such organizations (or sets of organizations) reduces the effort that must be spent building relationships and trust, and can greatly speed a broad-based organizing process. However, organizations often leave out some segments of the community, such as renters, smaller block clubs, and minority groups in diverse communities. Reaching out directly to individuals is more difficult and time-consuming but, especially in fragmented communities, can result in the mobilization of a more inclusive, representative group.

Whatever the chosen strategy, some residents become deeply involved in working for the community (and often receive leadership training to support and enhance their intensive engagement). However, the goal is generally not to enlist the ongoing participation of masses of people; rather, it is to engage a relatively small core group of committed leaders, as well as to develop a pool of other stakeholders who can be called on for large projects or actions and who can supply replacements for the core group as needed. In addition, "pure" strategies (e.g., straight conflict, or simultaneous pursuit of multiple issues) are rarely observed, although a single snapshot of the initiative may create that impression. Periodic observations (a "movie") will typically show modulation over time—a consensus-style initiative occasionally resorting to conflict, or the sharpening of a broad issue to mobilize energy around a particular action.

Collaborations, Partnerships, and Organizational Networks

In the context of community capacity building, developing relationships between and among organizations depends both on the ability of participating organizations to negotiate the costs and benefits of partnership and collaboration and, often, on the association's success in establishing itself as a legitimate actor on behalf of the community.

Strategies for building organizational collaboration in a community fall into three broad categories: establishing "broker" organizations, creating ongoing coalitional arrangements, and engaging in more limited partnerships focused on specific goals and activities. Broker organizations are promising mechanisms for fostering interorganizational relations if they can establish trust and legitimacy among potential partners and if they possess the capacity and resources to act without being perceived as competitors. Structured coalitions offer potentially greater reach and flexibility, can have significant influence within and beyond the community, and can provide a useful forum for the development and expansion of informal networks among organizations. Over time, however, it can be difficult to maintain consistent member engagement and contribution. More specialized organizational partnerships are somewhat less complicated to develop and are likely to be more immediately fruitful for producing defined outcomes, although their reach is, by definition, not as broad. However, relationships built during limited, concrete activities can sometimes become institutionalized over time or provide the building blocks for developing broader networks.

Whatever the strategy, interorganizational cooperation is most successful when each organization has a clear contribution to make and anticipates gaining a clear benefit from it. This situation occurs when the responsibilities of all parties are clear and agreed on, when the participating organizations are all competent to perform their responsibilities, and when participants have crafted some reliable mechanism for sharing both risk for failure and recognition for success.

Linking Strategies

Connections among the four major strategies for creating community capacity are potentially important: Individual leaders are central to increasing the capacity and effectiveness of organizations, and both organizational development and community organizing provide ready opportunities for developing community leaders. The impact of an organizing effort can and often does depend on the strength and "staying power" of the organization behind it. Productive interorganizational relationships require strong participating organizations. And the success of collaborative strategies frequently rests heavily on successful leadership development. Capitalizing on such connections increases the likelihood that efforts to build community capacity will make a lasting impact.

On the other hand, even such comparatively simple approaches as helping existing groups take on new roles can become quite complicated: Politics intrudes, people behave in unexpected ways, the timing of key program events becomes hard to adapt to changing circumstances in the community. Diagnosing a problem as it develops even in relatively simple interventions—never mind strategizing about how to resolve the inevitable difficulties—can test the skills of even a seasoned practitioner. This realization suggests the prudence of humility. Given the ample evidence showing the difficulty of implementing more comprehensive approaches, it makes great sense when undertaking a multifaceted intervention to perform a hard-nosed assessment during the program-design phase (with periodic revisits to the issue) of how the effort can best be managed with the money and skills available—especially since there has been little systematic thinking or experimentation to assess the pros and cons of various combinations of the strategies examined here. That said, however, it is undoubtedly a lost opportunity to maximize the impact of program resources if, in everything a community capacity–building initiative does, it does not strive to integrate complementary strategies into its primary capacity-building approach.

CROSS-CUTTING ISSUES AND LESSONS

Cutting across the accumulating experience and lessons gained through the four main strategies for building community capacity is a set of broader issues that speak both to the challenges of implementing community capacity–building efforts and to the factors conditioning their success.

Perhaps the most important of these issues is power and control. In one way or another, each of the cross-cutting issues we will explore involves the question of power and how it is negotiated, since each concerns the relative abilities of different actors to effect change and influence change in others. In some cases, the issue of power is explicit; in others, it remains beneath the surface. Either way, it shapes the expectations and actions of the participants within a target community, as well as those of the external sponsors of capacity-building efforts. In addition, the distribution of power in the surrounding macroenvironment both opens opportunities and sets limits on what community-change efforts, by themselves, can accomplish.

Power and Control

Efforts to strengthen community capacity in poor communities generally have multiple motivations. The most common one is to improve the quality of life in the community by increasing its ability to use its own resources more effectively. A second one, increasingly acknowledged and built explicitly into program designs, is to improve the community's ability to access or leverage external resources to augment those the community can muster on its own. A third motivation is about leveling the playing field—an idea conceived variously in terms of empowerment, or community control, or getting the community "a seat at the table" where the decisions shaping its future are made. Regardless of how the power issue is framed, however, at stake is giving the target community the same influence over decisions affecting it that other communities enjoy and the same opportunity to participate effectively in the larger democratic process. In short, this aspect of community capacity building is about the redistribution of power.

Power and control issues arise at two different levels in community capacity building. At the macrolevel, they concern the influence wielded by the target communities vis-à-vis external agents with authority and resources. At the microlevel, they concern the relative influence held by community members within the intervention itself and the challenges involved in managing changes in their influence over time.

The "p" word is rarely, if ever, used in polite company. Overt discussion of power would undercut the useful fiction that our society is egalitarian, that we are all equal. Beyond that, however, public acknowledgment that changes in power might be at stake would make efforts to build capacity in poor communities much more controversial, difficult to manage, and difficult to fund. Understanding this, and wanting to improve the well-being of poor communities without being disruptive (or disrupted), people who design and implement community capacity–building efforts are commonly silent, and perhaps uncertain, about how much change in the distribution of power and influence the effort can, or should, try to effect. Ironically, even those who are firmly committed to change of this sort may not fully understand how such change would require those outside the target community, including themselves, to change as well.

If capacity-building efforts are effective and sustained, however, the target community will not remain the only locus of change. Communities are part of social, political, and economic systems; successfully increasing a neighborhood's capacity, including its ability to link effectively to outside sources of resources and influence, eventually creates pressure for adjustments elsewhere in these ystems.

Within community capacity–building interventions, participants from target communities should, over time, come to exert greater power and influence over their circumstances. In most cases, the prospect of gaining greater control for the community is a powerful motivator for community stakeholders, especially residents.

Increasing the political leverage of residents in poor communities is a labor that must take place on several fronts. Residents typically need to learn about a variety of issues. This learning process is multidimensional and includes enhancing residents' self-efficacy, as well as raising their awareness of the role of elected leaders, the workings of the political system, and their rights and resources. In addition, participants in capacity-building efforts need to understand and acknowledge the specific political landscape in which they are working. Localities vary considerably in their receptivity to new people and ideas, tolerance for openly expressing opposing viewpoints, institutional responsiveness to local citizenry, and so forth. Developing a shared perspective on these issues, as well as on more specific issues (such as likely sources of support, resistance, or even opposition) and how to deal with them, can afford participants a much more sophisticated understanding of their political environment, build cohesion by consolidating a shared identity that is both community based and related to broader social arenas, and cultivate an appreciation of how long-run change can occur.

Resident leaders not accustomed to exercising power are likely to benefit considerably from targeted, respectful assistance in how to do so. This can be as "simple" as teaching the newly elected president of a community-based organization (CBO) board how to run an effective meeting, as surprising as coaching him or her on safeguarding the rights of the minority, or as delicate as helping him or her retain the active engagement of a senior pastor unaccustomed to working in groups where his or her opinion is viewed as merely one among many.

Exercising power and control must go hand in hand with assuming responsibility. But gaining power is risky: one can fail and be held accountable for that by the community. As several previous quotations attest, residents themselves are well aware of this danger—often more aware than program sponsors. Thus, residents are likely to experience occasional ambivalence about actually assuming control. Such ambivalence can sometimes be confusing to other participants, unless they understand that it is part of the development process.

Achieving a situation in which a community can actually exercise control—or even major influence—does not free nonresident participants (funders, services providers, technical advisors, professional organizers, etc.) to leave the table or otherwise abdicate their own responsibility for making the intervention a success. For example, it does not mean watching a newly empowered group make a serious mistake without voicing an opinion. Even empowered and well-organized residents of poor neighborhoods have a continuing need for friendly but tough-minded advice. Respectful power sharing by nonresident participants means having confidence that residents possess the self-esteem and capability to accept constructive criticism, to hear alternative points of view without being overpowered by them, and to be held accountable for meeting their commitments. Resident leaders can and should be held to high standards of performance. Failure to do so signals lack of respect and confidence in their ability, and it betrays a willingness on the part of outside agents to accept, that, once again, second best is good enough for the target community. Finally, it signals to the reflective practitioner that the program has not accomplished what it set out to do.

Participation, Legitimacy, and Consensus

Connected to the issue of power and empowerment is the question of participation. Much of the difficulty involved in applying and evaluating participatory strategies stems from ambiguities about what constitutes "legitimate" participation, why it should be engaged, and what can be expected from it. Opinions on these questions differ considerably. Often local government, private developers, and other actors view agencies and organizations located in the community as representatives of the community's interest, and they tend to be the dominant participants on broadly constituted community governance bodies. However, these local organizations and the capacity-building interventions that bring them together often succeed in engaging only a small number of residents in the effort, and they are usually the residents already most involved in neighborhood affairs.

There are several causes of this limited participation. Residents are often skeptical about whether their participation will be worth the effort. It is difficult to incorporate meaningful resident participation while showing near-term, tangible results. And in many cases, greater resident participation is not necessary for the effort to be seen as legitimately acting on the community's behalf. Legitimacy is always open to question (and challenge). But it is often enough for local organizations to present reasonable evidence of community connection to be treated by funders and local government as a (or even, for a given time or issue, *the*) legitimate neighborhood agent (Chaskin and Abunimah, 1999).

The reality of community participation as described here rarely reaches the goals that formal community capacity–building efforts set. There are several reasons for this discrepancy, ranging from lack of skill and resources on the initiative's part to residents' lack of skills or interest to get involved. Participation may also depend in part on the degree to which the change effort is externally conceived and driven. Finally, people use and ascribe meaning to neighborhoods differently. For some, it is a place to sleep and eat, with much of their social life occurring throughout the city or in multiple communities. Others perceive it as a space that is important for their identity and quality of life, and they are more likely to participate in community activities. Furthermore, people have families and jobs. The pressures of day-to-day existence frequently leave little time and energy for the added burden of active participation in a community-building effort. In particular, the poor have fewer resources and often less flexibility and discretionary time to devote to such participation.

Most formal efforts to build community capacity are sited in neighborhoods with clear resources on which to build, including some core number of engaged residents with both the inclination and the means to participate. In the most acutely disinvested communities—those that suffer neglect as well as numerous internal instabilities, such as high crime, isolation, and the lack of strong organizations or adequate services—residents may not be as optimistic about the capacity of external initiatives to leverage change. Thus, mobilizing even a small group of residents may require significant additional effort, and in order to take advantage of a neighborhood's existing resources, community-capacity building efforts need to understand the nature of those resources and how to modulate support (in degree and in kind) to develop them.

Even within the relatively circumscribed group that might be directly engaged in a community-building effort (a CBO board, a neighborhood council, the governance body of a comprehensive community initiative), consensus may not be easy to forge. The interests of some community actors may conflict with the interests—real or perceived—of others. Avoiding such differences is frequently made more difficult by the breadth of the agenda, and resolving the differences that do arise is often hampered by the difficulty of sustaining and managing broad participation, as well as by changing (and sometimes ambiguous) roles and expectations.

A lack of consensus (or even actual conflict) is not necessarily a barrier to building community capacity or to taking legitimate action. Disagreement may provide a catalyst to action that can exercise or even expand capacity within the community (for planning, advocacy, information dissemination, implementation). In fact, disagreements successfully resolved may constitute direct evidence of a community's capacity to solve problems. This can be the case even if some parties to the disagreement are disappointed in, and possibly unsupportive of, the outcome reached by and for the community—as long as the process for reaching that outcome is viewed as fair and legitimate. On that condition, "losers" can be retained as committed members who reengage on other occasions.

Establishing the ground rules and mutual trust for this kind of process, however, requires time and care. Initially, the desire for consensus is likely to be strong, especially if members of the group are just getting to know one another. Under those conditions, it is difficult for group members to know the intensity of one another's opinions, for example, or to gauge each other's willingness and ability to compromise. A variety of tactics can be used to cultivate a climate in which people feel less need for complete consensus. These include tackling early some issues on which there is widespread agreement (e.g., improving the community's appearance, providing opportunities for youth); establishing the norm that all viewpoints get a respectful hearing; seeking and cultivating common ground among those who clearly differ on some important issues (so the group does not divide into factions); and making sure that early "losers" (real or perceived, powerful or vulnerable) reengage in the group and are broadly supported in doing so.

Race, Class, and Culture

Issues of power and legitimacy are further complicated by the social dynamics of race. Community capacity–building efforts commonly target communities of color and attach positive value to the principle and practice of diversity and inclusion. Local cultures differ in how they treat and talk (or avoid talking) about social divisions: race, class, gender, power, experience, technical skills, and the like—but especially race. How issues concerning these divisions arise and how they can best be addressed will be shaped, at the margins, by the local context. But there are some basic themes.

One such theme is trust. Individuals and communities of color, especially individuals with strong personal experiences of discrimination and communities that have experienced a history of broken promises by government and others (funders, developers, researchers), may come to community capacity–building activities with a healthy skepticism concerning both the motives and trustworthiness of sponsors and selected partners. As one observer of community dynamics put it: "Questions about motives are always, at bottom, questions about the messenger." Conversely, members of the majority community may have reservations of their own. They may be concerned, for example, about whether they might at some point find themselves on the defensive in a racially charged situation. Or they may harbor doubts about what the minority community will actually be able to accomplish.

In short, trust cannot be assumed: it must be built. Building trust is possible but requires energy and thought, and it is likely to develop slowly. Special care to build a positive track record from the beginning is worth the effort. In the context of a community capacity–building intervention, there is clear value in having program staff take a lead role in modeling the behavior the intervention seeks to cultivate in participants, including diversity in membership, an inclusive and respectful style of working, and an ability and willingness to talk about race forthrightly when the issue arises.[1] Sensitive, respectful treatment of racial issues wins appreciation and helps to build trust—not only because it is desirable behavior, but also because it acknowledges and respects the importance of the issue to targeted communities of color. Constructive discussion of race-related issues is often difficult to introduce and to manage well, especially at first. It may not be any more difficult, however, than dealing with the problems and tensions that can arise when those issues cannot be talked about.

The more social divisions there are among participants in a community-building initiative, the harder the task of building bridges of trust is likely to be. Higher numbers of social divisions seem to increase the likelihood that differences of opinion about other issues will tap into preexisting stereotypes and fears that damage trust and respect. Thus, for example, other things being equal, bridges among culturally similar residents of a poor community are likely to be easier to build than bridges between them and powerful outsiders. The difficulty in this situation can be mitigated to a degree if participants from both groups are diverse along a variety of other dimensions, such as gender, educational attainment, and professional status.

External Stimulus to Building Community Capacity

Many formal community capacity–building efforts are catalyzed from outside the community, either by government initiatives or funding from private foundations. Consistent with the notion of capacity building, these sponsors tend to seek a "partnership" with the communities whose capacity they hope to help build. They attempt to support a locally driven process of deliberation and planning. Defining the nature of these partnerships has often been problematic, however, both because of assumptions at the community level about sponsors' motives and proclivities and because of the way the principle of grassroots action has interacted with the reality of top-down administration. Often, sponsors are seen as outsiders with power and resources, but without grounded knowledge of or legitimacy in the communities they seek to support.

Because the communities targeted by most capacity-building efforts are impoverished and largely populated by people of color, issues of race, concerns with social justice, and mistrust of paternalistic approaches play an important role in defining this dynamic. Some sponsors sensitive to this issue have been overly cautious in their approach, declining to state clearly their assumptions and expectations for fear of being perceived as too controlling. Or they have been reluctant to make their own funding priorities and processes clear. In other cases, sponsors have been perceived as arrogant, overbearing, or unrealistic in dictating rules, expectations, and procedures or in allowing their own objectives to dominate by promoting them through their control of resources. In still other cases, sponsors have been inconsistent, sending mixed signals or failing to follow through on stated or implied commitments. Because of the relative power that comes with resources, even small actions (or inactions) on the part of sponsors can sometimes be overscrutinized by community actors trying to interpret their meaning and what it implies for securing or losing potential support.

Partnership in community capacity building may be strengthened if, on the one hand, sponsors are both clear and consistent about their objectives and expectations and open and flexible with community participants, and, on the other, if local stakeholders are involved in the early development of an intervention, including its design and the way it is presented locally. Individuals and organizations that are active in their community are not only useful for recruiting participants but also may have purchase for establishing, early on, the legitimacy of the effort. This type of early enlistment differs from the approach of an external funder who conceives a program and then enters the community to solicit "partners," since it gets the community "on board" and providing input into the design and goals of the initiative before it is publicized. As in all partnerships, this approach involves the danger of making enemies (especially of those not chosen and their allies) or of inadvertently co-opting the partners (or appearing to do so in the eyes of local observers). This danger underlines the need to allow sufficient time to allow for broad and meaningful community participation from the outset of the initiative.

Further, community capacity is more likely to develop when sponsors think of themselves as investing in capacity and invite local participants to exercise that capacity in a variety of ways valued by the community (including, but not limited to, responding to funding opportunities). In this approach, sponsors will use not just program outcomes, but the production of capacity and strengthening of the mechanisms through which it works—individuals, organizations, and networks—to define and assess the success of their effort. If they understand capacity in this way, sponsors will have a framework to explain and guide investments in its development. They are also likely to do a more thorough capacity inventory before jumping in, since it is much easier, and more respectful of the community, to build on existing assets than to start fresh.

Resident Mobility and Leadership Turnover

Community development and other place-based strategies to help the poor always confront the dilemma posed by household mobility: the real goal is to help people, not pieces of geography. Help to people-in-places, however, can enable the people assisted to leave those places for greener pastures. This is an inevitable risk. What, then, is a community developer to do?

First, accept the risk as real, and then reframe the issue. Making the possibility of upward mobility a reality in seriously disadvantaged communities in which multigenerational poverty is becoming more common is hardly a bad outcome. Many would argue that upward mobility is a sign of real progress, because all healthy neighborhoods should be avenues to opportunity. From this perspective, the goal is to make the community a launching pad to better things *and simultaneously* a place that is attractive enough to draw in "replacements" for whom the target neighborhood is a step up (or at least not a step down).

Second, understand that it is possible to mitigate the risk by increasing positive engagement in the community and by publicizing and celebrating accomplishments. Most people like to feel that what they do makes a difference. They enjoy the feelings of efficacy that come with accomplishment and are pleased if their contributions are acknowledged and appreciated. People who become engaged in community life are typically those who already have a commitment to the neighborhood. They would like to see it improve, because they care about it and, by implication, would like it to be a nicer place to live. And many residents will experience a deeper commitment to the community if they can contribute successfully and if they can see their efforts and accomplishments linked to larger victories that they could not have achieved on their own. Fostering a climate in which residents have these kinds of experiences can encourage them to stay in the neighborhood to reap the fruits of their labor. Further, if the community supports and celebrates those who leave for new opportunities, those who remain may feel better about staying because they can see that residents have real choices: they are not trapped. At the same time, fostering this climate enables the community to present a more positive image that would possibly attract others to the neighborhood.

Finally, it is instructive to note that resident mobility does not appear to have arisen as an important issue in the community capacity–building efforts examined in this volume. Insofar as the issue has surfaced for discussion, it appears that although a few resident leaders moved from their communities, they did so for personal reasons and their numbers were too few to create serious problems for the efforts. Indeed, some continued to be involved in the efforts after their move. Although further attention to this issue is in order, it may turn out to be of little consequence.

Organizations participating in capacity-building activities face a similar dilemma. Investments in the skills of individual staff members make those staff members more attractive to other employers, including employers who offer better salaries, benefits, or promotion opportunities than the typical CBO. This is especially the case when staff gain technical skills that are in demand in the local economy. Since many community organizations run on tight budgets and rely on relatively few leaders, member and staff turnover can be detrimental to organizational capacity and effectiveness.

Reframing the issue provides perspective here, too. Staff may leave to use newly honed skills elsewhere, but good staff members are also likely to leave if their organization is not providing them with opportunities for growth. Over the long haul, building an organization that has a compelling mission and is good at what it does—so that staff feel their work makes a difference—provides a counterbalancing incentive for staff with increasing competence to stay. Such an organization also has an edge in attracting good staff, especially if it has a reputation for helping staff advance professionally.

Nevertheless, the risk of losing newly trained staff is real, and the costs to an individual organization of turnover in key leadership positions can be high, especially in smaller organizations with limited leadership depth. Indeed, while the mobility of resident leadership in the capacity-building examples we reviewed was not a significant problem, in several cases staff turnover was. Screening prospective leaders for commitment, as well as formal qualifications, may help reduce the frequency of the problem, but it does nothing to diminish the severity. In the event of senior staff turnover, it may be necessary to undertake short-term damage control efforts, such as renegotiating time lines, reallocating responsibilities among participants, securing financial support for a thoughtful search process, providing coaching for whoever assumes interim responsibility for the duties of the vacated position, and acknowledging that this process is likely to produce uncertainty and anxiety among other participants. In some cases, it may become necessary to secure additional resources and structure incentives to attract and retain suitable leadership. In the longer term, it is likely to be helpful to focus on building, institutionalizing, and reproducing a broader pool of leadership in the community (and within the organization) at a scale that can withstand the impact of mobility.

Exogenous Influences and Constraints

The political, social, and economic contexts at the metropolitan, regional, national, and even global levels can have a profound impact on what is possible at the community level. Shifts in policy, migration, and investment (both public and private) that originate well beyond the boundaries of the local community can condition what is possible to change or maintain. For example, a community capacity–building effort by itself is usually powerless to affect the system of resource allocation to schools, to create neighborhood-based economies that are self-sufficient, or to reverse systemic discrimination in housing markets or mortgage lending.

Nevertheless, many aspects of action and production *can* be profitably engaged at the local level. The community provides an organizing locus for action, planning, and advocacy. It is an important context of opportunity and constraint for those who live there—particularly for children, the elderly, and those who are less well off and less well integrated into the larger society and therefore more reliant on what their local community has to offer. Addressing basic needs—affordable housing, accessible and responsive human services, quality goods, the safety and availability of public space—can often be best done in local communities, planned and delivered based on the stated priorities of community members and with reference to the specific circumstances and dynamics at work in specific places. Organizations and strengthened networks among individuals can act as conduits for residents to learn about and gain access to opportunity beyond the community. And an organized community can provide a necessary foundation for effective advocacy to effect change in broader policy arenas and in the practice of external actors such as developers and government service agencies.

But much of what will be necessary to maintain some ongoing community capacity will require a broader shift in power, resources, and influence that allows communities to take advantage of opportunities and buffer themselves against calamity born of actions by government and business at the metropolitan level and beyond. This is one sense in which building community capacity is ultimately about putting disinvested communities on a more even par with those that are more fortunate economically. This suggests additional action—beyond activities to build community capacity locally—at broader policy levels, by connecting local communities to communities that share their interests and needs through constituency-building activities, and by employing broad-based organizing, legislative advocacy, and political mobilization to influence changes in state and national policy.

Reasonable Expectations

The foregoing discussion begins to outline the importance of crafting reasonable expectations for community-building efforts. Many formal efforts—large-scale community development corporations, comprehensive community initiatives, the federal Empowerment Zone / Enterprise Community program[2]—state their goals in sweeping and ambitious terms. They speak of neighborhood transformation, community revitalization, and the alleviation of poverty. Yet the extent of the interventions and the scale of resources allocated are small compared with the magnitude of change sought. The circumstances of the communities they seek to change did not develop overnight; they are the product of decades of public and private disinvestment. Both official policy and unofficial practice have supported segregation of the population by race and class, concentrating poverty and diminishing resources and access in poor communities. Significant change will take time, will be incremental, and will require action at both the community level and beyond, including a focus on policies that address more fundamental questions of education, income equality, racial discrimination, and access to opportunity. This is not to imply that support for community development activity is misplaced or that community capacity building is not crucial. It does, however, indicate the need for careful consideration of what can be done, how long it will take, and what resources it will require.

Such caution, though, creates a dilemma: In order to garner support for a social change agenda, the promise of benefits needs to be made clear and provocative; policy rhetoric that far outstrips likely outcomes commonly leads to disillusionment and withdrawal of support. Crafting reasonable expectations at the outset, or adjusting expectations in light of evidence provided by experience, can mitigate this problem.

Once the issues of exogenous influences and the scale of the intervention have been taken into account, two additional (and interrelated) perspectives can help shape reasonable expectations. One is a consideration of short-term versus long-term outcomes. Building community capacity is a slow process that requires sustained investment. Developing leaders and building strong organizations are labor-intensive activities that happen over years, not days. The same is true for the relationships forged through organizing and collaboration—building trust, finding a common agenda, and taking action on that agenda all require a significant time investment, the results of which may only show up in the quite distant future. Building community capacity is an ongoing process: new leaders must continually be nurtured, organizational development promoted, and new ways of linking individuals and organizations around common aims advanced. This process and the mechanisms it leaves in place—active leaders, strong organizations, and networks of association—are the essence of community capacity, the foundation on which change can be built and sustained. To say that this all takes time does not mean that no benefits may accrue in the near term. Indeed, fostering successful processes is one such outcome, and there is a range of short- and mid-term changes that can and should be defined, based on the nature of the activities pursued and the particular goals identified. A series of modest but meaningful accomplishments gives people a sense of what might be a reasonable positive trajectory toward their long-term goals. In that context, slow and often hard-won, short-term gains can be understood as part of a larger cumulative process that can gain momentum and generate a sense of collective efficacy.

Another perspective that informs reasonable expectations distinguishes between individual and collective outcomes and notes the differential advantage that is likely to accrue to various segments of the community. Benefits may accrue to particular people who are directly involved in the effort, to particular organizations that are engaged, to social networks among discrete sets of actors, and to the community as a whole in terms of its physical space (housing, safety, infrastructure), economic circumstances, access to goods and services, and connections to the broader community and the opportunities it provides. Those closer to the center of action are likely to benefit sooner and more obviously than those at the periphery. Although efforts to promote community capacity ultimately seek change at the broadest level, the early achievement of some benefit valued by those at the center—leaders, volunteer workers, staff members, and other participants—is also important; they are part of the community, they interact with others and have a symbolic presence in the community, and their ongoing efforts are key to the intervention's progress. In addition, their involvement can lead to new kinds of supportive networks and relationships that bring further benefits. Understanding the social organization of a community is important here. Each neighborhood houses multiple "communities" whose capacities are likely to be enhanced in different ways over time. And although it is possible that collective capacity may ensue by "trickling out" from those at the center to others by virtue of their residence in the community, it is more likely that concerted effort will be needed to translate developing capacity among one group within the community into a viable building block for others.

Measurement

The issue of crafting reasonable expectations about outcomes leads to the equally important issue of devising ways to recognize and measure those outcomes. Our definitional framework is intended to provide some clarity about the components of community capacity; the dimensions of context and strategy that relate to building such capacity; the kinds of "other outcomes" such efforts hope to achieve; and how these various dimensions relate to one another. In this, as in other areas of social science inquiry, clear concepts and definitions must precede real progress in refining measures.

Measuring community capacity on the ground, however, presents a number of particular problems. Some approaches have attempted to enumerate the factors that need to be present but without specifying measures or methods (National Civic League, 1996; Aspen Institute, 1996). Others have suggested ways to map community "assets," defined as the organizations that are operating locally and the skills and experience of community residents. Related constructs, such as a community's "collective efficacy," have been measured through survey instruments that combine indicators of social cohesion and an expressed willingness to act, but without tapping information about actual action (Sampson, Raudenbush, and Earls, 1997).

Some analysts have begun the task of measuring particular characteristics of community capacity (as defined in our framework) or related constructs. Sense of community, for example, has been measured, largely through survey instruments (Chavis and Wandersman, 1990). Commitment can be measured in part by the number of residents participating in local organizations. Access to resources can be measured in part through the analysis of capital flows and measures of political influence. Mechanisms of problem solving can be measured with reference to the levels of agency at which they work; that is, through attendance to individual capacities, organizational effectiveness and connection, and a host of measures of network structure and functioning. Recognizing the importance of being able to measure progress along these various dimensions, the Aspen Institute's Roundtable on Comprehensive Community Initiatives is developing a database of measures used to assess changes in communities. Some of these are indicators of outcomes generated in several functional areas (e.g., housing, public safety, community economic development); others seek to measure the components of community capacity directly (Aspen Institute, 2000).

Measuring the progress of interventions that seek to *build* community capacity adds another layer of difficulty. Such efforts are notoriously difficult to evaluate for methodological reasons (see Connell, Kubisch, Schorr, and Weiss, 1995; Aspen Institute and Fulbright-Anderson, Kubisch, and Connell, 1998). Moreover, sponsors commonly make multiple demands of evaluation that exacerbate the challenges, asking both that the research capture the process and outcomes of community capacity building and that it be directly useful to those attempting to do the work and learn from its experience. Other factors complicate the task further—the limitations of available neighborhood-level data, the fact that neighborhoods are "open systems" for which it is often difficult to establish comparisons to support causal attribution of neighborhood changes to initiative efforts, and often a lack of initial clarity about measurable expected outcomes (Rossi, 1999).

Operational and financial constraints are significant. Evaluation is expensive. Sponsors and their partners often lack clear expectations for evaluation and consequently do not provide dedicated funding to support it. Funds for evaluation are often seen as funds "taken away" from programs, and the focus of much evaluation activity—on housing starts and numbers of job referrals rather than on less tangible but more informative outcomes such as capacity—is often seen by those working in community capacity–building efforts as inappropriate.

We have tried to illustrate the fact that community capacity is not unobservable. In principle, one can structure approaches to measuring changes in community capacity by monitoring specific progress on strategic activity (to build leadership, develop organizations, mobilize residents, foster interorganizational relations), monitoring change at the community level in the several dimensions of our framework, and then relating the one to the other. However, this is more easily said than done. Reliable and workable measures need to be developed, and the field needs further work on methods and approaches that are applicable within the constraints—financial, temporal, political—of such efforts. Developing these measures and methods is likely to require some targeted efforts in which the usual constraints are relaxed to allow for experimentation and testing that might complicate, or be compromised by, an ongoing community intervention.

Finally, efforts to build community capacity sometimes seek to build a local capacity for research, data analysis, and evaluation. This is not the same as doing an outcome evaluation. Rather, the focus is on developing the skills, tools, knowledge, and resources to allow local actors to gain access to data on existing community circumstances and dynamics and to collect new information where data do not exist, in a timely and cost-effective way. Some work is being done in this regard, including the development of technologies for culling and integrating administrative databases; methods for geocoding and mapping data on service provision, demographics, and social dynamics; and neighborhood drive- and walk-through protocols to guide observation. Beyond the tools themselves, however, this task requires that the research process be demystified so that posing researchable questions and reviewing available data becomes a useful part of local assessment and planning. It often also requires support for management information systems that allow community organizations to collect information on the conduct and impact of their programs as part of the normal course of their administration. And it requires sponsor support for access to information relevant to community actors that is held by agencies and organizations outside the community, as well as assistance in using such information in the service of community activities.

CONCLUSION

Community capacity tends to be spoken of as a unitary thing, a generalized characteristic of a neighborhood as a social system. "Opening the black box" reveals that community capacity has component characteristics, operates through individuals, organizations, and networks within the community and between it and other systems, and performs varied functions toward various ends (see Figure 1). Efforts to build community capacity can focus on many possible combinations of these elements and thus can assume many forms.

The strength of each of the elements of capacity differs among communities and may not be evenly distributed within them. An important rationale for a focus on capacity building is an expectation that it will lead to a more equitable distribution of the benefits capacity bestows on communities and their members. But key questions remain unanswered: How much and what kinds of capacity can be built by externally stimulated change efforts? And how much of what *can* be built can be integrated into the social fabric at the community level? Helping individuals and organizations enhance their capacity to engage, either singly or in concert, in development activities is a more straightforward endeavor than incorporating that capacity into the broader context of the *community*. It is tempting to hypothesize that many public and philanthropic efforts to support normative activities and primary services (libraries, congregations, youth programs)(Wynn, Costello, Halpern, and Richman, 1994) and human service agencies might have greater impact if effected in ways that consciously sought to strengthen and enlarge *community* capacity.

Communities are nested in complex economic, social, and political systems; our framework suggests that this fact presents additional capacity-building opportunities. One is to work on structural barriers to the production of social capital by addressing such issues as resident stability (e.g., through home ownership and tenant-management programs), safety (through community policing and other efforts), and physical revitalization—efforts that promote the social interaction and sense of safety that are the foundation of community (Sampson, 1999). Another is to strengthen ties (e.g., through associational networks, organizational partnerships, or interlocking board memberships) that connect community members and organizations not only to one another but also to institutions (corporations, local government, and nonprofit organizations) beyond the neighborhood.

Successfully building community capacity within a neighborhood can increase that neighborhood's ability to produce certain public goods locally, connect residents and organizations to opportunity and resources, and enhance the influence of community actors on public policy, service delivery, and development activities driven by exogenous actors. But it is not a panacea. Important macrolevel structural issues are not susceptible to microlevel change strategies. They require policy changes at the metropolitan, state, or federal levels to affect broader issues of racial and economic segregation, to reduce the concentration of poverty, and to foster equity of educational and economic opportunity. However, building community capacity can help communities provide what can be provided locally, by crafting mechanisms for responding to local problems and opportunities. And it can help consolidate locally based constituencies to influence policy and practice at higher levels of action.

NOTES

1. For an extended discussion of the issues of race and power in CCIs, see Stone and Butler (2000) and Lawrence (2000).
2. See note 1 of Introduction.

Appendix A
Core Case Study
Descriptions

Empirically, efforts to build community capacity in urban neighborhoods focus on a range of strategies (generally stressing one or more of the four principal strategies detailed in this book) and operate under a number of different auspices. These include comprehensive community initiatives (CCIs), community development corporations (CDCs), and other community-based organizations (such as neighborhood associations, community-based service providers, and settlement houses), and intermediary organizations (from those supporting organizing efforts, to those that run programs and provide technical assistance on a range of issues).

The three core case studies at the center of the book are all multifaceted interventions that have engaged in some combination of the four principal strategies and that together represent a cross section of the field of community capacity–building efforts. The Neighborhood and Family Initiative (NFI) is a multisite CCI centered on the creation of neighborhood collaboratives as mechanisms to promote resident participation and organizational collaboration for a broad-based process of planning and project implementation. The Glades Community Development Corporation (GCDC) is a single-site effort focusing on the creation of a community-based organization to act as a local intermediary serving three rural communities. The Consensus Organizing Demonstration Program (CODP) is a multisite organizing effort spearheaded by a national intermediary to identify and train local leaders and develop local CDCs that can endure as community problem-solving and capacity-building mechanisms. What follows is an overview of each of these core case studies, followed by brief descriptions of the additional efforts most frequently or extensively referred to.

NEIGHBORHOOD AND FAMILY INITIATIVE

Among the earliest of the current generation of CCIs, NFI was launched in 1990 by the Ford Foundation as a four-site demonstration of a broad approach to community development defined by two fundamental principles. The first principle is that community development strategies need to address the interrelations among the social, physical, and economic needs and opportunities within the neighborhood. This principle includes notions of *comprehensiveness* (addressing the full range of needs and circumstances) and *integration* (weaving together individual strategies that, as a whole, foster synergistic, sustainable change). The second principle is that neighborhood residents must participate actively and meaningfully in both planning and implementation, and organizational collaboration must be fostered among relevant institutions in both the public and private sectors. This range of participants is to make use of available resources (and seek new ones) both inside the neighborhood and throughout the larger community.

A major impetus for NFI was the realization that community development focusing on housing and, to some extent, local economic development (which had come to characterize most CDCs and much of Ford's support in this area) was developing increasingly independently from work that focused on human services in poor neighborhoods. Although this functional separation allowed for some concentrated successes, particularly in the area of low-income housing, it was failing to significantly transform poor neighborhoods or the quality of life of their residents or to build a broader community capacity to effect and sustain change. In addition, a renewed emphasis on notions of "empowerment" and resident participation shifted the focus away from established organizations toward an attempt to catalyze broader-based and more embedded processes to guide community change efforts. Finally, as part of its interest in developing intermediaries to help drive and sustain community development processes, Ford looked to shift the focus of community foundations toward becoming important agents, catalysts, and supporters of local change and to build their capacity to do so.

Structure and Operations

NFI was given similar form in each of four participant sites: Detroit, Hartford, Memphis, and Milwaukee. Each local NFI effort was required to focus on a geographically defined target area, plan for comprehensive development, engage in asset-based strategic planning, and involve significant community participation in the planning and implementing of development activities. In each city, Ford chose a community foundation as the local intermediary charged with identifying a target neighborhood, hiring a staff director, and creating a neighborhood "collaborative" to govern the conduct of the initiative. In turn, the collaboratives were charged with identifying neighborhood needs, identifying connections among them, and developing strategies to address these needs.

The membership of each of the four collaboratives was structured to include residents of the target neighborhood, neighborhood-based organizations and businesses, and representatives of the city's public, private, and nonprofit sectors. The notion was that by bringing together participants with a wide range of expertise, experiences, and access to resources, around the same table and on "equal footing," the group would be able to catalyze broad-based and sustainable neighborhood change that was both grounded in the needs and priorities of residents and connected to the broader systems that influence the neighborhood's operation. The intent was to promote an ongoing capacity within the neighborhood for governance, planning, implementation, and informed interaction with actors and resources beyond the neighborhood.

How such a capacity would ultimately be organized and sustained was not prescribed at the outset. One option was for the collaborative to "work itself out of a job," leaving in place either a set of new, independent organizations to carry out components of the collaborative's strategic plan or a more connected network of stronger, already-existing organizations and associations. Another option was to institutionalize the long-term presence of the collaborative through its formal incorporation as a nonprofit organization. In practice, both options have been exercised with different emphases and to different degrees across sites. Three of the collaboratives (in Detroit, Hartford, and Memphis) ultimately chose to incorporate as independent nonprofit organizations. The collaborative in Milwaukee continued to operate throughout the course of the initiative under the umbrella of the community foundation, but has been responsible (wholly or in part) for the creation of two independent nonprofit organizations in the neighborhood. Ultimately, the collaborative disbanded, leaving the continuation of its work (and the remainder of its funding) to these organizations or to other CBOs.

The NFI effort in each of the four sites is organized within a national initiative that provides some common institutional support and mechanisms for cross-site information sharing and collaboration. The Ford Foundation is the principal funder and architect of the general framework for the initiative. Over the course of the effort, the foundation has provided funding in grant periods of between nine months and three years, and since 1990, each local effort has received about $2.5 million for operations and program support. In addition, Ford has established a program-related investment (PRI) fund of $2 million, managed by Seedco (a national intermediary and technical assistance provider based in New York), for the local initiatives to draw on to promote particular development projects in their communities.

Operationally, Ford's influence was most critical during NFI's principal planning phase, during which it made the fundamental decisions regarding target cities, major objectives, participating institutions, and central goals that would set the strategic context for action. The Center for Community Change (CCC), a national intermediary and technical assistance (TA) provider based in Washington, D.C., provided general technical assistance to all sites and facilitated communication among them for the first five years of the initiative. Thereafter, cross-site technical assistance was provided only for particular issues (e.g., PRI funding, computer networking) by different TA providers, and sites engaged their own TA providers as specific needs were identified.

Local Context

The cities chosen to participate in NFI were identified using a few loosely defined factors. First, the Ford Foundation was interested in targeting cities in which neighborhoods were important units of action that could be identified and mobilized, in which there was both a clear need for the intervention and some set of clearly identifiable assets on which to build, and in which relatively few initiatives were already in place. Second, it wanted a certain degree of diversity—in size, politics, economy, geography—across the cities. Finally, it wanted to choose cities in which there was a community foundation with both the interest in and capacity for acting as the local intermediary for the initiative. The cities ultimately chosen differed in size, location, history, ethnic composition, and economic structure.

Each neighborhood targeted in NFI was chosen by the local community foundation, based on its own calculations of the neighborhood's need, assets, and responsiveness to racial and political dynamics in the city. Although they hold several characteristics in common—each is principally African American, located close to the city center, and poor but with some significant resources upon which to build—the neighborhoods are quite diverse along several dimensions.

The Lower Woodward Corridor, Detroit. The Lower Woodward Corridor is the least typical of the four NFI neighborhoods and is unique in several respects compared with other neighborhoods in Detroit. Covering a large geographic area and home to about seventeen thousand, the corridor includes a number of distinct subneighborhoods. As a whole, the corridor has relatively few children and families and a correspondingly larger elderly population, as well as households comprised of single individuals. Approximately 64 percent of the population is African American, and about 52 percent lived below the poverty line at the initiative's inception. It is less densely settled than other neighborhoods in Detroit and has a more transient population overall.

The institutional presence in the corridor is significant and unique among other neighborhoods targeted by NFI. Several major hospitals, a large university, and a number of cultural institutions dominate the organizational landscape. In addition, the corridor is home to about fifty nonprofit organizations and more than thirty churches, many of which provide various social services including counseling, advocacy, child care, meals programs, job training, substance abuse programs, and health and medical care. The corridor is located just north of downtown Detroit and was included in 1994 as part of the city area to receive federal funding under the Empowerment Zone/Enterprise Community (EZ/EC) Program.

Harambee, Milwaukee. Of the four NFI sites, Milwaukee's Harambee neighborhood comes closest to the Lower Woodward Corridor in terms of size, poverty, and the richness of the organizational infrastructure (without the range of large institutions present there). But it differs significantly on a number of dimensions. Physically, Harambee is made up primarily of residential wood frame single- and two-family houses, and three-story rowhouses, with fewer multiunit dwellings. Commercial real estate exists in various locations, concentrated particularly along the main north-south thoroughfare and on the eastern boundary of the neighborhood. There is also a tract of low-rise industrial space, mostly vacant at the initiative's inception, that has become a cornerstone of activity for NFI through its engagement in a multiorganizational partnership developed to renovate the property as an industrial park.

Like the other NFI neighborhoods, Harambee is primarily African American (83 percent). It has a history as a center of African-American culture, commerce, and social life in Milwaukee, but its cohesion was disrupted by the events that followed urban renewal, the withdrawal of manufacturing from the city, and the race riots of the early 1970s. Harambee also has a sizable Latino population (about 7 percent of the residents), which is concentrated for the most part along the eastern fringe of the neighborhood.

Of the four NFI neighborhoods, Harambee has the youngest population, as well as the greatest disparities in education, income, and labor force participation between the neighborhood and the city in which it is located. Yet Harambee has several important assets as well, including its location near the city's central business district, the existence of viable organizations, and a strong identity and history of involvement among its residents. In 1994, it was also included as part of the geographic area chosen to receive federal EC funds.

Orange Mound, Memphis.   Orange Mound in Memphis has the longest history as a coherent community of any of the NFI neighborhoods, and is one of the oldest and largest African-American communities in Memphis. About 94 percent of its sixteen thousand residents are African American.

The neighborhood is largely residential, primarily divided into small lots that in many cases still accommodate the small, single-family "shotgun" houses that were first built there, so named for their narrow structure, which permits looking from the front door straight through the back door, as though through the barrel of a shotgun. The combination of this predominance of single-family houses and a relatively high degree of residential stability among the elderly population helps to support a level of informal interactions among residents through a "porch culture," in which neighbors can talk in passing and keep an eye on block-level activities. Although fear of crime has had some impact on this tradition (as evidenced in part by the heavy security doors and barred windows that now adorn house fronts in the neighborhood), porch front activity is still a common sight.

In contrast to other NFI neighborhoods, there are fewer (and fewer kinds of) community-based organizations (CBOs) or institutions in Orange Mound. The major institutions are churches and schools, and both types of organization have historically played a significant role in the neighborhood's history. A few civic associations and block clubs are active in the neighborhood. Commercially, some small businesses serve the neighborhood, and a larger concentration of commercial activity exists at its fringes. As in Milwaukee, the area chosen in Memphis to receive federal EC funding included this NFI neighborhood.

Upper Albany, Hartford.   Upper Albany in Hartford is the smallest of the NFI neighborhoods, consisting of thirty-one blocks and home to just under ten thousand people. The neighborhood is a narrow, well-defined, primarily residential area surrounding an active commercial artery. Building stock is mostly residential, predominantly two- and three-family wood frame houses. On one side, the neighborhood is bounded by a large public park containing woods, play lots, hiking paths, playing fields, and outdoor basketball courts. On the south and west sides, its borders are defined by a railroad line, which limits through traffic except at a few underpasses. The neighborhood lies between (and within blocks of) affluent neighborhoods and suburbs and downtown Hartford. The central artery and main commercial strip, Albany Avenue, is a major thoroughfare to downtown.

Upper Albany has the highest concentration of black residents in Hartford. They comprise a total of 82 percent of the population, including a significant number of West Indians (about 15 percent). It also has a sizable minority Latino population, primarily Puerto Ricans (also about 15 percent), who for the most part are clustered at the neighborhood's southeast end, which borders on the primarily Latino neighborhood of Clay Arsenal. Upper Albany's organizational infrastructure is smaller than that of Harambee and the Woodward Corridor, but the neighborhood has several key organizational assets, including a public library, several schools, a large health clinic, and the city offices of the Urban League, as well as smaller CBOs and civic groups (the latter being particularly strong among the West Indian population).

Program Agenda and Principal Strategic Foci

Whereas all four NFI efforts share a comprehensive focus, each has taken a somewhat different approach to organizing its work within a strategic framework that orients and, to an extent, guides planning and implementation. Within these broad frameworks, the local efforts have pursued a range of activities including housing, education, youth development, leadership development, economic development, community organizing, and child and family services, as well as employment generation, training, and placement.

In Detroit, the strategic framework centers on "strengthening linkages" among the organizations and institutions in the Lower Woodward Corridor and fostering greater connection between these organizations and residents of the neighborhood. Much of NFI's work in Detroit revolves around three ongoing projects. A job-training and placement program called New Beginnings was initially developed by the Detroit Medical Center (DMC), adapted by the collaborative in partnership with DMC, and implemented in collaboration with Wayne State University and other local medical and educational institutions. The program engages neighborhood residents in a twelve-week training course to prepare them for jobs in the health care industry, then places them in positions at one of the participating heath centers. It also focuses on graduates' continuing education and training, through arrangements with the hospitals and Wayne County Community College. Another project is a service providers' collaborative known as the Back to the Basics Partnership, whose principal goal is to facilitate communication and strengthen working relationships among the different service organizations operating in the corridor. In addition to regular meetings for joint planning and information exchange, the Partnership provides small grants of up to $5,000 to neighborhood service providers for discrete projects and for facilitating client access or provider collaboration. With the third project, the NFI collaborative [eventually incorporated as a nonprofit organization known as DNFI (Detroit Neighborhood Family Initiative)] acts as the lead agency to develop and operate a Community Self-Sufficiency Center, one of three funded under the city's federal EZ program. The Self-Sufficiency Center in Detroit trains residents for employment in targeted sectors, such as banking or health care, places them in jobs locally, and provides support services such as child care, counseling, and transportation to individuals in the central region of the EZ. Through its access to PRI funds provided through Seedco, DNFI has also supported several physical revitalization projects, including building renovations for commercial purposes and for low- and mixed-income housing.

In Milwaukee, NFI has focused on providing a "living wage" for Harambee residents, and its strategy has largely centered on the creation and support of new organizations in the neighborhood to enhance the community's capacity to solve problems and produce particular goods and services. Two such organizations are central to this agenda. The Martin Luther King Economic Development Corporation (MLKEDC) began as a community financial institution created by the collaborative to establish a revolving loan fund to provide venture capital to residents and local businesses for whom traditional lending institutions were not a viable option. MLKEDC also provides some training and support to applicants who are turned down for funding and has expanded its activities to include a focus on housing and employment. Among its numerous projects is a commercial-development project (the Cluster Project) being developed in partnership with two community organizations (a CDC and a community housing and advocacy organization), the city's Business Improvement District, and several other government agencies, as well as local banks, foundations, and corporations. It also runs two job-training and placement programs, one focusing on janitorial services and the other on training workers for employment in the health care field.

The second organization, the Northeast Milwaukee Industrial Development Corporation (NMIDC), was formed by five partner organizations (including the NFI collaborative) to plan and manage the revitalization of an industrial park (Riverworks) adjacent to Harambee. After purchasing the land, NMIDC sold a number of lots to businesses (service, commercial, and light manufacturing) newly locating in the area, engaged in environmental reclamation activities, and developed a number of support services for businesses and employees.

As in Detroit (but to a smaller extent), the NFI collaborative in Milwaukee has used PRI money from Seedco to fund some physical revitalization projects. In addition, it has attempted to focus on leadership development activities through a combination of specific training sessions, community engagement, and youth development projects.

In Hartford, the NFI collaborative incorporated itself as a community organization and has largely followed an organizing strategy with three principal components. One focuses on developing a network of block clubs in the neighborhood and connecting them organizationally to the initiative through the creation of a joint planning body, the Collaborative Community Committee. This has entailed both the creation of new block clubs and outreach to existing ones, as well as working with the Problem Solving Committee, a forum created by the city's police department to support community policing and provide a mechanism for community-city interaction. Another component centers on engaging with a recently established state-sponsored neighborhood planning process that mandated the creation of local committees in several neighborhoods (Neighborhood Revitalization Zones) to create a comprehensive development plan for the neighborhood. The third component focuses on linking the NFI collaborative to a broader revitalization process through participation with other north-end CBOs in the development of a collaborative organization, the North Hartford Initiative. These three organizing efforts have connected the NFI collaborative in some way to much of the specific programmatic activity in Upper Albany. For instance, advocacy activities engaged in by the collaborative have contributed to revisions in a magnet school plan developed by the city school board and the placement of a police substation in the neighborhood. Through similar relationships, the NFI collaborative has also contributed to home repair programs, youth training and employment programs, neighborhood festivals and health fairs, parent organizing for school reform, and a project to install security lights on neighborhood houses (which was eventually taken up by the city as a program to be implemented in other neighborhoods with public funds).

In Memphis, the focus has been on housing, leadership development, and community outreach, communication, and convening. To pursue the housing part of its agenda, the collaborative in Memphis (like that in Milwaukee) created a new organization, the Orange Mound Development Corporation, to spearhead activity in home ownership programs, home repair and renovation, and neighborhood beautification. Its leadership development activities have revolved around offering neighborhood residents a series of training classes, which have also been used as a recruitment tool to engage participants in collaborative planning and other community activities. The collaborative has also attempted to structure itself as a conduit for information and a facilitator of interorganizational relationships, roles that are often focused on building school-neighborhood relations. It has, for example, produced a community newspaper (for a time in partnership with teachers and students at the local high school), helped establish a family resource center and computer lab at a neighborhood elementary school, and involved high school students in a project to create a geographic information system on housing code violations and neighborhood conditions (the project eventually became an ongoing program in the high school).

Challenges

The four NFI efforts have faced some common challenges that have affected the conduct of the initiative and the shape and outcomes of its approaches to community capacity building. There have also been some circumstances particular to each effort, in which local variations in strategy, process, or context have contributed to different ends.

Governance and Resident Participation.   The challenges of governance in NFI stem from a tension between democratic ideals of neighborhood-based associational action and more instrumental, bureaucratic approaches to decision-making and implementation. The challenges are reflected in a number of aspects of internal operations: control, membership, representation, decision-making, and organizational structure and function. Initially, residents made up a relatively small proportion of collaborative membership, and there was a disjunction between them and the professionals who sat on the collaboratives in terms of priorities, goal orientations, and ways of communicating and solving problems. In addition, there has been ambiguity around the nature and intent of representation: Who speaks for whom (based on what sources of legitimacy), what are participants expected to bring to the table, and what can they expect to take away? Although these tensions have continued to influence collaborative operations over time, relatively more residents have been recruited to participate, and the resident "voice" has grown stronger in most of the collaboratives. At the same time, there has been a trend toward greater formalization of collaborative rules and processes, with collaboratives increasingly taking on the protocols of formal committees and attempting to clarify staff-collaborative relationships. (This trend has culminated in the incorporation of three of the four collaboratives as independent nonprofit organizations.) Throughout this process, there has been an enduring tension between whether the collaboratives are to operate as "working boards," in which members are actively engaged in all aspects of decision-making and implementation, or "policy boards," in which they provide broad guidance to collaborative staff who are responsible for implementation and the day-to-day management of initiative activities. As a consequence, a good deal of the collaboratives' energy has been spent on trying to "fix" internal operations and on negotiating internally among competing claims for legitimacy and purpose.

Legitimacy and Resident Connection.   A second but related challenge looks outward, to the ways in which the collaboratives have engaged with residents in their communities, beyond those involved in the organizational framework of the collaborative itself. Here, variation in approach is significant across sites, with most collaboratives focusing principally on broad information-dissemination strategies, such as community forums, festivals, or newsletters. Connection with a broad base of residents in such cases is episodic and largely unidirectional, with the collaboratives providing information to residents for their use. Some sites have engaged in different types of door-to-door outreach, combining information dissemination, solicitation of input, and recruiting. In a few cases such outreach has aimed at expanding resident involvement in the decision-making process for the initiative. The absence of a focus on broader, more-integrated resident involvement has opened some collaboratives to charges of isolation and nonrepresentativeness. On the other hand, an increased focus on such involvement has involved a trade-off in which efficiency and organizational protocol are frequently disrupted by demands to clarify, explain, and reorient decision-making and activity for the benefit of a growing, shifting, increasingly vocal neighborhood constituency.

Organizational Niche, Collaboration, and Partnerships. Beyond the question of neighborhood connection defined by resident awareness and involvement, collaboratives have struggled to define and fill an organizational niche that allows them to add value to the range of resources and capacities already in place in the community. Although all have engaged in a degree of direct program implementation, they have ultimately defined themselves as "brokers" and "facilitators"—local intermediaries that can organize information, constituencies, and organizational resources for collective planning and action. The challenges of pursuing such an agenda include both internal and external dynamics. Internally, the struggle was one of both definition and capacity: Consensus on mission and the parameters of such a role required long negotiation among members, and the emphasis on clarifying internal roles and expectations complicated efforts to build an organizational capacity to operate as an intermediary among existing organizations. Externally, each collaborative was brought to life within different organizational contexts. In some cases, the collaborative that emerged in NFI was well placed to fill an organizational void. In others, its emergence was seen as a threat by existing organizations, which saw themselves already performing the role the collaborative wished to adopt. Where partnerships were developed for the implementation of certain programmatic agendas, collaboratives encountered the need to reconcile different timelines, sources of support, and organizational agendas; to adapt to shared roles and responsibilities; and to appropriately attribute credit for accomplishments.

Comprehensive Development. Although the NFI efforts have thought broadly about needs and responses across a range of strategic areas, there has been little integration of strategies. To some extent, the notion of comprehensive, integrated development has provided a useful lens through which collaboratives view their planning. Each collaborative has developed a different strategic focus (some more clearly defined than others), and some individual projects have attempted to combine social-, economic-, and physical-development strategies. In general, however, projects have been developed in response to emerging opportunities in the local environment and through the collaborative's access to such opportunity, based largely on the networks of members. Thus, program development often has not been well integrated but has tended to followed parallel streams of categorical activity.

Funding Relationships.   Beyond collaborative- and neighborhood-level challenges, the attempt to build community capacity through NFI was complicated by the structure of funding relationships and the role played by the collaboratives' local and national sponsors. As with many CCIs, NFI required participants to plan for long-term change within the constraints of short-term grant periods. This tension, along with a perception of funder ambiguity regarding expectations, long-term commitment, and criteria for decision-making, influenced the conduct of collaborative deliberations, as well as the collaboratives' approach to strategic planning and, to a degree, their implementation choices. These issues were further complicated by significant staff turnover at the Ford Foundation and by the complexities of the range of roles played by CCC, which in part mediated between Ford and the four NFI efforts. At the local level, relations between the collaborative and the community foundation were critical in shaping collaborative structure, operations, and strategic choices. Questions of control, autonomy, credit for accomplishments, and the appropriate structure of a collaborative-foundation "partnership" have been at issue throughout the initiative. These issues have been negotiated most successfully where early conflicts were aggressively resolved and a role was crafted for the foundation in which it provides strong, dedicated staff and additional resources but plays a relatively unobtrusive role in collaborative deliberations. In other cases, the balance has been struck less effectively, and the move to incorporate the collaboratives as independent organizations has been embraced, to a large extent, to address that imbalance.

Accomplishments

Some of the challenges outlined above have been negotiated more successfully than others, and some of the NFI efforts have had more success negotiating challenges than have others. Regardless, the four efforts exhibit a range of accomplishments, which vary in terms of objective, impact, and the array of local players engaged in their development and implementation.

Programs and Collaboratives.　The collaboratives in each of the four neighborhoods targeted by NFI have developed a number of programs and funded their implementation. In some cases, these have been quite small (a small-grants program, a community garden, a food distribution effort). Although the impacts of such efforts have often been confined to the (much needed) direct provision of time-limited services to a relatively small portion of the neighborhood's residents, occasionally such activities have leveraged considerable additional activity, both in the neighborhood and in other parts of the city. A project to provide exterior lighting to homes as a crime reduction strategy in Upper Albany, for example, was adopted and implemented as a citywide effort by the city of Hartford, and the involvement of the local block club that initially spearheaded the effort had a significant impact on the composition of the collaborative and the focus of its community-organizing activities. Similarly, a modest program to support school beautification, which involved some planting and landscaping of the three neighborhood schools in Orange Mound, contributed to what became a much broader collaboration between the schools and the NFI collaborative, as well as greater communication and cooperation among the schools themselves. In other cases, programs have been large and capital intensive, providing new housing, creating new organizations, providing career path employment for residents, or redeveloping the physical infrastructure and commercial activities in defined portions of the neighborhood.

Organizational Partnerships.　Except in cases where new organizations have been created as mechanisms for program implementation, most of the programmatic strides made by the NFI collaboratives have been implemented through the agency of local organizations with which they have developed instrumental relationships. Some of these partnerships have been institutionalized in new organizational forms (such as NMIDC in Milwaukee); others are more informal but broad ranging (such as the network of service providers represented by the Back to the Basics Partnership in Detroit); still others are more program specific (such as the school-based family resource center in Memphis). Although in a few cases the organizational relationship was defined simply through funding (in which the collaborative provided resources for program implementation already being engaged in by a local organization), in most cases the partnerships entailed both new activities and new (or renewed or strengthened) interorganizational relationships.

Leveraging Resources and Catalyzing Activity.　Both the direct work of the NFI collaboratives and their work through partnerships with existing organizations have contributed to leveraging additional resources beyond those provided by Ford and to catalyzing additional community development activity beyond that connected with the collaboratives. Additional resources have been leveraged from both public and private sources, generally to support particular programmatic activities. The extent to which collaboratives have done this varies from site to site, and the resources leveraged have ranged from in-kind support of staff time or equipment to several hundred thousand dollars to support job training, land acquisition, service delivery, housing rehabilitation, loan fund capitalization, or commercial redevelopment. There has also been additional development activity across sites, as well as a heightened focus on addressing neighborhood needs and making neighborhood planning processes more inclusive. Although it is often difficult to tease out the extent to which the NFI collaboratives have been generative rather than merely supportive of or unconnected to such work, there is a clearly growing body of activities in each locality that reinforce each other to a great extent. Where such activity has clearly been generated independently of the NFI effort (for example, as a result of EZ/EC funding), collaboratives have tended to play some role in the planning process and to be incorporated in some way into implementation plans, though the extent and impact of such work varies significantly across sites.

Neighborhood-City Connections.   Beyond its own instrumental partnerships, such as those that successfully leveraged Community Development Block Group (CDBG) or Community Housing and Development Organizations (CHDO) funds for particular projects, NFI collaboratives have in at least a few cases contributed to a fundamentally positive, more active relationship between the neighborhood and the city and, in some cases, to a greater neighborhood focus on the part of certain city departments. In Milwaukee, for example, the city approached the NFI collaborative to lead a community planning process that would help govern the availability and use of CDBG funds, and has been a partner in the redevelopment of the major commercial district in the neighborhood.

Leadership Development.   Leadership development is an explicit programmatic focus in some of the NFI efforts, but it is also a central component in all four efforts through the engagement of residents, businesspeople, local agency professionals, and other neighborhood stakeholders in the collaboratives' governance, planning, and implementation processes. Such engagement has provided a number of participating individuals with new skills, a greater understanding of neighborhood resources and needs, experience with planning and development processes, and access to funders and local officials with whom they have had little or no prior contact or influence. In some cases, the effect of this participation has been dramatic, particularly in the case of a small, core set of residents across sites who have used the NFI collaboratives as a foundation for further education and career development and have become increasingly involved in community organizing and development work.

GLADES COMMUNITY DEVELOPMENT
CORPORATION

The Glades Community Development Corporation (GCDC) began in Florida as the Glades Community-Based Development Project in 1991 as a project of the Community Foundation for Palm Beach and Martin Counties, with support from three additional foundations: the John D. and Catherine T. MacArthur Foundation, the Charles Stewart Mott Foundation, and the Bernard van Leer Foundation. The project changed its name to GCDC in 1993 and was incorporated in 1995 with its own bylaws and board of directors. It has been operating in the Glades since then with an annual budget of $350,000 to $450,000 and a staff of six.

The impetus for GCDC came from several sources. In 1989, the Community Foundation's assets reached $7 million, and its board and staff felt that the foundation could now afford to initiate some grantmaking, rather than focus entirely on responding to requests. At the same time, community leaders were beginning to speak up about the plight of the Glades, a predominantly agricultural region in the western part of Palm Beach County that includes the municipalities of Belle Glade, South Bay, and Pahokee. The Glades was portrayed as an island—isolated physically, socially, and economically from the dynamic growth and prosperity in the rest of the county and from the private and public power brokers concentrated in the part of the county along the Atlantic coast whose decisions affected the nature of opportunity in the Glades.

Over the next two years, foundation staff made numerous visits to the Glades, developing relationships with different segments of the community while bringing potential funders and other resource people to the Glades to get a firsthand picture of the community. Building trust and a stake in this exploration was not an easy process. Based on past experience, people in the Glades had little reason to believe that those from the coast would not come in, tell them what to do, and then disappear in a year. Funders and others from outside the Glades were often overwhelmed by what they perceived as the intransigence of the problems and the low probability of addressing these problems effectively. Negative media coverage continued to stigmatize the people in the Glades and reinforce the cultural and psychological separation of the area from the rest of the county. Racism, poverty, hopelessness, and vested interests all contributed to resistance to change, both inside and outside the Glades.

Slowly, however, a core planning group developed a proposal for a planning grant. With funding from this grant, an office was opened in the Glades in 1990 and staffed by an executive director and a community resource coordinator who oversaw a community assessment process. A central feature of this process was a survey that asked residents and service providers about their ideas for improving life in the Glades. With the help of the preexisting Glades Interagency Network, a consortium of public and nonprofit health and human service providers, project staff designed the survey and carried it out in a significant proportion (over forty) of the area's neighborhoods using local residents as interviewers. This survey and related data collection from provider agencies and community leaders, served to introduce the project to the Glades and to involve citizens in an initial participatory planning process. The final product was a proposal to create the Glades Community-Based Development Project, a comprehensive and integrated approach to development. According to its mission statement, the project's goal was "to enable people in the Glades communities to design and implement sustainable solutions to their problems and to mobilize financial, human, and political resources, both within and outside the Glades, to support these efforts."

The Glades initiative officially began in 1991 when each of the four funders accepted the proposed plan and awarded the project a three-year grant that would be administered through the Community Foundation. The core principles that would drive the project's approach were described in the proposal:

• It must take a holistic approach, encompassing health, education, economic, and social development and the relationships between and among these domains.
• It must engage the community in defining, designing, and implementing solutions.
• It must build institutional capacity and leadership.
• It must build relationships and public dialogue among the diverse constituencies that make up the Glades.
• It must be informed by and leverage resources from county, state, national, and international bodies.

Local Context

The three Glades cities are located on Lake Okeechobee, about sixty miles west of Palm Beach. About thirty-six thousand people live in this predominantly agricultural region, whose fertile soil (a deep layer of rich organic matter over sand and limestone) is known as black gold.

The Glades population is roughly 60 percent black, 29 percent white, and 11 percent of other racial origin. Hispanics, primarily of Mexican and Cuban origin, constitute about 21 percent of the population, and Haitians are estimated to constitute a significant minority of about 5 percent. During the harvest months, migrant workers from various backgrounds increase the numbers residing in the Glades. The diverse population of the Glades is characterized by significant poverty, health problems, and limited economic opportunity, both historical and current. Only 40 percent of Glades residents have a high school education.

Agriculture in general and sugar in particular serve as a substantial employment anchor in the Glades. The Florida Department of Labor estimates that nearly 70 percent of all jobs in the Glades area relate directly to the agricultural industry. Yet even the apparently robust sugar economy faces serious challenges: Some predict that the soil will be exhausted in a decade or so; environmentalists seek to enact strict regulatory legislation about the nature of runoff from the fields of sugar cane; substantial federal subsidies of sugar are threatened; and if it becomes accessible, foreign sugar is likely to sell for significantly less than U.S. sugar. In 1994, the U.S. Sugar Corporation's decision to close South Bay Growers, its vegetable farming and marketing subsidiary, resulted in layoffs for more than 1,300 full-time and seasonal workers. This decision created significant dislocation for South Bay, whose next-largest business had only thirty year-round employees. It also underscored the already-pressing need to diversify the economic base of the area and develop a more skilled workforce. Prisons and correctional facilities represent a significant growth industry in the Glades, accounting for an estimated eight hundred jobs. But many of the jobs they generate—like middle-income administrative and professional jobs in other sectors—are filled by skilled workers who live outside the community.

In sum, the Glades is characterized by abundant fertile agricultural land, a magnificent lake, and a population that is racially, ethnically, and economically diverse, as well as by significant poverty, limited opportunities, and isolation. These sometimes contrasting characteristics pose important challenges for designing an effective community development strategy.

Structure

A local or community-based intermediary, like GCDC, is a vehicle for engaging diverse community stakeholders in the process of planning and implementing change. It aims to *build the capacity for development* across all sectors and at all levels (i.e., individual, organizational, and associational levels). As it builds this capacity, the intermediary acts as a catalyst and coach to help community stakeholders identify and act on strategic opportunities to advance the community's agenda. Both stakeholders and opportunities may lie within or outside the community. A local intermediary must be embedded in the community, and it must have strong ties with actors, resources, and decision-making processes outside the community. While there is no uniform template for such an organization, there is some consensus about the functions it can perform, including:

• Convene and stimulate productive and informed dialogue among diverse community constituencies.
• Demonstrate the value of and strategies for engaging community residents, particularly those who traditionally have not had a significant voice, in all aspects of community problem solving.
• Build the institutional infrastructure of the community by strengthening existing organizations, helping start new organizations as needed, and promoting new relationships and collaborations among organizations within the community and between those in the community and outside.
• Broker access to previously untapped resources and opportunities, both within and outside the community.
• Integrate leadership development into every action it undertakes.
• Champion the community's interests and ensure that the community's voice is heard in forums outside the community.

The local intermediary model seemed particularly appropriate for the Glades. Its relatively undeveloped institutional infrastructure, its insufficiently strong and visible leadership, and its physical and social isolation from the rest of the county all limited the Glades' ability to obtain its fair share of resources. Significant racial, ethnic, and economic divisions within the community, as well as the historic lack of cooperation among the three municipalities, meant that there had been little tradition of public dialogue and little sense of common interest. These factors limited the Glades' political capital and its access to philanthropic assistance. Those foundations that were receptive to funding in the Glades frequently had difficulty identifying "good" projects in which they could have confidence that their investments would be used effectively or would make any lasting difference.

Under these conditions, any substantial new enterprise in the Glades would need to build confidence, both within the community and externally, that broad-scale development was possible: An agenda for change could be developed among diverse constituencies, capacity could be built and resources identified to implement this agenda, and the process of change could itself be sustainable over the long run. These were the hopes expressed at the inception of the Glades Project, and these were some of the factors that led those involved in designing the project toward an intermediary model.

As it evolved from the Glades Project, GCDC developed a board that to-day is diverse in terms of race, ethnicity, gender, economic status, and ge-ography. Members come from the African-American, Haitian, Hispanic, Arab, and white communities and from all three municipalities. They are involved in different aspects of community life, such as law, health, bank-ing, education, and agriculture, and operate in the commercial, govern-ment, nonprofit, and religious sectors. Most of the board members either live now or have spent most of their lives in the Glades. The board's com-mitment to improving the quality of life for *all* residents has helped the organization weather the threat of divisive forces that could have under-mined its work. Because race relations have such a powerful historical legacy, the board members have found that it is important both to recog-nize that there is more that unites them than divides them at the same time that many issues do contain racial dimensions that need to be acknowl-edged and addressed on a regular basis.

Organizational Development

The process of developing the initial Glades Project board into a strong board for GCDC was complicated by the fact that the project was being in-cubated by the Community Foundation, whose own board had ultimate fiscal and legal responsibility for it. The project was managed by the Com-munity Foundation through the liaison committee of its board, two mem-bers of which served as nonvoting members of the Glades Project board. Technically, the project's director reported not to the Glades Project board but to the executive director of the Community Foundation. These arrangements led to a difficult period in the incubation process in 1993, when the project was moving toward greater independence, in part, to em-power its own board (the project and its board assumed the GCDC name in 1993).

Although the long-term vision for the Glades Project supported the eventual creation of an independent nonprofit organization in the Glades, there had been little discussion about the timing or the form that such a de-velopment would take. On the one hand, all acknowledged the commit-ment and patience that the Community Foundation had brought to and sustained over the life of the initiative. Very simply, without the founda-tion's support through tough times, GCDC would not exist. This support was especially impressive because GCDC represented not only an oppor-tunity for success through bold action, but also a high-risk potential liabil-ity for a funder as small and new as the Community Foundation. On the other hand, the growing strength of GCDC's board and its desire to make decisions and control resources locally rather than be governed by an en-tity outside the community contributed to pressures for separation.

Good intentions existed on all sides, but that did not preclude misunderstanding as the parties moved through this sensitive period of organizational restructuring. Sometimes demands were shrill and patience short. Occasionally individuals reverted to old roles and patterns of interaction that were characteristic of the historical relationships between the Glades and the coast, which involve issues of race, class, history, wealth, and access to power. These dynamics are not unusual in the relationships between foundations and the community initiatives they support. One vehicle that helped to address these tensions and support the restructuring process was the Transition Management Board, a committee made up of GCDC board members and representatives of the Community Foundation. Established in 1994, the Transition Management Board helped GCDC create procedures for managing its own finances, ensuring that sound accounting and monitoring functions were in place, and addressed other organizational development issues, such as personnel policies and procedures.

The Community Foundation transferred organizational responsibility and all remaining project funds to GCDC when it received its nonprofit designation from the Internal Revenue Service in 1995. The relationship between the two organizations emerged from the transition period intact. Foundation staff continued to provide valuable and appreciated informal support, to broker connections for GCDC with donors and other important contacts on the coast, and to publicize the challenges confronting development in the Glades and the importance of GCDC's work. GCDC board members increasingly felt comfortable calling their Community Foundation counterparts directly, a sign not only of the continuing strength of the relationship between the two organizations, but also of the foundation's commitment to GCDC and the GCDC board's maturing capacity and confidence.

Program Agenda

GCDC's program agenda focuses on three primary areas: economic development, health and human development, and capacity building. As an intermediary, it has operationalized this agenda through multiple activities aimed at fulfilling its mission of enabling people in the Glades communities to "design and implement sustainable solutions to their problems." The most important of these activities are summarized below.

Organizational Support and Development.   A survey in 1990 found that about forty-five organizations provided health care, child care, counseling, and other social services to residents of the Glades, one organization developed and provided affordable housing, and none focused primarily on economic development. A consortium of these agencies, the Glades Interagency Network (GIN), tried to promote information sharing and coordination among the organizations, but services still tended to be fragmented and categorical in nature. Overall, the institutional infrastructure of the community was underdeveloped, underfunded, and not well connected to the resources of the larger county. Many of the professional jobs in these organizations were filled by people from outside the community.

In its efforts to build strong local organizations, GCDC's technical assistance to emerging groups and more-established institutions has taken a variety of forms: assistance in developing bylaws and applying for nonprofit tax status, free meeting space and access to a fax machine and computer, individualized help and workshops to identify funding opportunities and develop proposals, and a willingness to act as a fiscal agent for organizations that do not have their nonprofit tax status or as a fiscal conduit for managing resources coming into the community that involve collaborations or cross-city initiatives.

When GCDC identified a significant gap in the array of organizations working in the Glades, it worked to fill this gap, sometimes by incubating a new organization itself, sometimes by stimulating new collaborative efforts, sometimes by brokering external resources with existing organizations in the Glades. Two independent organizations that GCDC helped found are the Med-Mobile, a mobile medical provider now operated by the Palm Beach County Health Care District, and a small-business incubator, the EDGE (Enterprise Development for Glades Entrepreneurs) Center. Examples of programs that GCDC helped bring to the Glades include the Business Loan Fund, the Home Instruction Program for Preschool Youngsters (HIPPY, which is administered by Head Start), and the Western Communities Tourism Alliance, a collaborative effort by GCDC, the three local cities and chambers of commerce, and the county's Tourist Development Council to improve the opportunities for tourism development in the area.

In some cases, GCDC's organizational development efforts aimed at fostering collaborative efforts among existing organizations, for example, by helping establish a youth council made up of the many organizations serving youth so that programs could be coordinated and resources used more efficiently. In other cases, the emphasis has been on creating more accountability among organizations receiving resources to serve the people of the Glades. Toward this end, GCDC participated in an Empowerment Evaluation project, sponsored by the National Civic League, which focused on providing citizens with the resources and tools necessary to eval-uate the efficacy and effectiveness of such organizations.

Another way in which GCDC staff and board members have reached out to many state, county, and local organizations operating in the Glades is by serving on their boards, committees, and task forces. Examples of these organizations include HIPPY, 100 Black Men (a chapter of a national civic and service organization), the Business Loan Fund, and the Workforce

Development Board. This effort has enabled GCDC to assist these groups, as well as to reach into new networks and become further acquainted with the issues and perspectives of different groups.

Community Outreach and Public Forums.   Since its inception, GCDC has found many ways to reach out to different people and groups in the community and promote forums where different segments of the community can meet and talk with each other. This approach is seen as essential in a community with little tradition of civic dialogue, many long-standing divisions among groups, and large numbers of people whose voices were seldom heard. The following illustrate the kinds of forums that GCDC played a key role in generating:

• Citizen Planner Series: forty to fifty people went through training courses designed to provide them with planning and community development information and skills.
• Local City Charrettes: diverse groups of citizens and other stakeholders participated in visioning and strategic planning sessions.
• Rural Initiatives Conference: residents were presented with information and a process through which they established priorities in four areas—tourism, agriculture, enterprise development, and workforce preparation.
• Youth Speak Out: three hundred youth from the three cities participated in meetings between youth representatives and the three city councils.
• Economic Summit: public officials and citizens came together for the first time in 1993 to explore different ways to address the region's economic problems.
• Family Forum: a diverse group of more than four hundred people representing families and youth discussed their concerns in areas such as health, family support, public safety, and adolescence; prioritized the issues that this discussion generated; and presented them to a panel of public and nonprofit officials.

GCDC found that these and other public forums represented meaningful steps toward building a regional perspective and a sense of common interest and developing new collaborations and partnerships. For example, when the federal EZ/EC applications were announced the year following the Economic Summit, the three Glades cities ended up preparing a joint application, an event few think would have occurred without the cities' having worked together and engaged in these issues previously through the Economic Summit. Similarly, the Youth Speak Out meetings began to lay the groundwork for the creation of the youth council described earlier.
Two important principles have guided GCDC's promotion of public di-

alogue, principles that are also central to most community-organizing efforts. First, GCDC staff work assiduously to avoid representing or speaking for the community, paying particular attention to developing opportunities for residents with the least voice to be heard by the larger community. Whether they are youth speaking at a local chamber of commerce meeting, people on welfare testifying at a hearing on welfare reform, or residents affected by HIV / AIDS voicing their concerns about the quality and availability of services, GCDC aims to facilitate a process that organizes and positions people in different sectors of the community to speak for themselves. Second, staff assume that information is power, an assumption that leads them to spend considerable effort promulgating information so that people will have the knowledge and tools to provide input. For example, much of the agenda at the Rural Initiatives Conference was devoted to explaining various rural development strategies to participants so that they could make informed choices about which to pursue. Although these principles have tended to slow down the pace of program implementation, GCDC staff consider them critical to building long-term capacity in the community.

Leadership Development.   Leadership development is not a separate program at GCDC. Rather, it is a lens through which all its activities are viewed and potentially exploited for their potential to enhance leadership. GCDC staff and board members frequently identify emerging leadership and provide support ranging from informal assistance to nominating individuals for board positions throughout the community and engaging them in various community initiatives. When GCDC starts a new organization or develops a new initiative, it aims to engage residents and other stakeholders from the beginning and insists on their representation in formal governance positions. A somewhat more formal approach to leadership development was taken with the Vision to Action Forums that were carried out in partnership with MDC, an organization in North Carolina that has significant experience with community planning. The Vision to Action Forums exposed thirty-two people to a year-long series of intense retreats designed to help individuals from diverse backgrounds and philosophies listen to each other, discuss the issues, and reach consensus on the vision, goals, and specific strategies that would comprise a long-range strategic plan for the Glades. The group assignments required participants to work together between sessions to gather, analyze, and synthesize information. Once a set of strategies was agreed upon, the group spent months reaching out to various parts of the community to solicit input and build support for the agenda, which is now being implemented through a follow-on program (Acting on the Vision) with the help of an additional 150 to 200 volunteers.

Community Identity and Pride.   Much of GCDC's work aims to reinforce a sense of community identity and pride. Community clean-ups,
teacher appreciation weeks, elementary school art contests, and the creation of opportunities to honor individuals who have made contributions
to the community are examples of such efforts. Similarly, community festivals and events at which residents eat, celebrate, and have fun together
help create social ties that promote a sense of belonging and shared interest. A recent initiative sponsored by GCDC, Potluck in the Muck, involved
a diverse group of people in a community theater production. Friends and
neighbors became actors, singers, musicians, and dancers as they told the
stories of their community. Besides building a shared sense of history
among the different groups that live in the Glades, the individuals involved hope that Potluck in the Muck can become a valuable tourist at-
traction.

Challenges

Building a local intermediary as a key strategy for community revitalization is not easy, especially for a new organization in a community whose
pressing needs may be more immediately apparent than the assets on
which to develop a revitalization strategy. GCDC experienced significant
challenges in trying to implement a local intermediary approach.

Pressure to Deliver Products Rather Than Build Capacity.   As a new
enterprise, GCDC felt strong pressures to produce tangible results in a
short time frame to generate credibility—internally and externally—and
to attract additional resources. Under these conditions, there was a temptation to devote all the organization's energy to producing something
(such as housing units or day care slots) to show funders, community
members, and evaluators at the expense of taking on the difficult, often be-
hind-the-scenes role of building the capacity of others to generate these
much-needed products. GCDC staff have had to resist the impulse to do
for rather than *with*. They have had to resist the temptation, for example,
to facilitate a meeting that a community person, with support, could lead;
to generate and implement a new idea rather than take the time to involve
the relevant constituencies; or to do all the outreach and make all the
arrangements for an event rather than engage the efforts of others.

Difficulty Establishing Realistic Benchmarks of Progress.   Setting clear
expectations and benchmarks of progress within particular time frames is
difficult in any comprehensive community initiative. Without a consensus
among funders and participants about what success should look like at different stages in GCDC's development, the organization was vulnerable
early on to questions about pace and effectiveness. As its agenda matured,

however, GCDC was increasingly able to articulate specific goals and outcomes for its work.

Difficulty Identifying GCDC's Contribution.   Much of GCDC's work has involved facilitating, brokering, and assigning the credit for accomplishments to others. Under these conditions, GCDC has been hard pressed to demonstrate the impact of its role to funders and other observers. Some events or accomplishments, such as the Med-Mobile or Potluck in the Muck, were clearly the primary result of GCDC's work. GCDC's role was semivisible in other events, such as the Economic Summit, which involved GCDC but in partnership with other players. In many cases, however, GCDC's contribution was more indirect and difficult to assess. The establishment of better dialogue among the three cities in the Glades or an increase in tourism in the area represented more indirect input on GCDC's part. GCDC staff assistance to organizations—for example, in developing proposals—may have led to these organizations' getting funded or simply to building their capacity in ways that will pay off in concrete or visible terms only several years later. Investments in outreach and relationship building made at one point may position GCDC to take advantage of opportunities that arise some time later. Even when a definite link could be made between GCDC's contribution and a particular accomplishment, GCDC had to be careful that in taking credit it did not undermine the position and growth of other organizations in the community.

Risks and Limitations of Partnerships.   In brokering and collaborating with other organizations rather than operating programs itself, GCDC was subject to the strengths and limitations of its partners. As GCDC assumed an increasingly active brokering role, it was faced with an increasingly complex set of choices about how to implement its agenda. Although partnerships and collaborations had the potential to bring new resources to the Glades and to help GCDC establish connections with new constituencies and new audiences, they also had the potential to drain GCDC's resources and divert its staff. Incubated projects often took longer than expected to become independent. Or once they did, they foundered and needed GCDC's continued attention. Quality control problems appeared with activities that GCDC catalyzed but over which it had no formal authority. GCDC once avoided another potential partnering problem by refusing an opportunity to broker external resources because these resources were so large they had the potential to define GCDC's identity in the eyes of people in the Glades. Thus, each partnership brought with it potential challenges that needed to be assessed and carefully managed.

Problem of Perception as a Gatekeeper.   A gatekeeper is a conduit through which funds, resources, and contacts must be accessed. A gatekeeper connects organizations in the community to outside contacts or funds and channels these outside resources to individuals and organizations in the community. The role of gatekeeper is antithetical to building the capacity of different segments of the community to have their own voice, both within the community and externally. When GCDC received its first grants, it encountered some resentment from other CBOs that were volunteer-led or had small staffs and little connection to outside resources. This dynamic is not uncommon in communities that have experienced substantial disinvestment. But GCDC was faced with the challenge of dispelling any notion in the community that it had exclusive access to external funders or that it intended to compete with other nonprofit organizations for outside funding. The fact that both the Community Foundation and the MacArthur Foundation made grants to other nonprofit organizations in the Glades helped to dissipate this concern somewhat.

Difficulty Diversifying Its Core Funding Base.   Most funders hesitate to provide general operating support to their grantees. They prefer to fund specific programs with their own goals, outcomes, and budgets. Categorical funding puts a great deal of stress on an organization that aims to develop an integrated agenda responsive to the changing needs of the community. It is particularly difficult for an intermediary because its program is essentially the time its core staff devote to various capacity-building and catalytic activities that do not fall neatly into specific project categories. Without funding for its core budget, an intermediary cannot carry out its mission effectively. GCDC has not yet diversified its sources of core support beyond the three foundations that have provided core funding since its inception. These foundations, along with GCDC, continue to face the difficult task of educating other funders about the critical importance of this type of funding.

Accomplishments

The initial charge to GCDC was to "build relationships, leadership, and institutional capacities," all of which are necessary ingredients in a comprehensive revitalization project. GCDC has struggled with the challenges of operationalizing this role, challenges that are familiar, if often unresolved, in other community-building initiatives around the country. Notwithstanding, the intermediary strategy adopted by GCDC has yielded some important signs of early success.

Strong Multiracial, Multiethnic Board.   GCDC has built a strong multiracial, multiethnic board, which is a testament to the organization's commitment to find its roots in and derive its legitimacy from the Glades communities. Despite the endless meetings and frequent turmoil of the early years and despite the historical forces that sometimes threatened to divide the group, GCDC board members maintained a willingness to stay engaged with each other to do the hard work of developing an organization.

Multiple Relationships.   GCDC has relationships with multiple constituencies and sectors. Although it is not tracked on a systematic basis, the number of individuals and groups that know about GCDC has grown significantly. The frequency with which it has been asked to be a broker or fiscal agent, the number of working contacts it has in the governments of the Glades cities and Palm Beach County, and the number of residents who have participated in a survey, activity, or community forum sponsored by GCDC all indicate the degree to which GCDC has become embedded in the life of the Glades. Each initiative in which GCDC has been involved has widened the organization's network of relationships, which can be mobilized to promote additional development in the community.

Credible Convener.   GCDC is a credible convener of diverse parties. It has achieved the credibility and legitimacy to bring together a cross section of the community in multiple forums and venues. It has maintained its political independence while vigorously and carefully cultivating relationships throughout the community. It has also provided neutral turf for initiatives, such as the Western Communities Tourism Alliance, that require a nonpartisan home. In a politically divided environment like the Glades, the ability to convene across boundaries of race, age, geography, and economic status has been central to taking on an effective intermediary role.

New Community Ethos of Debate and Problem Solving.   GCDC has sparked a new community ethos of debate and problem solving in the Glades. It has worked hard to create many different kinds of forums at which people can voice their goals and concerns and listen to those of others. These forums have given individuals with little experience in civic involvement an opportunity to develop and practice new skills and to identify the ways in which their own interests and those of others converge. These experiences have often moved individuals to further engagement and action. In public meetings to describe the Vision to Action process and agenda, for example, community residents demanded more information, action, and inclusion. In addition, some participants in one-time events, such as the Family Forum or a city charrette, have moved on to participate in ongoing projects, help with community surveys, or represent the Glades at a public hearing.

Responsive Agenda.   GCDC's agenda continues to respond to the community. The organization's fundamental commitment to citizen engagement and education has been one of its defining characteristics. Its agenda has been responsive to community priorities that are expressed through a range of formal and informal vehicles. Despite production pressures, GCDC staff have internalized the value of soliciting community voices that might not otherwise be heard.

Influence on Use of Resources.   GCDC has influenced the use of existing resources (a function central to the intermediary approach to community development) in a number of ways. Through the Empowerment Evaluation workshops, various constituencies have been encouraged and taught to raise questions about the allocation of resources in community organizations of interest to them. This development has led to overall growth in the community's capacity to hold local organizations accountable for their use of resources received or directed on behalf of the community. In addition, GCDC staff have participated on various committees, such as the state-designated Enterprise Zone board, which constitute important vehicles for influencing the use of existing resources.

New Resources.   The Glades have secured both public and private development resources that would not have been brought into the community had GCDC not played the role of broker, incubator, or advocate for these resources. New public resources have supported the spinning off of HIPPY with three years of funding, the small-business incubator (EDGE) project, and the Western Communities Tourism Alliance. The county has also requested GCDC to administer the Core Regions Grant Fund for the Glades, through which $25,000 was secured for each of the three municipalities for community improvements. New private resources have come from the W. K. Kellogg Foundation's support for Acting on the Vision, the Joseph and Florence Roblee Foundation's grant for an entrepreneurial training curriculum, and the Lost Tree Village Charitable Foundation, which has generally restricted its funding to northern Palm Beach County but made an exception for GCDC's youth-related work in the Glades.

New Capacities.   GCDC has built new capacities, individually and organizationally, by using a leadership development and capacity-building lens for all its projects. At every opportunity, people have been engaged to advise, monitor, implement, and evaluate activities so that a high degree of ownership has developed for much of GCDC's work. The parents reached through the HIPPY parent training program, the youth learning to be entrepreneurs, the residents trained to administer community surveys, and the citizens involved in Acting on the Vision have developed new skills, as well as new opportunities to exercise these skills. In addition, GCDC's technical assistance to emerging organizations, its staff participation on various organizational boards, and its efforts to promote new collaborations and partnerships, such as the youth council or the Med-Mobile, have increased capacity at the organizational level, thus strengthening the institutional infrastructure of the community.

Conclusion

GCDC's evolution has not taken place in a vacuum. Certain propitious conditions have cultivated its growth, including the existence of three active funders who supported GCDC in multiple ways beyond funding, consultants from all over the country who provided valuable technical assistance, and strong community leaders who were willing to work with funders and each other to build the organization. Absent these particular conditions, GCDC's course would likely have been much less successful. And even with its progress, GCDC faces both internal and external challenges. The need to secure core funding for the foreseeable future continues to demand significant effort. Similarly, because an intermediary requires an enormous array of talents and skills in its staff, ongoing staff development is required to ensure staff's ability to grow with the complicated and changing demands of GCDC's work.

To maximize the effectiveness of its role as an intermediary, GCDC has committed itself to trying to shape policies that affect the Glades, including those that influence how welfare reform gets implemented in the Glades and how state and county resources for economic development get spent. These issues are all natural extensions of GCDC's current work. GCDC's board and staff see the organization's challenge as reflecting its relationships with multiple and diverse community constituencies and grounding its policy voice in the support it gets for the day-to-day work of the organization. These relationships and this support are what give GCDC its legitimacy and potential power.

CONSENSUS ORGANIZING
DEMONSTRATION PROGRAM

The Local Initiatives Support Corporation (LISC) is one of several national intermediaries serving the community development field. Founded in 1979, LISC by 1990 was active in almost thirty areas of concentration, the majority of which were metropolitan areas in the Northeast, Midwest, and on the West Coast. These were localities where established CDCs with a "track record"—having the capacity to qualify for and use LISC's core grant and loan development programs—were most numerous. LISC, however, was interested in expanding. It recognized the value, both in providing services to low-income communities and in advocating on their behalf, of extending its network to make it more truly national. But it needed new strategies for moving into areas, like the cities of the South and Southwest, that did not already have seasoned CDCs with which it could work.

One organizational response to this strategic problem was the inauguration in 1991 of the Consensus Organizing Demonstration Program (CODP) in three localities (Little Rock, New Orleans, and Palm Beach County) with little history of effective community development. The purpose of CODP was to test the efficacy of "consensus organizing" in developing community-based capacity and forming new CDCs in neighborhoods that had not spawned them spontaneously.

The consensus-organizing approach was conceived and piloted in the Monongahela Valley, Pennsylvania (Mon Valley), in the mid-1980s under the auspices of the Allegheny Conference on Community Development, a group of corporate and civic leaders in the greater Pittsburgh area. The conference staff were disturbed by the deterioration of economic and social conditions in the Mon Valley. The economy of the valley depended on jobs and tax revenue derived from steel manufacturing facilities owned, operated, and ultimately closed by companies headquartered elsewhere. There was little history of locally initiated economic or community development effort, and public programs at the county and municipal level had been ineffective.

The conference hired Michael Eichler, a highly regarded community organizer in Pittsburgh, to develop a strategy to improve conditions in the Mon Valley, where the closing of the steel mills had left many small towns economically depressed. Eichler devised a plan to (1) generate fresh community-based organizational capacity throughout the valley and (2) foster collaborative relations between valley residents and the support community in Pittsburgh. His strategy was to use the LISC program in Pittsburgh as an organizing tool for both the residents and the corporate community of the Mon Valley. His consensus-organizing approach was widely regarded as a success. The effectiveness of using the core LISC program to mobilize community members and supporters was clear, both to him and to LISC. He joined the LISC staff, and a partnership was born.

Fundamental Goals and Guiding Principles

CODP's stated objective was to expand the national community development industry into localities where it previously did not exist. At the same time, the program was also a test of the general efficacy and applicability of the consensus-organizing approach in furthering that objective. LISC's national track record of accomplishment and reputation for insisting on high project and organizational quality standards were expected by all parties to extend to CODP. Also emphasized from the beginning was Eichler's commitment to building new organizations that were rooted in and controlled by local community residents.

The demonstration attempted to achieve its main objectives through core strategies and activities modeled on Eichler's work in the Mon Valley. The core strategies included:

- Developing broad involvement based on consensus and the promise of delivering tangible products (i.e., housing production).
- Breaking the complex real estate development process into relatively simple, straightforward activities.
- Engaging carefully selected residents of targeted neighborhoods and individuals from the support community.
- Developing leadership, both among neighborhood residents on CDC boards and in the corporate sector, to advocate for community development.
- Parallel organizing of residents in multiple neighborhoods and members in the support community, using progress in each of these two "spheres" to foster effort and progress in the other.
- Linking residents of low-income neighborhoods to resources and individuals in the support community.
- Managing risk, for example, by selecting primarily sites and neighborhoods where CODP had a good chance of success.

Structure and Operations

CODP implemented a core set of activities, in sequence, in three sites. *Site assessment* involved LISC staff determining the feasibility of operating a successful demonstration effort in a particular locality that had expressed interest in the program. The assessments included extensive interviews both with potential funders and program supporters and with community leaders in prospective target neighborhoods.

When a selected site neared its fund-raising target, Eichler *assembled a staff*. He hired a local coordinator, who in turn hired three community organizers and recruited local area professionals to serve as technical consultants to the neighborhood groups. The coordinator and the organizers became known as the development team. Initial training highlighted the six neighborhood networks—renters, home owners, businesspeople, social service providers, religious organizations, and prominent neighborhood institutions (such as hospitals and schools)—in which the organizers were expected to assess leadership potential, willingness to volunteer, commitment to the community, and attitudes toward community development.

The primary objective in assembling the staff was to assure a team that could deliver the program at a high level of quality and integrity. This required, first and foremost, identifying individuals who could demonstrate that they understood and were strongly committed to the program's methods (the consensus-organizing approach) and its core values and concerns, including honesty, diversity, responsiveness to local concerns and needs, and improvement of conditions and capacities of targeted populations. The strong representation of people of color was critical to building local credibility for CODP, especially in the target neighborhoods, since it helped to undercut the distrust of some in the African-American community who saw LISC as a white, New York organization. It also gave the program credibility for serving as a model of the inclusive behavior it expected of others.

The development team in each site selected six target neighborhoods. Each community organizer identified potential volunteers in two neighborhoods and helped the volunteers *establish new CDCs* that had broad-based representation. Each new CDC held an open town meeting to discuss community priorities. The town meeting, along with *technical training and assistance,* was meant to help board members identify projects that had potential to benefit the community as a whole. Then, by undertaking *real estate development projects* under the development team's aegis, the CDC volunteer board members were expected to learn about the development process, expand their organization's capacity, establish its credibility, and gain control over their community's development.

Each site had a planned date to *transition* (reflecting the period for which program funding was raised, initially two years in Little Rock and Palm Beach County and three years in New Orleans) from a development team to another arrangement. However, the exact form (institutional structure, staffing, funding, governance) that transition would take was left unstated, except for a commitment that local stakeholders would make those decisions when the time came.

Eichler and Richard Manson (a vice president at LISC) managed CODP. Eichler—first as national LISC program director and then as director of the Consensus Organizing Institute (COI), which he founded after leaving LISC in 1994—had primary responsibility for hiring and supervising local development teams and for working with the local coordinators on strategy. He also selected a local host organization to house and officially administer the development team (a highly regarded local home gave the new staff instant credibility). Manson was responsible for establishing local advisory committees, which are made up of representatives of all major LISC contributors in the locality. Typically chaired by a prominent corporate leader, they function much like boards, meeting quarterly to review the progress of the local program, set policy, and review funding applications. They must approve all grants and loans made to local CDCs. Manson was also responsible for working with the CDCs and their committees on their first real estate development projects and hiring and supervising a local CODP program director.

A national consultant with legal training and extensive community development experience assisted the development teams in all three sites. He was primarily responsible for project development support and technical training of both development team staff (including technical consultants) and CDC board members in such topics as finance, marketing, and project development. He employed a well-structured project development model that helped CDC volunteers identify target areas, form working committees (e.g., marketing and counseling, finance), and undertake technical analysis.

As program implementation moved forward in the targeted neighborhoods, CODP staff at all levels invested in building relationships with the local support community, particularly members of the local private sector who sat on the local advisory committee. The goal was to create a knowledgeable, cohesive support community for the CDCs by the time they had completed their first housing developments.

Local Context

The CODP design called for a development team program in three sites, with six neighborhoods targeted in each. CODP's approach to demonstrating broad program efficacy was to be sure that each site clearly needed community development assistance of the type CODP could provide *and* also had the raw materials that would enable the program to succeed. In addition, to show the breadth of the program's possible applicability, sites were sought that differed from one another in important respects (e.g., size, political context, socioeconomic and demographic characteristics).

Assessing need was relatively straightforward. Site assessments relied on two primary indicators: (1) the presence of neighborhoods with significant physical and economic problems, and (2) limited existing community development capacity, both in the neighborhoods and at the metropolitan-area level.

Assessing the likelihood of success was more complex and entailed three main elements. First, program success hinged on the presence of an interested and supportive private sector. Most obviously, private-sector support would provide a strong likelihood that local funding for the program, one of CODP's core requirements, would be forthcoming. As important, however, sites were sought in which a group of highly regarded private-sector leaders would give CODP strong general support, as well as specific financial help, and thereby give the program visibility and credibility.

Second, critical to program success was the presence of a pool of potential community volunteers. In sites that had genuinely needy neighborhoods, program staff sought localities that contained a critical mass of committed residents and other stakeholders who would be willing to volunteer and support neighborhood-based CDCs.

Finally, since CODP relied on consensus-style organizing, the likelihood of success was greater if there were no local groups likely to oppose or compete with the program. Some localities had such limited prior experience with community development that they literally presented a clean slate—the simplest program setting. Other localities presented more complex environments. Some were home to ineffective or nonrepresentative nonprofit development entities, discredited past efforts that had tarnished community development's image, or existing groups that relied on conflict-style organizing. In such places, CODP looked for signs that existing community-organizing or development organizations were ones with which the consensus-organizing effort could coexist (in essence, going separate ways). In other places, nascent community organizations showed signs of genuine volunteer engagement and commitment. There, CODP sought an explicit affirmation that the emerging group(s) supported the development team's approach to community development and shared the program's goals and values; these groups were asked to reconstitute themselves using the guidelines followed by CODP-initiated CDCs. Together, these three criteria helped to identify sites that would likely benefit from CODP's efforts.

Within each site, the objective of the neighborhood selection process was to identify a set of neighborhoods that would allow the program to demonstrate its value. This meant identifying neighborhoods that clearly needed community development, but that also possessed the attributes CODP needed to succeed. The principal criterion used in making the judgment about the likelihood of success was the prospect of recruiting a diverse, committed group of volunteers who would be interested in engaging in a new community development effort working with the development team. The community organizers were instructed to assess the leadership potential of local residents, their commitment to improving their neighborhoods, and their willingness to volunteer for an organized group effort and work together.

In addition to considering the characteristics of individual neighborhoods, the development teams sought neighborhoods in which, as a group, people of color had a strong presence, and that represented a range of problems and related program risks. Variations in neighborhood physical, economic, and social conditions allowed CODP to include neighborhoods where there was a real possibility of failure (especially small, isolated African-American communities in unincorporated areas where the public sector was unlikely to invest), without jeopardizing the program as a whole. This made CODP less vulnerable to criticisms of "creaming," that is, helping the neighborhoods that least needed assistance. Nevertheless, CODP did rule out some prospective sites that faced problems so severe that the program would clearly have been an inadequate remedy—places such as the Glades in western Palm Beach County and large, distressed public housing developments in New Orleans.[1]

The three chosen sites shared many of the characteristics of the Mon Valley: a substantial number of neglected and declining older neighborhoods, little community-based development capacity, and a lack of concerted local community development effort and experience. At the same time, they varied significantly in scale, extent, and severity of poverty; in prior community development experience; in robustness of the local economy and housing market; and in history, political culture, and climate of race relations. In other words, they were diverse enough to show whether the approach was feasible in a variety of settings:

• Palm Beach County, one of the fastest growing large metropolitan areas in the country, was the largest of the three demonstration sites (population 863,500). The local economy was strong, but income disparities were great. Minorities (13 percent of the population) were increasingly concentrated in the older communities along the railroad that parallels the Intercoastal Waterway. Housing prices were rising steadily, and local government regulations made production of affordable housing difficulty.

• Little Rock is the hub of a relatively small urban area (population 350,000) that was growing, but much more slowly than Palm Beach County. The integration efforts and civil rights activism of the 1960s, including the federally enforced integration of Central High School in Little Rock, had spurred the movement of white families to the growing suburbs and had left their mark on race relations in the city. Older neighborhoods in the inner city had experienced substantial population declines accompanied by significant housing decay and rising crime rates. African Americans made up 34 percent of the population and had per capita incomes less than half those of white residents in Pulaski County.

• New Orleans presented the most difficult challenges, including racism, a long history of political corruption and neglect, and the second-highest urban poverty rate in the country (32 percent). With almost 500,000 residents, the city's population had declined by 21 percent since 1960, while the nonwhite portion of the population had risen to 65 percent (ranking fifth among all large cities in the United States). Several neighborhoods were dominated by large, distressed public housing projects with many vacant units. With a high vacancy rate and substantial blight, housing was clearly an important issue—to which city government was paying little attention.

The neighborhoods chosen for participation in CODP in each city were clearly neighborhoods with significant community development needs. All had average household income at least 25 percent below their county's average, all had problems with their housing stock (creating the basis for an initial set of housing development projects), and all lacked the organizational resources to undertake development activities. Most were predominantly African American, but each site had at least one neighborhood that was racially and ethnically mixed. As a group, the chosen neighborhoods in each site had lower income (and hence presumably greater need) than those nominated but not chosen.

Challenges

Creating new organizations from scratch is always a demanding exercise, and it was especially so in the context of a program that required those new organizations to begin their work by completing a technically complex activity: housing development. In carrying the program forward, staff experienced a variety of challenges, both expected and not.

Adapting to Different Local Contexts.   From the outset, differences in local context influenced program strategy and tactics, including the choice of a host organization, a coordinator (local versus nonlocal, race), and people selected to screen candidates for that job (to build legitimacy for the coordinator choice). In New Orleans, for example, it was especially important that staff be recruited locally, since residents have a tendency to be suspicious of outsiders. Hiring local community organizers was a priority in Little Rock for the same reason, though this was not an issue in Palm Beach County, where immigration is very high. In all sites, the diversity of the staff (the result of a labor-intensive staff recruitment process in each site) helped build credibility, particularly in skeptical minority communities that had previously been disappointed by community development, particularly efforts initiated by outsiders.

Variations in the political settings also provoked program adaptation. In Palm Beach County, the new CDCs were spread across six local jurisdictions, requiring staff to spend considerable time cultivating relationships with all the individuals whose work would affect the CDCs' projects. In New Orleans, city government was viewed as corrupt, and the program avoided contact with the city as much as possible until a new mayor was elected. In Little Rock, community development was so new— the Arkansas State Finance Agency had never worked with a low-income housing tax credit development—that public-sector staff had to be assisted by senior LISC staff in learning how to handle development-related issues.

Supporting Technically Complex Work Done by Volunteers.   The program strategy of segmenting the real estate development process into discrete steps, presented when volunteers were ready to undertake them, proved central to CODP's initial success. In providing this training, the national TA provider left volunteers with valuable tools (checklists, worksheets, examples, etc.) critical not only for keeping a complex set of tasks organized and moving forward, but also for managing the organizing portion of the program. The organizers used this strategy to motivate volunteers, to build volunteer confidence and skill, and to keep forceful individuals from dominating the boards. The strategy was easiest to implement in the early stages of the program, when many tasks needed to be performed simultaneously (making it possible to spread the work broadly and keep many people involved), but became more difficult when the CDCs entered the construction phase of development, when the CDCs hired professional builders and there was little for the volunteers to do, other than the few required to monitor the project's progress.

CODP had anticipated recruiting local professionals knowledgeable about the development process to work with each new CDC when the national TA provider was not available. This approach worked well in Little Rock, where the program coordinator was able to recruit at least two professionals to work pro bono with each new group; this accomplishment is the primary reason that housing production proceeded on schedule in that site. In the other sites, persistent efforts to recruit architects, developers, brokers, planners, and other local TA providers were unsuccessful. CODP staff had neither the skills nor the time to substitute for these trained professionals, and staff efforts to come to grips with the seriousness of this problem came too late. The CDCs' real estate projects lagged badly in most neighborhoods as a result, ultimately costing the program credibility with local funders.

Maintaining Broad Volunteer Participation. CODP sought to organize CDCs with a commitment to broadly based participation. In a few of the CDCs, one or two individuals assumed most of the responsibility for "making things happen," but most boards had at least a small core of people (six or eight in most cases) taking active leadership roles, at least through the time that the CDCs got predevelopment funding from their local advisory committee. After that point, many boards replaced their initial committee structures (which spread responsibility broadly) with a small cadre of volunteers who assumed responsibility for all CDC activities and administration. In all three sites, boards had a tendency to become less participatory, mostly out of expediency (i.e., to speed housing production). Some boards consciously decided to consolidate decision-making activities within a core group, and many of these boards became the most active real estate developers. This decision commonly resulted in lower levels of volunteer participation and commitment. The boards that shared responsibility more broadly were characterized by leaders who valued participation and diversity; however, their development projects made slower progress, and some ground to a halt. Technical issues, for example, could be addressed only at the pace of the least technically capable member of the board, and efforts to make decisions by consensus frequently bogged down and led to postponement of important choices.

Although the CDCs' approach to managing their real estate projects contributed to declines in participation, "natural" attrition (e.g., by individuals who initially overestimated the amount of time they could commit or who experienced some type of personal emergency) also took its toll. Both the number of volunteers who left the boards and the extent to which they were replaced by other members of the community varied considerably, both across sites and within each site. Maintaining board size and diversity clearly called for ongoing community organizing, but this activity flagged in Palm Beach County and New Orleans as program staff struggled to support the technical needs of the residents as best they could. For their part, few volunteers internalized the importance of remaining broadly grounded in the community. As a result, when they did recruit new members, they did so using their preexisting networks; consequently the boards tended to become less diverse over time.

Managing the Transfer of Control to the Volunteers.   The core promise made in recruiting volunteers was that participation in CODP would gain them a meaningful degree of collective control over the development of their neighborhood. They would gain this control because the program would support them in acquiring the skills needed to exercise it competently, thereby winning the respect of influential people in the public and private sectors who could provide development resources. From the outset, the community organizers understood that the residents, not the organizers, were responsible for doing the work that had to be done; the organizers were only to provide guidance and support and link the CDCs to TA when they needed it.

Implicit in the assumption that residents were to learn by doing is the reality that the residents did not have the knowledge and skills they needed to do the work, even though the objective was for them to be in charge. CODP's challenge was to transfer responsibility and control to the volunteers as quickly as they could be prepared to handle it. For example, it was clear that the CDCs' leadership, especially the board presidents, would play key roles in maintaining broad participation and board diversity, as well as in assuring production. The program's success hinged on the residents making good choices when they voted for officers. But many volunteers had never served on a board and did not know what the officers needed to be able to do—and, in any case, they did not know one another very well yet. The organizers' job was to carefully guide the officer selection process, helping residents to understand the qualifications the officers needed, to quietly assess one another's strengths and weakness, and thus to be in a position to make wise choices. This delicate process had to be repeated many times as the residents faced new tasks and challenges.

Phasing Out the Program. The transition period, when a structured intervention phases out, is the most visible aspect of many such programs, as it is a natural point for national and local observers and participants to assess what has been accomplished. Good program design and management of the transition are therefore quite important if the program is to have a strong legacy. Developing a good transition strategy entails thinking of transition as a *process*. The transition may appear to be an *event*, described in terms such as "now the CDCs have a coalition and are in charge." But effecting a smooth transition requires the same care and thought required for good program start-up, such as attention to learning and practicing skills, teamwork, careful timing, and follow-through.

In Palm Beach County and Little Rock, the virtually simultaneous formation of new coalition organizations (to which all the CDCs belonged and which were to provide them with staff support) and the departure of the development teams increased the work demands on volunteers. They needed (for the first time) to hire and supervise staff, to negotiate more complex power and organizational relationships, and to exercise the authority needed to hold staff accountable. As the development teams prepared to leave, alternative supports for participants needed to ratchet up, but they did not. As a result, both coalitions got off to a less-than-ideal start, making poor choices in hiring executive directors, among other missteps. Most volunteers did not fully understand how to make the coalitions work for them and their CDCs. As a consequence, the coalitions were not productive, and support for them faded among both volunteers and funders.

Educating Supporters and Managing Expectations. CODP was an ambitious program. It sought simultaneously to create new organizations under the meaningful control of resident volunteers and to have those new organizations complete technically demanding real estate development projects—all within a relatively short time. In two of the three sites, the program's relationships with its funders (primarily corporate) frayed when funders' expectations about housing production were not met. The program had sold the private sector on housing development as the primary indicator of developing organizational capacity in the neighborhoods. Thus, sustained private-sector support for leadership and organizational development objectives depended on the accomplishment of real estate objectives, but this happened only in Little Rock. When the CDCs in Palm Beach County and New Orleans failed to reach their housing development goals, that failure was obvious, and funders were understandably unhappy.

In retrospect, given most funders' lack of prior experience with community development, the program should probably have given greater emphasis to enhancing their understanding of the work. In particular, funders needed more help in learning how to think about and assess community development program performance. The logical steps of the real estate development process provided more detailed indicators of "hard" progress than is often available, and local advisory committee members heard reports on them. But the development team also had other indicators of progress that they used to gauge both organizer performance and the CDCs' organizational progress. This information could have helped the support community develop a more sophisticated understanding of community development's requirements and opportunities. Greater engagement by program supporters with volunteers and program staff (e.g., visiting with volunteers at development sites in neighborhoods) could have enabled supporters to understand and consider broader measures of program performance, including progress on such intangibles as enhanced volunteer knowledge of community development, increased volunteer commitment to their neighborhoods and CDCs, and developing neighborhood leadership.

Accomplishments

The initial organizing component of the program worked well in all three sites. In each site, the development team organized broadly based CDCs with at least ten members and guided them as they applied for nonprofit tax status, hosted town meetings, elected officers, selected initial real estate projects, conducted marketing surveys, and met with lending institutions. Of the nineteen neighborhoods targeted by the development teams, all formally organized a CDC, and all but one successfully petitioned its local advisory committee for predevelopment funding.

The process of organizing new CDCs generated a significant increase in the level of citizen participation and commitment in the targeted neighborhoods. Prior to CODP, resident involvement in community development in these communities was quite limited. In response to the program, approximately three hundred volunteers across the three sites agreed to serve as founding board members of the newly formed CDCs. This number is particularly impressive because of the character of the commitment volunteers were asked to make. Volunteer board members were expected to assume responsibility for actually *doing the work* required to identify, plan, and oversee a low-cost housing development. In addition, about a third of the CDCs chose to engage in non–real estate activities (neighborhood clean-ups, fund-raising events such as car washes, etc.) that involved other members of the community. The demands on their time were therefore heavy and sustained.

This pool of volunteers produced an impressive number of capable and energetic local leaders, many of whom had not previously been active in community service. Some served as officers of their CDCs, others as committee chairs. Volunteer board members included significant numbers of African Americans (more than 70 percent of the initial group of volunteers), and they assumed the key leadership roles in a majority of the CDCs.

By mid-1996—almost five years after the first CDCs were organized in Palm Beach and four years after the first groups formed in New Orleans—the number of CDCs had fallen to fifteen. Of the original CDCs, five in Palm Beach, six in Little Rock, and four in New Orleans were involved in real estate production, that is, they had acquired and begun work on at least one property. Three of these CDCs were quite fragile organizationally, and their future was less certain than that of the remaining twelve. These twelve each appeared to have a base of volunteers that was solid, but typically smaller and narrower than what the CDCs had planned and originally enjoyed. Of the four inactive CDCs, one had dissolved, one had engaged in some non–real estate activity, and two had yet to begin a housing development or other significant development effort. Two Little Rock communities not originally selected by the development team, but impressed with what the CODP-assisted CDCs were able to accomplish, had formed their own CDCs with the local coordinator's help, and a third seemed likely to follow suit.

Efforts to leave in place a coalition of CDCs were ultimately unsuccessful in all three sites. In both Palm Beach County and Little Rock, coalitions were established but then experienced difficulties. In Palm Beach County, the process of choosing an executive director was difficult and divisive. In both sites, the persons hired as executive director were not right for the position. The ensuing problems ultimately led to diminished support for the coalition by both funders and volunteers and to disagreement between CODP's parent rganizations (LISC and COI). In the end, both coalitions were disbanded. This outcome was the product of poor program design for managing the phase-out transition, a series of implementation shortcomings, and disagreement between LISC and COI about priorities. In New Orleans a coalition was never formally organized. Nevertheless, all three locations remain active LISC sites.

NOTE

1. Staff at both LISC and the MacArthur Foundation felt that the problems in the Glades were too acute and multifaceted to be addressed in a serious way by the CODP program design; some of these problems, especially those concerning health and environmental quality, are unique. The institutional infrastructure in the Glades is much less developed than in the rest of the

county, and the area is isolated both physically and socially. This is consistent with the rationale for the need for an intermediary—to help build institutional infrastructure and ties with the rest of the county. The Glades thus needed a customized program, which MacArthur was in the process of developing in collaboration with other major foundations, and which soon became GCDC.

Appendix B
Other Efforts

In addition to the core case studies described in Appendix A, a variety of other efforts have been referred to throughout the book to illustrate one or more of the four principal strategies used to build community capacity. Following is a brief description of each of those efforts referred to most frequently, in alphabetical order. These descriptions are intended only to provide enough background to make our examples useful, and are not intended to give a complete picture of the efforts.

ASSOCIATION OF COMMUNITY ORGANIZATIONS FOR REFORM NOW (ACORN)

The Association of Community Organizations for Reform Now (ACORN) is a national organizing movement with more than five hundred neighborhood chapters in thirty cities. It raises 80 percent of its operating funds internally through member dues and fund-raising events.

ACORN grew out of the National Welfare Rights Organization (NWRO). It began in 1970 in Little Rock as the Arkansas Community Organizations for Reform Now, working with welfare recipients on welfare rights issues. It then broadened to include issues of unemployed workers, veterans, and parents and, moving beyond Little Rock, tackled issues of concern to farmers. The result was a geographically broadened and racially integrated movement consolidated around a common, economically based agenda.

ACORN also developed a role in electoral politics, originally in the form of candidate forums, then local election endorsements, then building to national activity. For example, in an effort to increase the representation of low- and moderate-income people in the 1980 presidential nominating process, a contingent of forty-two ACORN members was elected as delegates or alternates at the Democratic National Convention. This broadening scope of activity reflected a broadening organizational base, with

ACORN organizations present in twenty states by the beginning of the 1980s.

From a classic strategy of "outsider" pressure organizing, ACORN has broadened its approach by building its capability to engage in such tactics as legislative lobbying. This dual focus is apparent in many important ACORN campaigns. For example, ACORN organized a "squatting" campaign in which abandoned housing was occupied by people at the margins of the housing market—low-income renters and homeless people—while at the same time lobbying Congress to preserve and enforce existing legislation such as the Community Reinvestment Act, which requires financial institutions to reinvest in local communities through such activities as mortgage lending to lower-income home buyers.

ACORN lists accomplishments within the areas of community reinvestment, housing, schools, living wages, jobs, voter participation, health and environmental justice, and neighborhood safety. ACORN has helped create affiliate organizations to focus on specific agendas. These include the United Labor Union, now an AFL-CIO affiliate organizing low-wage service workers, FM radio stations in Dallas and Little Rock, and the ACORN Housing Corporation with offices in twenty-seven cities across seven states, which is working to increase low-income home ownership. ACORN also pursues coalition politics.

BLOCKS TOGETHER

Blocks Together is a grassroots organization that emerged in the early 1990s from an effort aimed at organizing residents to fight crime and drugs in the West Humboldt Park and North Garfield Park neighborhoods in Chicago. An organizer trained and supported by the National Training and Information Center (NTIC), an organizing intermediary in Chicago, made the initial door-knocking organizing forays within the neighborhood, recruiting a base of neighborhood residents who were assisted in learning basic organizing skills. Working with the NTIC organizer, residents established a number of issue-oriented block clubs. Through NTIC, the block clubs received a grant from the Mott Foundation's Intermediary Support Organization program, giving them organizational development support that enabled them, in 1994, to formally incorporate as Blocks Together, a nonprofit organization. A governing board of up to fourteen local residents is elected at a neighborhood membership convention every two years. Anybody who "lives, works, or worships" in the neighborhood may join Blocks Together for a $5 annual membership fee. The group maintains a paid staff of six—all organizers—and is hiring two more organizers.

Blocks Together organizes residents to address issues of local concern.

Often this includes identifying people in relevant positions of power, arranging for them to attend community meetings where residents present their concerns and ask for commitments to act on them, then following up to make sure resident concerns are addressed. The organization has worked successfully to persuade local officials and bureaucrats to pave streets, more effectively target criminal activity, and improve local schools. Blocks Together was also successful in getting a railroad company to repair its crumbling viaducts—a public safety problem endemic to Chicago because of its status as the nation's primary railroad transshipment hub. This success was so extraordinary that the group was contacted by the mayor's office for strategic advice on how to replicate the agreement in other areas of the city.

COMMUNITIES ORGANIZED FOR PUBLIC SERVICE (COPS)

Communities Organized for Public Service (COPS) of San Antonio, Texas, was organized in 1974 by Ernesto Cortes, Jr., now the regional director for the Industrial Areas Foundation (IAF) in the Southwest. COPS is the anchor of the robust, statewide Texas network of IAF organizations.

The IAF organization movement was begun in Chicago by Saul Alinksy. In a neighborhood behind the livestock yards of Chicago's storied meatpacking industry, Alinsky organized the Back of the Yards Council in 1939. Alinsky worked through the institutional structures of the local Catholic parishes to reach the working class, mainly Catholic industrial workforce of the neighborhood. This general approach became the model by which the IAF began building a national network of organizing efforts. The IAF network now includes about forty local organizations in eight states and the United Kingdom.

COPS leadership represents twenty-seven congregations and eight schools on the largely Mexican and Mexican-American west side of San Antonio. In 1984, Metro Alliance was organized on the north and east side of town representing twenty-five congregations and six schools. While institutions join and help support COPS and Metro Alliance through institutional membership, leaders are developed to address issues of the community as a whole rather than only those of their particular institutions. The organization's professional staff includes four full-time organizers and two support staff.

At the grassroots level, COPS and Metro Alliance are developed institution by institution and block by block using the energies and talents of interested leaders to organize house meetings of their neighbors. The organizers teach leaders how to organize house meetings to identify the issues that are important to the community, how to use research to inform problem-solving strategies, how to identify responsible individual and institutional actors, and how to organize assemblies with public officials to address their concerns. This organization also creates a broad-based constituency to ensure the accountability of responsible actors to the community.

Because San Antonio's West Side has been historically neglected by the city government, early COPS activities focused on winning improvement of the area's roads, sewers, and storm drainage. That ultimately successful campaign involved a classic strategy of organizing residents and bringing pressure to bear on responsible city leaders. COPS and Metro Alliance are now regularly consulted in the process of making civic decisions and policy, retaining their power base through continual neighborhood organizing. As part of a statewide IAF network, COPS and Metro Alliance also participate in broader campaigns (such as a "living wage" campaign), but each local IAF affiliate is organizationally autonomous.

The initial funding for COPS was raised by a committee of parish priests and Protestant clergy. COPS and Metro Alliance now raise all of their money through church membership dues, foundation grants, and investments from local business. The organizations do not accept any government funding.

COMMUNITY BUILDING INITIATIVE

The Community Building Initiative (CBI) was a program of the Local Initiatives Support Corporation (LISC) that ran from July 1994 to June 1997. CBI provided modest technical and financial support to selected CDCs in eleven cities to help them expand activities enhancing the social and physical infrastructure of the low-income communities they serve. Rather than act as service providers, CDCs were encouraged to act as intermediaries, coordinating local institutions and resources in order to effectively address locally defined issues. In two cities, CBI worked with a single CDC, while in the other nine cities, it worked with groups of CDCs, organizing them into collaborative relationships intended to enhance their overall impact.

CBI funding helped CDCs carry out community planning processes to identify key areas of need and then, typically, supported hiring an organizer or TA provider to help coordinate solutions. Examples of activities CBI supported include organizing block clubs and family and youth development programs in order to reduce crime and increase the sense of community in CDC-owned housing developments; training low-income residents to work in the home health-care field; developing community-based primary health-care services; and working to increase local business development and employment opportunities. All told, CBI provided funding and assistance to forty-four CDCs.

COMMUNITY DEVELOPMENT
PARTNERSHIP STRATEGY

The Community Development Partnership Strategy is a Ford Foundation program that began in 1983. Its purpose is to pool the resources of banks, local foundations, government, business and industry, and national non-profit funders in support of neighborhood revitalization efforts and to shift the support of local CDCs from direct funding to funding through local partnerships or intermediaries. Not only does this help strengthen CDCs, but it helps direct banks and others to the most sound investment opportunities in the community and reduces the risk of the investment that any one of the partners must carry.

The strategy targets cities where LISC and the Enterprise Foundation, both of which pool funds for individuals CDCs and provide them with TA and training, do not operate or where their work could be augmented. The Ford Foundation has invested $30 million in this strategy and leveraged more than $400 million for community development projects. These funds have helped create public-private partnerships in seventeen sites (mainly cities). Some of these partnerships are administered by local LISC offices or a community foundation, while others are independent.

Through these partnerships, resources from local and national funders have been channeled to more than 150 CDCs for general operating and technical support grants, which have helped them provide a wide range of services to their communities, including the construction or rehabilitation of affordable housing and the development of commercial, industrial, and retail space.

COMPREHENSIVE COMMUNITY
REVITALIZATION PROGRAM (CCRP)

In the 1960s and 1970s, residents, jobs, and community organizations migrated out of the South Bronx and many of the buildings were abandoned or destroyed by arson. In the 1980s, CDCs took the lead in physically redeveloping the area. Although these efforts were very successful, by the 1990s it was clear that the services and infrastructure in the neighborhoods also needed to be rebuilt. The Comprehensive Community Revitalization Program (CCRP) was an effort to address this need in four neighborhoods within the Bronx. Initiated by the Surdna Foundation in 1991, it ultimately received support from twenty-one corporations and foundations. The project chose a strong CDC in each of the four neighborhoods to act as the lead organization. Most of CCRP's resources were focused on providing staff—a project director to oversee the demonstration program, a CCRP manager at each CDC to run CCRP-related programs, and funding for an outreach worker at each site. A smaller amount of program money was also available, which could be committed quickly to pursue new opportunities. This flexible and easily accessible money enabled the CDCs to attract over $60 million in additional funds from other sources and ensure the stability of programs after the demonstration ended.

Each CDC created a neighborhood quality-of-life physical plan and strategic action plan for the future through focus groups, task forces, and annual community planning events. The CDCs implemented new programs as quickly as possible to ensure that the community saw tangible results and to maintain momentum toward the larger goals of the plan. New programs resulted in new primary health care practices, economic development, a Beacon school, employment resource centers, green space projects, and improved quality of life, while the CDCs continued to build and manage housing. In implementing these programs, the CDCs formed new relationships with one another at the local level and citywide.

In addition to having an impact on the target communities, CCRP fostered change in the way the participating CDCs work. As their role expanded, the CDCs grew substantially. To help alleviate the organizational pressures this created, CCRP funded technical assistance and made consultants available to the CDCs to help them with organizational development, as well as to analyze and undertake new program areas, to build their skills as conveners of the different community stakeholders, to build partnerships to help implement programs, and to keep community residents engaged in the CDCs' activities. In 1998, the initiative officially ended; the four CDCs created a new independent entity—CCRP, Inc.—to continue the work.

DEVELOPMENT TRAINING INSTITUTE

Founded in 1981 in Baltimore, the Development Training Institute (DTI) works to strengthen communities across the country by providing training and support to those engaged in community development and community building, including community-based organizations, financial institutions, foundations, and government. They offer a variety of training programs that range in intensity from single-day classes to workshops that meet regularly over weeks or months. They also provide personalized consulting and technical assistance on organizational development, personnel management, strategic planning, project development, and a variety of financial issues related to housing and economic development. Most of this is done on-site, but increasingly they offer on-line skills-building and training options. Through their Community Building Investment Program, community-based organizations and HUD-certified Community Housing Development Organizations (CHDOs) can apply for grants of up to $15,000 for organizational development uses such as purchasing computer equipment, sending staff to training, or hiring marketing, legal, or other professional services.

The Advanced Project Development Program is a five-week, twenty-five-day workshop designed to help staff of community-based organizations develop their skills at managing housing development. The Asset Management workshop helps participants assess possible housing development opportunities and maintain the value of their organization's existing properties. The Bank of America Leadership Academy meets for thirty days in four workshops over nine months. Also designed for managers of community-based organizations, the academy covers a wide variety of topics including leadership development, community planning, community building, community organizing, organizational development, board development, and fund-raising. In collaboration with the Philadelphia Neighborhood Development Collaborative and Eastern College, DTI is testing a local version of this national leadership academy in Philadelphia, called the Greater Philadelphia Leadership Academy, Management and Leadership in Community Building Certificate Program, which was launched in 1999.

DUDLEY STREET NEIGHBORHOOD
INITIATIVE

The Dudley Street Neighborhood Initiative (DSNI) is a neighborhood-based organization that formed in 1984 in response to widespread devastation and disinvestment in the Roxbury / North Dorchester area of Boston. Its core purpose is resident-led planning and organizing to realize the community's vision of a vibrant urban village. Its 1986 Don't Dump on Us campaign was DSNI's first communitywide organizing effort and resulted in action by the City of Boston to clean up vacant lots, enforce antidumping laws, and tow abandoned cars. As a result of DSNI's Take a Stand Own the Land organizing campaign, in 1988 the city granted eminent domain authority over vacant land within the central Dudley area known as the Dudley Triangle to the community. A $2 million low-interest Program Related Investment (PRI) loan from the Ford Foundation in 1992 allowed DSNI to use this authority to assemble parcels of private and city-owned land for new affordable housing development. From 1990 to 2000, primarily through partnerships with developers based on a DSNI-conducted community planning process, over two hundred units of new affordable housing have been built. DSNI has conducted extensive community processes around land use, planning and then partnering for development of community gardens and food production lots, parks and playgrounds, community facilities, parking lots, and commercial space.

DSNI created Dudley Neighbors Incorporated (DNI) as a community land trust to exercise the community's eminent domain authority and to acquire, own, and manage land on behalf of the community. DNI is separately governed by a board composed of six DSNI appointees and five representatives of public officials, two of whom are nonvoting members.

DSNI has developed a Resident Development Institute as well as various information and community thinking tools for informed resident decision-making. Its community change work includes youth development, organizing for better educational outcomes for neighborhood school children, community-building activities such as its annual Multicultural Festival, continuing campaigns to bring local trash transfer stations into compliance, urban agriculture, brownfields redevelopment, and other creative economic development activities.

DSNI is governed by a twenty-nine-member community-elected board. A total of sixteen seats are reserved for residents, with an equal number of seats designated for each of the neighborhood's major ethnic groups, African American, Cape Verdean, Latino, and white, with additional seats set aside for resident youth. Other elected seats are allocated to representatives of neighborhood stakeholders, human service agencies, CDCs, religious organizations, and small businesses.

DSNI's annual operating budget is over $1 million, a great proportion of which is provided by private foundations. DSNI is also one of the sites of the Annie E. Casey Foundation's Rebuilding Communities Initiative.

EMPOWERMENT ZONE AND ENTERPRISE COMMUNITIES

The federal government's Empowerment Zones and Enterprise Communities program (EZ/EC) began with legislation passed in Congress in 1993. This ten-year community development effort seeks to create jobs and business opportunities in the most economically distressed rural and inner city areas in the country.

One hallmark of the EZ/EC Initiative is its emphasis on community collaboration and decision-making and building relations among various levels of government and between government and communities. To this end, each community was encouraged to assemble community representatives, including residents, members of the nonprofit community, state and local government officials, and business people, to develop the application and complete a strategic plan. Each plan nominated one or more geographic target areas that met federally specified population and poverty criteria. Following a competitive selection process, the Department of Housing and Urban Development designated seventy-two urban areas and the Department of Agriculture designated thirty-three rural areas. Urban Empowerment Zones (Atlanta, Baltimore, Chicago, Detroit, New York, and Philadelphia/Camden) received $100 million each, while the rural Empowerment Zones (Kentucky Highlands, Mississippi Delta, and Rio Grande Valley) received $40 million each. As Supplemental Empowerment Zones, Los Angeles and Cleveland received a grant of $125 million and $90 million, respectively. In 1998, these two sites were made full Empowerment Zones with access to all of the tax incentives that that entails. Boston, Houston, Kansas City, and Oakland each received $25 million as Enhanced Enterprise Communities. The remaining ninety-three urban and rural areas were designated as Enterprise Communities and received $3 million each. In January 1999, a second round of fifteen Empowerment Zones was named, but full funding has not yet been allocated for them. In addition to grant monies, employers in the urban and rural Empowerment Zones are eligible for wage tax credits of $3,000 for every employee they hire who lives within the boundaries of the Empowerment Zone boundaries and may write off up to $20,000 more of equipment purchases than businesses not located in the EZ/EC.

Each site created a governance structure to oversee the implementation of the program. In some sites, this governance structure falls under the formal authority of an existing government agency. In other sites, a new organization was created or an existing nonprofit serves as the organizational auspice for governance of the zone. The structure and extent of resident and business participation in the governance of the Zones vary considerably.

Funded projects and activities differ widely across zones, but tend to focus primarily on economic opportunity, e.g., innovative financing strategies for business and real estate development, job and occupational skills training, and entrepreneurial and business support and assistance. Other common areas of focus include housing infrastructure, and children and senior care services.

HISTORICALLY BLACK COLLEGES
AND UNIVERSITIES INITIATIVE

The Historically Black Colleges and Universities program (HBCU) was initiated by Seedco in 1990. Seedco is a financing intermediary that provides funding and technical assistance to community development organizations, with a special focus on building community development partnerships between large higher education and / or health care institutions, and the low-income communities within which they are often located.

Seedco's HBCU program partnered Historically Black Colleges and Universities with CDCs to stimulate economic development in low-income Black communities through such activities as creating below-market housing, renovating historic structures, and working toward the creation of industrial parks to create manufacturing jobs for local residents. With funding from the Ford Foundation, the HBCU program initially supported five sites; by 1999 that number had grown to twenty-four. This program served as a model for a similar program sponsored by the United States Department of Housing and Urban Development (HUD).

HISTORIC EAST BALTIMORE COMMUNITY ACTION COALITION (HEBCAC)

The Historic East Baltimore Community Action Coalition (HEBCAC) is an umbrella organization serving neighborhoods in East Baltimore. In 1992, the mayor of Baltimore began an open community process to address issues of city redevelopment. A subcommittee was formed out of this process to focus on planning in East Baltimore. In 1995, this committee became HEBCAC.

HEBCAC is overseen by a sixteen-member board made up of representatives from different sectors of the community. Half of the members are residents who are elected to the board, including six residents representing twenty-four neighborhood organizations, a representative of the public housing tenant council serving the area, and a member of the council of neighborhood associations. The city is represented by the police commissioner, the deputy commissioner of the Housing Department, and the deputy commissioner of the Health Department because crime, housing, and health are areas of focus that are of particular interest to the board. In addition, the business association in the area elects a representative, the governor of Maryland appoints someone, and John Hopkins University fills three seats with a representative each from the school of medicine, the hospital, and the Kennedy-Krieger Institute. All of these representatives are full voting members and are viewed as speaking on behalf of their particular constituency. Board members sit on a variety of issues committees—such as land use, employment, economic development, and youth—and participate in a professionally facilitated annual retreat to determine the course of HEBCAC's work.

The role of the organization is to act as an intermediary between the community and outside resources as well as among the neighborhoods that make up its catchment area. It works to bring resources to the community, such as funding and technical assistance, that will help the community create and implement a strategic plan. Review by HEBCAC is part of the city's development and land use approval process. It negotiates among the different neighborhoods on the content of the community plan and the distribution of resources. It also identifies gaps in social services provided in the community and looks for agencies to fill those gaps. If there is no other agency available, HEBCAC oversees the service provision itself. For example, it manages a housing renovation program funded by HUD and a community policing program funded by the Department of Justice.

KANSAS CITY NEIGHBORHOOD ALLIANCE

The Kansas City Neighborhood Alliance (KCNA) was established in 1979 by the Civic Council of Greater Kansas City, an organization whose members are the CEOs of the city's one hundred largest corporations. The Council created KCNA to support Kansas City's communities by strengthening neighborhood associations and acting as an independent intermediary between them and the corporate, foundation, and public sectors. KCNA has four main goals: to develop and train grassroots leadership; to provide home ownership training for first-time home buyers; to develop affordable rental and for-sale housing units; and to implement geographically targeted community development efforts.

KCNA's Leadership Division offers a variety of programs and services to help build the skills of neighborhood leaders. A central piece of this work is the LeaderShip Program. The program, which began in 1991, works with six teams of leaders a year, each consisting of five members from the same neighborhood association. The organizations are expected to pay $25 per participant to cover materials. Organizations are chosen by KCNA staff based on their assessment of how representative the organizations are of their communities and of the organizations' ability to follow through on projects and produce results. Staff also try to choose organizations from different areas of the city for each session.

During the first year, participants develop the skills to manage their organizations and involve others from their community in their work. This training is structured around the process of developing a strategic plan for their organization. During the first quarter of the year, participants attend an overnight retreat and four Saturday morning sessions. Each team works on their strategic plan between these sessions, completing specific assignments in order to practice their skills. All of the teams report on their progress at each session. A final two-day retreat is held in the summer, during which teams present their completed plan, build additional leadership skills, and evaluate the training program. Graduates of the program, as well as staff, are available throughout to answer questions and provide support.

The teams are expected to implement their plan during the second year of the program and are encouraged to apply to the Neighborhood Self-Help Fund for money. More than twenty funders contribute to the Neighborhood Self-Help Fund, which provides grants to neighborhood-based organizations for small projects. In 1999–2000, the fund's sixteenth year, sixty-two neighborhood groups received a total of $134,000 in grants ranging from $380 to $4,600. Qualified proposals that come out of the Leader-Ship Program are given extra points in their review.

LOCAL INVESTMENT COMMISSION (LINC)

The Local Investment Commission (LINC) is a thirty-six-member citizen board founded in 1992 in order to reform the operations of the Missouri Department of Social Services (DSS) in Jackson County. Members are appointed by the DSS director and come from all parts of the region. They include business leaders, civic leaders, and neighborhood residents who serve as individual citizens, not as representatives of an organization or particular constituency. A Professional Cabinet made up of public agency staff and service providers plays an advisory role, but has no decision-making power. The day-to-day work is done by seventy full- and part-time staff and hundreds of volunteers who serve on ad hoc committees that work on program development.

In its work with DSS, LINC has reformed the agency's organizational structure, helped it connect to neighborhood resources, and established neighborhood-level DSS offices. It has since expanded its work into areas such as employment and training, health care, child care, housing, services for the elderly, and education. Two of these efforts are a Comprehensive Neighborhood Services initiative (CNS) and a number of welfare-to-work programs.

The goal of the CNS is to plan for and provide service delivery at the neighborhood level through a community-based site council made up of residents and service providers. This work involves sixty school sites. Schools are the hub of service delivery in each site. A large portion of the funding for CNS comes through Caring Communities, a statewide initiative that funds local community partnerships, which in turn fund selected schools and neighborhoods. LINC provides information, resources, and advice to the site council and works with them to raise additional funds to implement their programs.

LINC helped the Jackson County Division of Income Maintenance re-orient its work from income maintenance to employment assistance. Changes included providing support services to clients to help them keep the jobs in which they are placed and addressing transportation and child care issues when matching clients to jobs, rather than after placement. LINC also developed new performance-based contracts with local employment and training providers that expand the performance goals beyond the number of clients served to include indicators such as job retention.

In 1994, LINC formed a separate nonprofit organization called Greater K.C. LINC, Inc., which can apply for and receive a broader base of funding than LINC. This organization had a budget of $10.5 million in fiscal year 1999, most of which came from the state and provided both operational and project support. In addition, LINC provided monitoring and oversight for $2.63 million in funds from seven welfare-to-work contracts and three child welfare/domestic violence contracts. LINC calls this its "influence budget" because it does not have direct control over the monies, but can influence how they are spent. It also receives in-kind support from DSS in the form of space, equipment, and staff.

In 1995, the Missouri Family Investment Trust designated LINC as the state of Missouri's "community partner" for Jackson County. This designation allowed LINC to take a more comprehensive approach to its work while continuing to focus on children and families.

MDC, INC.

MDC, Inc. was established in 1967 to help North Carolina industrialize its economy and integrate its workforce. Since then, it has broadened its efforts and works with a variety of organizations and institutions in the South and nationally to design policies and programs that strengthen the workforce, foster economic development, and remove the barriers between people and jobs. MDC carries out much of this work by building the capacity of people in communities and institutions to conceive solutions for their communities themselves.

MDC's capacity-building work is designed and structured differently, depending on the communities and/or issues with which MDC is working. One form of this work is MDC's Rural Futures Program, a leadership development program that was launched in the 1980s in response to the need for new, rural economic development strategies in the South. The goal of the program is to develop cadres of leaders in rural counties or regions who understand how communities and economies work, and who have the skills to work across lines of race, class, and geography to make decisions collaboratively, to think and plan analytically, and to move from values-based vision to action. MDC implements the program in partnership with local or regional development organizations that continue to provide assistance to the leaders once the program is ended.

The structure of the program and MDC's role may vary significantly depending on the partners with which they are working; and MDC works with each to tailor the program to local needs and to identify and recruit community leaders to participate. Program partners have included the NC Rural Economic Development Center, the Penn Center for Preservation (St. Helena Island, South Carolina), the Glades Community Development Corporation (Belle Glade, Florida), Foundation for the Mid South, and Arkansas' Nonprofit Resources, Inc. MDC is currently adapting the program to an urban neighborhood setting in Fort Worth, Texas, in partnership with three community-based organizations and with support from the Burnett Foundation. MDC works intentionally to ensure that local partners are equipped with the capacity to continue ongoing support for the people who participate in the program and ideally are able to launch future "cycles" of the program themselves.

The program goes through a design phase during which MDC and its partner develop a conceptual framework that will help guide the program, a design that shapes the basic elements of MDC's approach to the scope and scale of the partner's needs, and a curriculum of specific training activities. The program begins with a multiday, off-site training session that focuses on team building, understanding the ideas outlined in the conceptual framework, and a discussion of the future direction of the program. Participants are given assignments to complete between sessions, and during the first phase they develop a multiyear plan. This portion of the work is structured by MDC's Moving from Vision to Action process, a nine-step planning process that begins with teams of community leaders identifying the underlying values that will guide the change effort. The teams then collect data on the current situation in their community and identify their strengths, weaknesses, opportunities, and threats. Using this information, they prioritize the issues that they believe are most urgent and create a vision for the future. The teams then set goals, identify the specific outcomes they want to achieve, and identify the actions they need to take to reach those outcomes. Next, they decide who needs to be involved, create a plan for implementing their actions, and define benchmarks to measure their progress. As groups are carrying out this strategic planning process, MDC is working with them intentionally to build their collaborative problem-solving skills within the community, and is exposing them to best practices in workforce and economic development. The goal is to produce plans that are both rooted in local creativity and informed by the best thinking nationally. As teams implement their plans, MDC and the local partner provide ongoing TA, which often focuses on negotiating the political environment in which their effort must take place.

NATIONAL COMMUNITY
DEVELOPMENT INITIATIVE

The National Community Development Initiative (NCDI) was inaugurated in 1991 through which a group of large philanthropic foundations and for-profit corporations sought to reinforce and expand the work of local CDCs. To date sixteen national funders and over 250 local partners have participated, including the United States Department of Housing and Urban Development. The funders recently decided to extend the program for an additional ten years.

NCDI seeks to boost the traditional CDC focus on community development by reinforcing the local institutional systems by which the work of CDCs is supported. Targeting specific CDC program goals is secondary to encouraging the development of diversified funding relationships for CDCs. NCDI has targeted twenty-three cities with multiple CDCs and seeks both to support the development of nascent CDCs and to reinforce and expand the scope of work of well-established CDCs. Such support has focused both on CDCs' capacity to develop housing and on efforts to diversify the work of CDCs to include other activities such as commercial retail development, child care, crime prevention, and moving from strictly rental housing production to owned housing production.

NCDI operates at three institutional levels: a national funding group, two intermediaries, and the CDCs. The funders' group maintains overall program oversight, sets broad funding principles, determines the total amount of funding to be allocated by each intermediary, and reviews the work plans of the intermediaries. Funders meet twice a year in a collaborative group with an annually elected chair. Decisions are typically made by consensus, but when consensus cannot be reached they are made on a one-vote-per-funder basis. Funding, in the form of grants and loan guarantees, has occurred over three phases with a planned ten-year funding level of $253.8 million: $152.5 million of that in loans and $101.3 million in the form of grants.

Rather than making grants and loans directly to CDCs, the funders work through two intermediary organizations, the Local Initiatives Support Corporation (LISC) and the Enterprise Foundation. Working through intermediaries eliminates the need to form a new organization for what was intended as a time-limited initiative, reduces overall administrative costs, and leverages the significant community development expertise, experience, and internal capacity of LISC and the Enterprise Foundation.

The role of the intermediary organizations is to translate the broad NCDI program goals established by the funders into specific programs tailored to the needs of each site. They do this in collaboration with local supporting institutions (banks, corporations, local foundations, and local government) with the goal of developing strong local systems of support for CDCs. The national funders approve intermediary work plans for each city. The intermediaries then identify and make grants and loans to suitable CDCs. Although local programs vary among the twenty-three sites, all incorporate efforts to build the capacity of participating CDCs and to diversify their funding base.

NEIGHBORHOOD DEVELOPMENT
SUPPORT COLLABORATIVE

Begun in 1986 as a five-year effort, the Neighborhood Development Support Collaborative (NDSC) is a program of LISC. Initiated by the Boston LISC office and other local funders, including the United Way, NDSC grew from the recognition that organizational development assistance was needed to help Boston's CDCs more effectively utilize the real estate loans that are the backbone of traditional CDC assistance.

In its first round of funding, NDSC made grants averaging $50,000 over three years to assist ten well-established Community Development Corporations in the Boston area. In 1991, similar assistance was extended to five more CDCs, bringing total funding for this round to $4.5 million.

NDSC initially worked with established CDCs to develop strategic plans, build organizational capacity to implement and manage larger and more complex housing development projects, and assist in establishing secure and diversified funding. In an effort to connect CDCs to local, secure funding streams, NDSC played a promotional and brokering role, educating potential funders about the work of CDCs in local communities, providing forums for funders and CDC staff to meet, and encouraging collaborations across funding and assistance sectors (i.e., government, private, and foundation). One success of this first round of activity was the establishment of direct United Way funding relationships for many of the CDCs that completed the program.

In 1993, a second round of funding was secured to build on the basic approach of Round One. In Round Two, NDSC evolved in scope and complexity. It expanded its intermediary role through a number of strategic partnerships that have allowed it to offer a broader range of assistance specifically tailored to the needs of a more diverse set of CDCs across a wider territory.

And NDSC has focused greater resources on the goal of helping CDCs target their activities to community needs and priorities, in part through better understanding and utilizing community organizing strategies.

With support from the federal Americorps program and the National Congress for Community Economic Development (NCCED), NDSC also introduced a Human Capital Development Initiative. It works to increase the pool of CDC professional talent by recruiting people, often recent high school graduates, from within CDC neighborhoods and employing them for a year doing staff work at the CDC. It also helps CDCs build staff capacity and recruit new staff, particularly staff of color. Through June 1998, the program supplied thirty Americorps volunteers to fifteen CDCs, fulfilling immediate CDC labor needs while introducing neighborhood people to careers in community development. And it offered capitalization grants and loans in order to increase liquidity and facilitate new programs and development.

NDSC, now in Round Three (1999–2001), continues the human capital and community-organizing programs. Capacity-building assistance is targeted to emerging CDCs and CDCs going through critical transitions. In this round, NDSC also encourages collaboration among CDCs with overlapping service areas and programming.

NDSC functions as an unincorporated collaborative of funders, with a subgroup of eleven core funders forming a steering committee. The steering committee sets overall policy and reviews operations. The entire collaborative is composed of close to twenty funders, including local and national foundations, the City of Boston, private lenders, and two other intermediary funding organizations. NDSC is operated by Boston LISC with full-time staffing provided by an NDSC staff director and program officer, and administrative and programming support shared with Boston LISC.

NEIGHBORHOOD LEADERSHIP CLEVELAND

Neighborhood Leadership Cleveland (NLC) is a training program for community leaders supported by the Center for Neighborhood Development at the Urban Center of Cleveland State University, in partnership with the Neighborhood Centers Association, which has twenty-one settlement houses and neighborhood centers across the greater Cleveland Area. The Center for Neighborhood Development provides technical assistance, information, training, and other services to neighborhood-based organizations. NLC has graduated a total of 197 community residents between 1994 and 2000. The program is funded by a variety of foundation grants, as well as through the Community Outreach Partnership Center, a HUD initiative, which provides support for residents of Cleveland's Empowerment Zone to participate in the program.

The objectives of the NLC are to build on the existing skills and experience of neighborhood leaders; to increase neighborhood leaders' knowledge of the critical issues facing Cleveland's neighborhoods, the city, and the region; to enhance the ability of neighborhood leaders to use conflict resolution and community organizing to resolve problems within their neighborhoods; and to help leaders establish networks among themselves, as well as with other neighborhoods and institutions.

Two classes of thirty to thirty-five neighborhood leaders participate in the program each year. Most participants are associated with at least one neighborhood organization, but participate as individuals rather than as representatives of particular organizations. Selection is on a first-come–first-served basis, with some reference given to those who are referred by program graduates. There is no fee charged to participants.

The program begins with an overnight retreat where participants get to know one another and begin to identify the issues they want to address in their community. The remaining three-hour weekly sessions focus on topics such as understanding a neighborhood's assets and setting goals for the neighborhood; the different roles and relationships that make up a community; a historical overview of Cleveland's neighborhoods; community organizing; the macrolevel forces that have an impact on Cleveland and its neighborhoods; community resources and technology; group process, public speaking skills, and meeting facilitation; and personal goal setting. Each participant is required to plan a forty-minute tour of his or her neighborhood, which is included in an all-day bus tour of participant neighborhoods in one of the later sessions. In addition, participants are divided into four working groups to prepare a presentation on the neighborhood issues that are important to them, and each participant is asked to identify his or her goals for the next year and submit a personal plan. The program coordinator is available to help participants implement their plan, even after the program has ended.

Two additional programs have emerged out of NLC. Neighborhood leaders meet monthly in the Greater Cleveland Neighborhood Forum, which was formed by graduates of NLC to exchange information about their community activities and participate in seminars. In addition, during June 1999 the Center for Neighborhood Development held a Summer Institute, a series of workshops and seminars for the staff and board members of local community development corporations and other nonprofit organizations, community volunteers, graduates of Neighborhood Leadership Cleveland, and other neighborhood leaders. NLC graduates could attend portions of the institute for half price.

NEIGHBORHOOD PARTNERS INITIATIVE

The Neighborhood Partners Initiative was launched in 1996 by the Edna McConnell Clark Foundation as part of its Program for New York Neighborhoods. The seven-year project aims to produce concrete, ongoing, sustainable improvements in living conditions within small targeted neighborhoods in New York City.

The initiative grew out of the foundation's research showing that a disproportionate percentage of homelessness in New York originates and is concentrated within certain low-income neighborhoods, including the South Bronx and Harlem. These neighborhoods are also beset by a deteriorating infrastructure, faltering schools, a lack of affordable housing, and a host of other persistent challenges whose roots lie in a tangle of failed policies and changing markets. To deal with the complex challenges facing urban neighborhoods, the initiative works with local agencies, strengthening their capacity to create specific, measurable improvements within geographically limited areas by improving their services and engaging in grassroots community organizing. The strategy is to make big changes in small communities.

Through a competitive application process, NPI selected five community-based organizations to lead the initiative: Abyssinian Development Corporation, a Harlem CDC; Rheedlen Centers for Children and Families, a multiservice agency in Harlem; Bronx ACORN, an organizing group in the South Bronx; Mid-Bronx Senior Citizens Council, a South Bronx CDC; and Highbridge Community Life Center, a South Bronx multiservice agency. Each organization works with residents and institutions in a three- to ten-block area in Central Harlem and the South Bronx, each having a population of 1,400 to 5,000, and a median income ranging from about $9,500 to nearly $16,000. With a high degree of resident leadership and participation, these agencies identify and implement strategies that target tangible, neighborhood-level results such as renovated housing, greater resident employment, decreased street crime, and more responsive public systems.

The work of the initiative is marked by three distinct phases. In Phase I, start-up, July 1996 through March 1998, the five lead agencies convened a broad group of residents and representatives from neighborhood institutions to identify priorities for neighborhood improvements and to develop effective local strategies for making those improvements. The goals and strategies articulated by these groups serve as a plan for future action at each site.

During Phase II, capacity building, which began in April 1998 and is expected to continue through spring 2001, the lead agencies are implementing neighborhood improvement strategies. At the same time, resident groups are developing their capacity to perform community-led community-building work.

Phase III, completion, begins in 2001 and concludes in 2003. During this phase, the lead agencies will continue to work to bring about the improvements sought by their communities while strengthening their own institutional capacity. By the conclusion of the program, these agencies should have the organizational capacity to continue the work of community building in the future and to sustain that work with effective community support, and resident groups are expected to have become robust and effective in working to improve neighborhood conditions.

The foundation supports the work of the initiative through grants to the lead agencies, enabling them to fund staff positions for the project, to better manage and implement their programmatic and resident-organizing strategies, and to address key organizational issues that will help them to work more effectively in their neighborhoods over time. Additional NPI grants provide technical assistance, fund documentation and evaluation efforts, and advance the priorities of the five neighborhoods.

NEIGHBORHOOD REVITALIZATION PROGRAM

The Minneapolis Neighborhood Revitalization Program (NRP) emerged out of a growing concern with the decline of Minneapolis neighborhoods in the mid-1980s. In 1987, the mayor and City Council launched a task force charged with identifying potential new funding sources for neighborhood revitalization. This task force, made up of business and community and civic groups, with significant representation from private and nonprofit developers, estimated the cost of physically redeveloping neighborhoods in Minneapolis at $3 billion and recommended that the problem be addressed through a citywide planning effort, initiated by the city with the intense involvement of neighborhood residents.

In May 1989, the Implementation Advisory Committee presented a Twenty-Year Revitalization Plan that outlined a detailed neighborhood planning process. Based on this plan, the Minnesota Legislature and the City Council established the NRP and dedicated $20 million a year for twenty years to fund it. Funding for the program comes from the revenue of several tax increment financing districts, which is pooled together and managed by the Minneapolis Community Development Agency, the housing and economic redevelopment arm of the City of Minneapolis.

NRP is governed by a nineteen-member Policy Board made up of representatives from the neighborhoods, the five governing jurisdictions of NRP (the city, the county, the public schools, parks, and libraries), and other community interests. This group provides the overall direction for the program and has primary responsibility for the review and approval of Neighborhood Action Plans. The Management Review Team, made up of neighborhood residents and senior managers from the five jurisdictions, coordinates staff involvement and manages the review, approval, and implementation of Neighborhood Action Plans.

NRP has four primary goals in addition to redeveloping neighborhoods. First, neighborhoods work to build the knowledge and skills of community residents so that they can organize themselves and meet their community's needs. Second, the program provides a forum for neighborhoods to voice concerns to public officials and government staff, particularly about budget priorities and service delivery. Third, NRP provides a mechanism for better communication and coordination of services among the five local government jurisdictions. Finally, by creating a place for neighborhood residents to work together, NRP hopes to enhance the residents' sense of community.

NRP began with six neighborhoods in February 1991. In January 1995, seventy-nine of the city's eighty-one neighborhoods were involved in the program. Participating neighborhoods work with NRP staff to develop and implement their Neighborhood Action Plan. First, the neighborhood must submit a Participation Agreement to the NRP that outlines the work plan and budget for the neighborhood's planning process. The agreement must detail how the neighborhood will elect an NRP steering committee, involve the community in the planning process, gather information, define neighborhood issues and opportunities, and structure the meetings and events through which they will develop their plan. When the agreement is accepted, the neighborhood begins its planning process. Once a draft plan is completed, it is submitted to neighborhood residents and other stakeholders for approval, and then to the NRP's Management Review Team and the Policy Board. The neighborhood steering committee, working with NRP staff, government staff, businesses, and nonprofit organizations in the community, implements the plan.

NORTHWEST BRONX COMMUNITY
AND CLERGY COALITION

The Northwest Bronx Community and Clergy Coalition (NWBCCC) is a formal affiliation of ten neighborhood associations. The coalition's mission is to "provide structures through which neighborhood residents can define and act upon common problems." The sixteen-member NWBCCC board is composed of one representative from each of the member neighborhood associations and six at-large clergy seats. NWBCCC provides administrative and coordinating functions for issues of relevance across neighborhood association jurisdictions, but important decisions around key campaign issues are made by the residents involved in campaign committees and in the neighborhood associations. Resident (primarily tenant) organizing around particular issues provides NWBCCC's power base. One-to-one recruitment (such as knocking on doors) forms the leading edge of the organizing strategy; institutional outreach, through such groups as religious congregations and parent associations, augments individual-level outreach.

NWBCCC conducts long-term work, organized by standing committees, on issues such as safety, housing, education, and environmental justice. For example, the Housing Committee works to ensure that local rental properties are well maintained and up to code. Code enforcement activities include assisting residents in clearly articulating housing complaints to New York City's Department of Housing Preservation and Development (HPD) and following up to make sure that HPD responds with effective enforcement. Enforcement monitoring includes meeting with HPD senior administrators to communicate needs and expectations, and then following up to make sure that commitments made result in action. The Housing Committee has also brought pressure to bear on landlords by organizing pressure on the banks holding landlords' mortgages to enforce the "good repair clauses" of their mortgages. Such pressure is sometimes achieved by arranging resident meetings with bank officers and sometimes involves working through political officials at all levels.

NWBCC is also a member of the Parent Organizing Consortium (POC), which is working to create a citywide group of parent leaders to whom public officials feel accountable and who are able to effect policy change around education issues such as class size reduction, overcrowding, and facilities improvement and construction. POC uses strategically designed direct actions and campaigns to pressure public officials and politicians to change policy, in particular where it affects low-performing schools in low-income neighborhoods.

NWBCCC's ability to successfully address such issues is the result of ongoing attention to resident organization, issues education, and leadership training, as well as actively maintaining relationships with the public and private officials.

PARTNERSHIP FOR NEIGHBORHOODS
INITIATIVE (PNI)

The Partnership for Neighborhood Initiative (PNI) was a five-year demonstration project that began in 1995 in Palm Beach County, Florida. The purpose of the initiative was to engage in community development by involving residents and neighborhood groups in reforming the delivery of health and human services within the pilot communities. The initiative was governed by a Steering Committee composed of representatives from each of thirteen funders, including both private foundations and a variety of public agencies, in an effort to integrate these different funding streams. A project director oversaw the day-to-day operations of the initiative, including the work of three organizers and an administrative assistant.

The communities for the initiative were chosen through a competitive application process that involved both the staff and the Steering Committee. Low-income neighborhoods with no fewer than five hundred and no more than five thousand residents were eligible to apply. The communities selected were chosen based on the level of resident involvement in the application process and the proposed plan, the extent to which they have a broad base of community representation, the quality of their plan for outreach and consensus-based decision-making, the level of collaboration among participants, and the strength of the existing networks among residents and groups in the neighborhood.

Three communities were chosen in Palm Beach County. An unincorporated area west of the City of Lake Worth, with a population of approximately one thousand, is the smallest site; Delray Beach targets the southwest section of that city; and the South Bay site encompasses that entire city, with a population of just over four thousand.

The activities of the initiative varied across the communities. In Lake Worth, there was a focus on crime, particularly drug activity and prostitution. Delray Beach focused largely on the needs of senior citizens, such as providing access to transportation, and on youth development. Employment, education, and a gathering place for children, youth, and families were identified as needs in South Bay.

PEOPLE UNITED FOR A BETTER OAKLAND (PUEBLO)

Formally named in 1990, PUEBLO emerged from a 1989 organizing campaign of parents seeking a more aggressive county level public health agency response to an outbreak of measles. In 1999, PUEBLO became a legally independent nonprofit organization. It is one of two affiliate organizations [along with Denver Action for a Better Community (Denver ABC)] of the Center for Third World Organizing (CTWO), an organizing intermediary that seeks to improve the life conditions of low-income people of color through community organizing, addressing grievances arising from a broader foundation of racial and ethnic oppression.

PUEBLO is involved in a long-term effort to increase police accountability to the community through civilian review procedures, including organizing to strengthen this process. A citizens' review board, in place since 1981, now has subpoena power, has a full-time investigator on staff, and operates through open, public meetings. It successfully organized residents living near two large manufacturing businesses, winning agreements from American Brass and Iron Foundry and the Owens Brockway Glass Company to significantly reduce airborne emissions. And it emphasizes youth inclusion and leadership development, with the auxiliary group Youth of Oakland United (YOU) devoted to organizing activities among those ages of twelve and twenty-one. YOU was central to one of PUEBLO's recent, major campaigns, the Kids First ballot initiative (Measure K) through which Oakland voters agreed in 1996 to set aside 2.5 percent of the City's general fund (above and beyond the existing youth budget) over twelve years for youth programs.

PUEBLO's general membership numbers over six hundred families who pay annual membership dues of $24 for adults or an entire household and $12 for youth and seniors. Regular meetings can count on a core of about fifty regular participants. General membership meetings occur every other month in concert with the meeting of the PUEBLO board in order to emphasize board accountability to the general membership. The eleven-member board meets monthly. At least five of the eleven board members are drawn from low-income communities, and criteria of racial, ethnic, generational, and gender diversity are considered in constituting the board.

Because PUEBLO works with racially and ethnically diverse constituencies, the general membership meetings provide occasion for developing intercultural experiences and coalitions. Toward that end, meetings sometimes feature cultural learning around the experiences and traditions of one of the ethnic communities present. For example, the Mexican Day of the Dead may open a discussion about how death is understood and ceremonially elaborated within the cultures of other PUEBLO members present.

STEANS FAMILY FOUNDATION

In 1995, the Steans Family Foundation (SFF), located in Chicago, decided to target a single neighborhood for its grant-making and community revitalization efforts. The west side community of North Lawndale was chosen for its high, unmet need and significant assets upon which to build: the neighborhood's strategic location west of downtown, combined with available transportation, a large, untapped labor force, and plentiful vacant land contribute to its vast potential for positive growth.

Once a thriving Jewish and, later, African-American community, North Lawndale underwent massive disinvestment in the 1950s and 1960s. Many residents and businesses, lured away by the GI Bill and other incentives, left the community, and the 1968 race riots and fires contributed to further population and commercial decline.

SFF's work in North Lawndale consists of a ten-year commitment (now in its fifth year) based on the following principles: fostering resident participation and ownership of neighborhood change; building on the individual and organizational assets that exist in the community; supporting and promoting leadership in the community; strengthening networks and connections among individuals and organizations; and strengthening the community's connections to outside resources.

To that end, the foundation works comprehensively in North Lawndale, with foci on Economic Development, Education/Youth, Family & Community Asset Building, Health & Human Services, Housing, and Quality of Life/Leadership Development. Grantees work to utilize and strengthen existing resources in the community.

Projects that have developed from these focus areas include the development of a charter school to serve motivated, college-bound students in North Lawndale, the opening of a second free tax preparation site in the community to assist residents in claiming the Earned Income Credit, and the establishment of a resident-managed community newsletter. In addition, SFF has been instrumental in the development of several networks, most notably the North Lawndale Learning Community, a coalition of local public schools, and the North Lawndale Employment Network, which works in partnership with employers, community-based organizations, service providers and residents to address the community's workforce development needs.

Because the foundation recognizes its ability to serve the community in a variety of ways, it functions as a capacity builder, convener/catalyst, community advocate, incubator, leverager, and grant maker. Program officers work directly with community-based organizations, public institutions, local government, and residents; unsolicited grant requests are not accepted. In calendar year 2000, the foundation plans to award over $2.5 million in grants, 97 percent of which will benefit North Lawndale's schools, institutions, CBOs, and residents directly.

UNITED NEIGHBORHOOD HOUSES

The settlement house movement in the United States began in 1886, with the establishment of the Neighborhood Guild (later renamed University Settlement) on the Lower East Side of New York City. Modeled after London's Toynbee Hall, American settlements sought to upgrade the quality of life in low-income, predominantly immigrant neighborhoods of the city by providing a range of social services related to such things as health, recreation, job training, and general American acculturation. In 1919, the United Neighborhood Houses of New York (UNH) was formed as an intermediary institution serving a federated group of dozens of settlement houses in New York City.

In 2000, with a full-time paid staff of over twenty, UNH supports the work of its thirty-seven member settlements by fund-raising, conducting public advocacy campaigns on shared issues, training staff, providing organizational development assistance, and engaging in program planning, assessment, and evaluation, including coordinating intersettlement programming.

UNH's advocacy work includes public policy and budget analysis, providing legislative testimony, working with other service and advocacy groups toward common goals, and meeting with public and elected officials. Current advocacy efforts seek to increase the availability of quality child-care services, create family centered welfare-to-work strategies, establish after-school and weekend places supporting the healthy growth and development of school-age youth, and enhancing immigrant support services, including citizenship programs.

UNH also prepares individuals to be active and effective citizens. In addition to voter registration drives, the UNH-assembled Civic Education Tool Kit explains the structure and responsibilities of different levels of government, provides information and strategies for contacting elected and public agency officials, and lists a range of other resources relevant to the local neighborhood participants.

UNH has addressed the need for quality child care affordable to low-income families by reaching out to the existing collection of small, independent, home-based child-care providers within low-income communities, helping them to meet and exceed the standards enforced by the New York state and municipal government. Through on-site technical assistance, UNH helps independent child care providers meet legal, health, safety, and nutrition standards, enhance educational offerings, borrow appropriate books and toys, participate with the children they care for in settlement house–based programs such as gym or arts classes, and upgrade their professional skills. By taking part in the UNH-sponsored assistance programs, the neighborhood-based, independent care providers become part of the UNH network, enabling them to enroll children whose parents or other caretakers have learned about the providers through settlement house referrals.

UNH enhances programs at individual settlements by coordination of resources across UNH members. For example, the Settlement Arts Consortium joins the efforts of arts staff across settlement houses in order to share ideas and programming, increase collaborations with other arts institutions, and provide a greater range and depth of arts programming across the UNH settlement neighborhoods.

Acronyms

ABC	Action for a Better Community, Denver
ACORN	Association of Community Organizations for Reform Now
ACT	All Congregations Together
BGCA	Boys and Girls Clubs in America
BUILD	Baltimoreans United in Leadership Development
CBI	Community Building Initiative
CBO	community-based organization
CCC	Center for Community Change
CCI	comprehensive community initiative
CCRP	Comprehensive Community Revitalization Program
CDBG	Community Development Block Group
CDC	community development corporation
CHA	Chicago Housing Authority
CHDO	Community Housing and Development Organizations
CNS	Comprehensive Neighborhood Services
CODP	Consensus Organizing Demonstration Program
COI	Consensus Organizing Institute
COPS	Communities Organized for Public Service
CRA	Community Reinvestment Act
CTWO	Center for Third World Organizing
DMC	Detroit Medical Center
DNFI	Detroit Neighborhood Family Initiative
DNI	Dudley Neighbors Incorporated
DSNI	Dudley Street Neighborhood Initiative
DSS	Department of Social Services, Missouri
DTI	Development Training Institute
EC	Enterprise Community
EDGE	Enterprise Development for Glades Entrepreneurs
EZ	Empowerment Zone
EZCC	Empowerment Zone Coordinating Council
EZGC	Empowerment Zone Governance Council
GCDC	Glades Community Development Corporation
GIN	Glades Interagency Network
HBCU	Historically Black Colleges and Universities

249

HEBCAC	Historic East Baltimore Community Action Coalition
HIPPY	Home Instruction Program for Preschool Youngsters
HOPI	Harambee Ombudsman Project Inc.
HPD	Department of Housing Preservation and Development, New York City
HUD	Housing and Urban Development, U.S. Department of
IAF	Industrial Areas Foundation
ISO	Intermediary Support Organization
JTPA	Job Training Partnership Act
KCNA	Kansas City Neighborhood Alliance
LINC	Local Investment Commission
LISC	Local Initiative Support Corporation
MDC	MDC, Inc.
MLKEDC	Martin Luther King Economic Development Corporation
NCCED	National Congress for Community Economic Development
NCDI	National Community Development Initiative
NDSC	Neighborhood Development Support Collaborative
NFI	Neighborhood and Family Initiative
NHI	North Hartford Initiative
NLC	Neighborhood Leadership Cleveland
NMIDC	Northeast Milwaukee Industrial Development Corporation
NPI	Neighborhood Partners Initiative
NRP	Neighborhood Revitalization Program
NTIC	National Training and Information Center
NWBCCC	Northwest Bronx Community and Clergy Coalition
NWRO	National Welfare Rights Organization
OMDC	Orange Mound Development Corporation
PNI	Partnership for Neighborhood Initiative
POC	Parent Organizing Consortium
PRI	program-related investment
PTA	Parent-Teacher Association
PUEBLO	People United for a Better Oakland Organization
SFF	Steans Family Foundation
TA	technical assistance
UANC	Upper Albany Neighborhood Collaborative
UNH	United Neighborhood Houses
YOU	Youth of Oakland United

References

Ackoff, R. (1994). *The Democratic Corporation*. New York: Oxford University Press.

Ahlbrandt, R. S. (1984). *Neighborhoods, People, and Communities*. New York: Plenum.

Alter, C., and J. Hage (1993). *Organizations Working Together*. Newbury Park: Sage Library of Social Research.

Aspen Institute (1996). *Measuring Community Capacity Building: A Workbook in Progress for Rural Communities*. Washington, DC: Aspen Institute Rural Economic Policy Program.

Aspen Institute (2000). Measures for community research. Available [on-line]: www.aspenroundtable.org.

Aspen Institute and Fulbright-Anderson, K., A. C. Kubisch, and J. P. Connell (Eds.) (1998). *New Approaches to Evaluating Community Initiatives*, Vol. 2: *Theory, Measurement, and Analysis*. Washington, DC: Aspen Institute.

Bass, B. M. (1990). *Bass & Stogdill's Handbook of Leadership: Theory, Research, and Managerial Applications*, 3rd ed. New York: Free Press.

Berger, P. L., and R. J. Neuhaus (1977). *To Empower People: The Role of Mediating Structures in Public Policy*. Washington, DC: American Enterprise Institute for Public Policy Research.

Berry, J. M., K. E. Portney, and K. Thomson (1993). *The Rebirth of Urban Democracy*. Washington, DC: Brookings Institution.

Briggs, X. N. D., E. R. Mueller, and M. Sullivan (1997). *From Neighborhood to Community: Evidence on the Social Effects of Community Development Corporations*. New York: Community Development Research Center.

Brown, P. (1995). *Settlement Houses Today: Their Community-Building Role*. Report for United Neighborhood Houses of New York. Chicago: Chapin Hall Center for Children at the University of Chicago.

Brown, P., A. Branch, and J. Lee (1999). *Neighborhood Partners Initiative: The Startup*. Chicago: Chapin Hall Center for Children at the University of Chicago.

Brown, P., B. Butler, and R. Hamilton (in press). *Review of the Sandtown-Winchester Neighborhood Transformation Initiative*. Baltimore: Annie E. Casey Foundation and the Enterprise Foundation.

Brown, P., and S. Garg (1997). *Foundations and Comprehensive Community Initiatives: The Challenges of Partnership*. Chicago: Chapin Hall Center for Children at the University of Chicago.

Brown, P., J. Pitt, and J. Hirota (1999). *New Approaches to Technical Assistance: The Role of the Coach*. Chicago: Chapin Hall Center for Children at the University of Chicago.

Brown, P., and P. Stetzer (1998). *Glades Community Development Corporation: A*

Chronicle of a Community Development Intermediary. Chicago: Chapin Hall Center for Children at the University of Chicago.

Bruner, C. (1998). *From Community-Based to Community-Staffed: The Experiences of Three Allegheny County Family Centers in Community Hiring.* Pittsburgh: Office of Child Development, University of Pittsburgh.

Burns, J. M. (1978). *Leadership.* New York: Harper and Row.

Burns, T., and G. Spilka (1984). *The Planning Phase of the Rebuilding Communities Initiative.* Philadelphia: OMG.

Bursik, R. J., and H. Grasmick (1993). *Neighborhoods and Crime: The Dimensions of Effective Community Control.* New York: Lexington.

Burt, R. S. (1992). *Structural Holes: The Social Construction of Competition.* Cambridge, MA: Harvard University Press.

Campbell, K. E., and B. A. Lee (1992). Sources of personal neighbor networks: Social integration, need or time? *Social Forces* 70(4), 1077–1100.

Center for Community Change (1993). Organizing around the church. *Community Change* (Winter, special issue), 1–4.

Charles Stewart Mott Foundation (1994). Neighborhood organizing: Nurturing strong, unified voices. *Charles Stewart Mott Foundation 1994 Annual Report.* Flint, MI: Author.

Chaskin, R. J. (1992). *The Ford Foundation's Neighborhood and Family Initiative: Toward a Model of Comprehensive, Neighborhood-Based Development.* Chicago: Chapin Hall Center for Children at the University of Chicago.

Chaskin, R. J. (1997). Perspectives on neighborhood and community: A review of the literature. *Social Service Review* 71(4), 521–47.

Chaskin, R. J. (2000). *Decision Making and Action at the Neighborhood Level: An Exploration of Mechanisms and Process.* Chicago: Chapin Hall Center for Children at the University of Chicago.

Chaskin, R. J. (forthcoming). Building community capacity: A definitional framework and implications from a comprehensive community initiative. *Urban Affairs Review.*

Chaskin, R. J., and A. Abunimah (1999). A view from the city: Local government perspectives on neighborhood-based governance in community-building initiatives. *Journal of Urban Affairs* 21(1), 57–78.

Chaskin, R. J., S. Chipenda-Dansokho, and M. L. Joseph (1997). *The Ford Foundation's Neighborhood and Family Initiative: The Challenge of Sustainability: An Interim Report.* Chicago: Chapin Hall Center for Children at the University of Chicago.

Chaskin, R. J., S. Chipenda-Dansokho, and C. J. Richards (1999). *The Neighborhood and Family Initiative: Entering the Final Phase.* Chicago: Chapin Hall Center for Children at the University of Chicago.

Chaskin, R. J., and S. Garg (1997). The issue of governance in neighborhood-based initiatives. *Urban Affairs Review* 32(5), 631–61.

Chaskin, R. J., and M. L. Joseph (1995). *The Ford Foundation's Neighborhood and Family Initiative: Moving Toward Implementation.* Chicago: Chapin Hall Center for Children at the University of Chicago.

Chaskin, R. J., and R. Ogletree (1993). *The Ford Foundation's Neighborhood and Family Initiative: Building Collaboration: An Interim Report.* Chicago: Chapin Hall Center for Children at the University of Chicago.

Chavis, D. M., and A. Wandersman (1990). Sense of community in the urban environment: A catalyst for participation and community development. *American Journal of Community Psychology 18*(1), 55–81.

Chrislip, D., and C. E. Larson (1994). *Collaborative Leadership: How Citizens and Civic Leaders Can Make a Difference.* San Francisco: American Leadership Forum Series, Jossey-Bass.

Clay, P. (1990, 1993, 1997). Unpublished reports for the Neighborhood Development Support Collaborative, Boston.

Coleman, J. S. (1988). Social capital in the creation of human capital. *American Journal of Sociology 94,* 95–120.

Community Building Initiative (1994). *Program Announcement.* Local Initiatives Support Corporation.

Connell, J. P., A. C. Kubisch, L. B. Schorr, and C. H. Weiss (Eds.) (1995). *New Approaches to Evaluating Community Initiatives: Concepts, Methods, and Contexts.* New York: Aspen Institute.

Crenshaw, E., and C. St. John (1989). The organizationally dependent community: A comparative study of neighborhood attachment. *Urban Affairs Quarterly 24*(3), 412–33.

Crenson, M. A. (1983). *Neighborhood Politics.* Cambridge, MA: Harvard University Press.

Cummings, T., and C. Worley (1997). *Organizational Development and Change,* 6th ed. Cincinnati, OH: South-Western College Publishing.

Davis, A. F. (1984). *Spearheads of Reform: The Social Settlements and the Progressive Movement, 1890–1914.* New Brunswick, NJ: Rutgers University Press.

Delgado, G. (1994). *Beyond the Politics of Place: New Directions in Community Organizing in the 1990s.* Oakland, CA: Applied Research Center.

DiMaggio, P. J., and W. W. Powell (1983). The iron cage revisited: Institutional isomorphism and collective rationality in organizational fields. *American Sociological Review 48,* 147–60.

Eichler, M. (1998). Look to the future, learn from the past. *Shelterforce* (September / October), 24–28.

Eichler, M., and D. Hoffman (n.d.). *Strategic Engagements: Building Community Capacity by Building Relationships.* Boston, MA: Consensus Organizing Institute.

Ellerman, D. (1998). *Knowledge-Based Development Institutions.* Washington DC: World Bank.

Fawcett, S., A. Paine-Andrews, V. T. Fransisco, J. A. Schultz, K. P. Richter, R. K. Lewis, E. L. Williams, K. J. Harris, J. Y. Berkley, J. L. Fisher, and C. M Lopez (1995). Using empowerment theory in collaborative partnerships for community health and development. *American Journal of Community Psychology 23*(5), 677–69.

Ferguson, R. F. (1999). Conclusion: Social science research, urban problems, and community development alliances. In R. Ferguson and T. Dickey (Eds.), *Urban Problems and Community Development* (pp. 569–620). Washington, DC: Brooking Institution Press.

Ferguson, R. F., and S. E. Stoutland (1999). Reconceiving the community development field. In R. Ferguson and W. T. Dickey (Eds.), *Urban Problems and Community Development* (pp. 33–76). Washington, DC: Brooking Institution Press.

Fisher, R. (1981). From grass-roots organizing to community service: Community organization practice in the community center movement, 1907–1930. In R. Fisher and P. Romanofsky (Eds.), *Community Organization for Social Change: A Historical Perspective* (pp. 33–58). Westport, CT: Greenwood.

Fisher, R. (1994). *Let the People Decide: Neighborhood Organizing in America.* New York: Twayne.

Ford Foundation (1964). *Public Affairs: Gray Areas Program.* Review Paper No. 002845. New York: Ford Foundation Archives.

Ford Foundation (1996). *Perspectives on Partnerships: A Report on the Ford Foundation's Community Development Partnership Strategy.* New York: Ford Foundation.

Freundenburg, W. R. (1986). The density of acquaintanceship. *American Journal of Sociology 92*, 27–63.

Frieden, B. J., and M. Kaplan (1975). *The Politics of Neglect: Urban Aid from Model Cities to Revenue Sharing.* Cambridge, MA: MIT Press.

Furstenberg, F. (1993). How families manage risk and opportunity in dangerous neighborhoods. In W. J. Wilson (Ed.), *Sociology and the Public Agenda.* Newbury Park, CA: Sage.

Gardner, John W. (1990). *On Leadership.* New York: Free Press.

Gittell, M., K. Newman, and I. Ortega (1995). *Building Civic Capacity: Best CDC Practices.* Paper presented at the Annual Urban Affairs Association Conference, Portland, Oregon.

Gittell, R., and A. Vidal (1998). *Community Organizing: Building Social Capital as a Development Strategy.* Thousand Oaks, CA: Sage.

Glickman, N., and L. Servon (1998). More than bricks and sticks: What is community development "capacity"? *Housing Policy Debate* 9.

Golab, C. (1982). The geography of neighborhood. In R. H. Bayer (Ed.), *Neighborhoods in Urban America.* Port Washington, NY: Kennikat.

Goodman, R. M., M. A. Speers, K. McLeroy, S. Fawcett, M. Kegler, E. Parker, S. R. Smith, T. D. Sterling, and N. Wallerstein (1998). Identifying and defining the dimensions of community capacity to provide a basis for measurement. *Health Education and Behavior 25*(3), 258–78.

Granovetter, M. (1985). Economic action, social structure, and embeddedness. *American Journal of Sociology 19*, 481–510.

Gray, B. (1985). Conditions facilitating interorganizational collaboration. *Human Relations 38*(10), 911–36.

Guest, A. M., and B. A. Lee (1983). The social organization of local areas. *Urban Affairs Quarterly 19*(2), 217–40.

Haar, C. M. (1975). *Between the Idea and the Reality: A Study in the Origin, Fate and Legacy of the Model Cities Program.* Boston: Little, Brown.

Halpern, R. (1995). *Rebuilding the Inner City: A History of Neighborhood Initiatives to Address Poverty in the United States.* New York: Columbia University Press.

Heifetz, R. A. (1994). *Leadership Without Easy Answers.* Cambridge, MA: Belknap Press of Harvard University.

Hirota, J., P. Brown, and B. Butler (1998). *Neighborhood Strategies Project: Report on Initial Implementation.* Chicago: Chapin Hall Center for Children at the University of Chicago.

Hirota, J., and O. Ferroussier-Davis (1998). *Putting Ideas to Work: Settlement Houses and Community Building.* Chicago: Chapin Hall Center for Children at the University of Chicago.

Hood, J. N., J. M. Logsdon, & J. K. Thompson (1993). Collaboration for social problem-solving: a process model. *Social Problems* (Spring), 1–17.

Jackson, M. R., and P. Marris (1996). *Collaborative Comprehensive Community Initiatives: Overview of an Emerging Community Improvement Orientation.* Washington, DC: Urban Institute.

Jackson, S. F., S. Cleverly, B. Poland, A. Robertson, D. Burman, M. Goodstadt, and L. Salsberg (1997). *Half Full or Half Empty? Concepts and Research Design for a Study of Indicators of Community Capacity.* North York, Ontario: North York Community Health Promotion Research Unit.

Jargowsky, P. A. (1997). *Poverty and Place: Ghettos, Barrios, and the American City.* New York: Russell Sage Foundation.

Johnson, K. (1999). ACORN branches out. *City Limits* (February), 24–27.

Kanter, R. M. (1997). *Frontiers of Management.* Boston: Harvard Business School Press.

Katz, M. B. (1986). *In the Shadow of the Poorhouse: A Social History of Welfare in America.* New York: Basic Books.

Kingsley, G. T., J. B. McNeely, and J. O. Gibson (1996). *Community Building: Coming of Age.* Washington, DC: Development Training Institute, Inc., and the Urban Institute.

Knauft, E. B., R. Berger, and S. Gray (1994). *Profiles in Excellence: Achieving Success in the Nonprofit Sector.* San Francisco: Jossey-Bass.

Knoke, D. (1990). *Political Networks: The Structural Perspective.* New York: Cambridge University Press.

Knoke, D., and J. Wood (1981). *Organized for Action: Commitment in Voluntary Organizations.* New Brunswick, NJ: Rutgers University Press.

Kramer, R. M. (1969). *Participation of the Poor: Comparative Community Case Studies in the War on Poverty.* Englewood Cliffs, NJ: Prentice-Hall.

Kretzmann, J. P., and J. L. McKnight (1993). *Building Communities from the Inside Out: A Path Toward Finding and Mobilizing a Community's Assets.* Evanston, IL: Center for Urban Affairs and Policy Research, Neighborhood Innovations Network, Northwestern University.

Kubisch, A., P. Brown, R. Chaskin, J. Hirota, M. Joseph, H. Richman, and M. Roberts (1997). *Voices from the Field: Learning from the Early Work of Comprehensive Community Initiatives.* Washington, DC: Aspen Institute.

Laumann, E. O., J. Galaskiewicz, and P. Mardsen (1978). Community structure and interorganizational linkages. *Annual Review of Sociology* 4, 455–84.

Lawrence, K. (2000). *Race and Community Revitalization.* New York: Aspen Institute.

Lee, B. A., and K. E. Campbell (1993). *Neighbor Networks of Blacks and Whites.* Unpublished manuscript.

Lee, B. A., K. E. Campbell, and O. Miller (1991). Racial difference in urban neighboring. *Sociological Forum* 6(3), 525–50.

Littell, J., and J. Wynn (1989). *The Availability and Use of Community Resources for Young Adolescents in an Inner-City and a Suburban Community.* Chicago IL: Chapin Hall Center for Children at the University of Chicago.

Logan, J. R., and G. Rabrenovic (1990). Neighborhood associations: Their issues, their allies, and their opponents. *Urban Affairs Quarterly 26*(1), 68–94.

Lorentzon, P. (1986). Leadership: Changing contexts, flexible concepts. *Bureaucrat* (Fall).

Manning, M. (1984). *Race, Reform and Rebellion. The Second Reconstruction in Black America, 1943–1982.* Jackson, MS: University of Mississippi Press.

Marris, P., and M. Rein (1982). *Dilemmas of Social Reform: Poverty and Community Action in the United States,* 2nd ed. Chicago: University of Chicago Press.

Massey, D. S. (1985). Ethnic residential segregation: A theoretical synthesis and empirical review. *Sociology & Social Research 69*(3), 315–30.

Massey, D. S., and N. Denton (1993). *American Apartheid: Segregation and the Making of the Underclass.* Cambridge, MA: Harvard University Press.

Massey, D. S., and M. L. Eggers (1990). The ecology of inequality: Minorities and the concentration of poverty 1970–1980. *American Journal of Sociology 95*(5), 1153–88.

Mattessich, P. W., and B. R. Monsey (1992). *Collaboration: What Makes It Work, A Review of Research Literature on Factors Influencing Successful Collaboration.* St. Paul, MN: Amherst H. Wilder Foundation.

Mayer, S. E. (1994). *Building Community Capacity: The Potential of Community Foundations.* Minneapolis, MN: Rainbow Research.

McDougall, H. A. (1993). *Black Baltimore: A New Theory of Community.* Philadelphia: Temple University Press.

McMillan, D. W., and D. M. Chavis (1986). Sense of community: A definition and theory. *Journal of Community Psychology 14*, 6–23.

Medoff, P., and H. Sklar (1984). *Streets of Hope: The Fall and Rise of an Urban Neighborhood.* Boston: South End.

Metro Denver Black Church Initiative (1994). Grant award announcement. Denver: Piton Foundation.

Milofsky, C. (1988). Structure and process in community self-help organizations. In C. Milofsky (Ed.), *Community Organizations: Studies in Resource Mobilization and Exchange.* New York: Oxford University Press.

Mitchell, C. (1969). The concept and use of social networks. In Clyde Mitchell (Ed.), *Social Networks in Urban Situations.* Manchester: University of Manchester Press.

National Civic League (1996). *The Civic Index: A New Approach to Improving Community Life.* Denver: National Civic League; Aspen Institute.

NMIDC (1997). *Strategic Planning Final Report.* Milwaukee, WI: Author.

Nonprofit Sector Research Fund (1999). Rethinking the potential of advisory groups. In *Snapshots.* Washington, DC: Aspen Institute.

Peterson, P., and J. D. Greenstone (1977). Racial change and citizen participation: The mobilization of low-income communities through community action. In R. H. Haveman (Ed.), *A Decade of Federal Antipoverty Programs: Achievements, Failures, and Lessons* (pp. 241–84). New York: Academic Press.

Pitcoff, W. (1997). Redefining community development, Part I: New partnerships. *Shelterforce* (November/December), 1–12.

Pitcoff, W. (1998). Redefining community development, Part II: Collaborating for change. *Shelterforce* (January/February), 1–16.

Portes, A., and R. D. Manning (1986). The immigrant enclave: Theory and empirical examples. In S. Olzak and J. Nagel (Eds.), *Competitive Ethnic Relations* (pp. 47–68). Orlando, FL: Academic Press.

Powell, W., and R. Friedkin (1987). Organizational change in nonprofit organizations. In W. W. Powell (Ed.), *The Nonprofit Sector.* New Haven, CT: Yale University Press.

Pressman, J. L., and A. Wildavsky (1973). *Implementation.* Berkeley: University of California Press.

Putnam, R. D. (1993). The prosperous community: Social capital and public life. *American Prospect,* 35–42.

Rossi, P. H. (1999). Evaluating community development programs: Problems and prospects. In R. F. Ferguson and W. T. Dickens (Eds.), *Urban Problems and Community Development* (pp. 521–67). Washington, DC: Brookings Institution Press.

Rubin, H. J. (1995). Renewing hope in the inner city: Conversations with community-based development practitioners. *Administration and Society* 27(1), 127–60.

Sampson, R. J. (1988). Local friendship ties and community attachment in mass society: A multilevel systemic model. *American Sociological Review* 53, 766–79

Sampson, R. J. (1991). Linking the micro- and macro-level dimensions of community social organization. *Social Forces* 70(1).

Sampson, R. J. (1999). What "community" supplies. In R. Ferguson and W. Dickens (Eds.), *Urban Problems and Community Development.* Washington, DC: Brookings Institution Press.

Sampson, R. J., S. Raudenbush, and F. Earls (1997). Neighborhoods and violent crime: A multi-level study of collective efficacy. *Science* 277(5328), 918–24.

Scheie, D., et al. (1991). *Religious Institutions as Partners in Community-Based Development: Findings from Year One of the Lilly Endowment Program.* Minneapolis, MN: Rainbow Research.

Schein, E. (1992). *Organizational Culture and Leadership.* San Francisco: Jossey-Bass.

Schermerhorn, J. (1975). Determinants of inter-organizational cooperation. *Academy of Management Journal* 18(4), 846–56.

Schon, D. (1983). *The Reflective Practitioner.* New York: Basic Books.

Scott, W. R. (1992). *Organizations: Rational, Natural, and Open Systems.* Englewood Cliffs, NJ: Prentice-Hall.

Senge, P., et al. (1994). *The Fifth Discipline Fieldbook: Strategies and Tools for Building a Learning Organization.* New York: Doubleday.

Skogan, W. (1986). Fear of crime and neighborhood change. In A. R. M. Tonry (Ed.), *Communities and Crime.* Chicago: University of Chicago Press.

Stack, C. B. (1974). *All Our Kin: Strategies for Survival in a Black Community.* New York: Harper & Row.

Stone, R. (Ed.) (1996). *Core Issues in Comprehensive Community-Building Initiatives.* Chicago: Chapin Hall Center for Children at the University of Chicago.

Stone, R., and B. Butler (2000). *Core Issues in Comprehensive Community-Building Initiatives: Exploring Power and Race.* Chicago: Chapin Hall Center for Children at the University of Chicago.

Suttles, G. D. (1972). *The Social Construction of Communities.* Chicago: University of Chicago Press.

Teitz, M. B. (1989). *Neighborhood Economics: Local Communities and Regional Markets,* vol. 3. New York: Sage.

Toney, M. (1997). *Tapping Community Vitality.* Oakland, CA: Applied Research Center.

Trist, E. (1985). *Intervention Strategies in Interorganizational Domains.* San Francisco: Jossey-Bass.

Venkatesh, S. (1999). Community-based interventions into street gang activity. *Journal of Community Psychology 27*(5), 551–68.

Venkatesh, S. (2000). *American Project: Gang and Community in a Modern Ghetto.* Cambridge, MA: Harvard University Press.

Waddock, S. (1991). A typology of social partnership organizations. *Administration and Society 22*(4), 480–515.

Wahl, E., M. Cahill, and N. Fruchter (1998). *Building Capacity: A Review of Technical Assistance Strategies.* New York: Institute for Education and Social Policy, New York University.

Walker, C. (1998). Personal Communication.

Walker, C., and M. Weinheimer (1998). *Community Development in the 1990s.* Washington, DC: Urban Institute.

Wallis, A. (1998). Social capital and community building: Part two. *National Civic Review 87,* 317–36.

Wellman, B. (1979). The community question: The intimate networks of East Yorkers. *American Journal of Sociology 84*(5), 1201–31.

Whetton, D. (1981). Interorganizational relations: A review of the field. *Journal of Higher Education 52*(1), 1–28.

Williams, M. R. (1985). *Neighborhood Organizations: Seeds of a New Urban Life.* Westport, CT: Greenwood.

Wood, D., and B. Gray (1991). Toward a comprehensive theory of collaboration. *Journal of Applied Behavioral Science 27*(2), 139–62.

Wynn, J., J. Costello, R. Halpern, and H. Richman (1994). *Children, Families, and Communities: A New Approach to Social Services.* Chicago: Chapin Hall Center for Children at the University of Chicago.

Wynn, J., S. Meyer, and K. Richards-Schuster (1999). *Furthering Education: The Relationship of Schools and Other Organizations.* Report to the Spencer Foundation. Chicago: Chapin Hall Center for Children at the University of Chicago.

Index